Recommended
COUNTRY INNS
West Coast

"Any inn-goer will find that this enticingly written book directs him to the finest in the West. It illustrates the tremendous variety of inns that are available in the West, and each write-up captures that individual spirit that innkeepers try to create."
—*Yellow Brick Road* newsletter

"The test of a good guidebook is whether the author's descriptions match your own experience. This guide passes that test with flying colors. Well designed, well written, and very informative."
—*Book Passage,* San Francisco, CA

"Julianne Belote has succeeded in producing a reliable reference packed with information . . . an excellent reference work for both travelers and innkeepers."
—*Travel Publishing News*

"If you plan to travel in the western states covered by the book, purchase a copy and make plans to stay at some of the inns mentioned. The pen and ink sketches are worth the price of the book."
—*Rota-Gene* newsletter, Sarasota, FL

"Beautifully written and useful, this will be of interest to those planning trips along the western coastline. Armchair travelers will like it. In fact, Belote's homey commentaries and earnest enthusiasm will encourage those without touring plans to pack their bags. It's a good guide at a fair price."
—*Small Press*

"Truly excellent."
—*Books of the Southwest*

"Recommended Country Inns" Series

"The guidebooks in this new series of recommended country inns are sure winners. Personal visits have ensured accurate and scene-setting descriptions. These beckon the discriminating traveler to a variety of interesting lodgings."
—Norman Strasma, publisher of *Inn Review* newsletter

The "Recommended Country Inns" series is designed for the discriminating traveler who seeks the best in unique accommodations away from home.

From hundreds of inns personally visited and evaluated by the author, only the finest are described here. The inclusion of an inn is purely a personal decision on the part of the author; no one can pay or be paid to be in a Globe Pequot inn guide.

Organized for easy reference, these guides point you to just the kind of accommodations you are looking for: Comprehensive indexes by category provide listings of inns for romantic getaways, inns for the sports-minded, inns that serve gourmet meals . . . and more. State maps help you pinpoint the location of each inn, and detailed driving directions tell you how to get there.

Use these guidebooks with confidence. Allow each author to share his or her selections with you, then discover for yourself the country inn experience.

Editions available:
Recommended Country Inns
New England • Mid-Atlantic and Chesapeake Region
The South • The Midwest • West Coast
Rocky Mountain Region • The Southwest
also
Recommended Island Inns
Recommended Romantic Inns

Recommended
COUNTRY INNS™
West Coast

California • Oregon • Washington

Fourth Edition

by Julianne Belote
illustrated by Olive Metcalf

A Voyager Book

The Globe Pequot Press

Old Saybrook, Connecticut

Library of Congress Cataloging-in-Publication Data

Belote, Julianne.
    Recommended country inns. West Coast : California, Oregon, Washington / by Julianne Belote ; illustrated by Olive Metcalf. — 4th ed.
      p. cm. — ("Recommended country inns" series)
    "A Voyager book."
    Includes indexes.
    ISBN 1-56440-091-3
    1. Hotels, taverns, etc.—California—Guidebooks. 2. Hotels, taverns, etc.—Oregon—Guidebooks. 3. Hotels, taverns, etc.—Washington (State)—Guidebooks. I. Title. II. Series.
TX907.3.C2B45 1992
647.947901—dc20
                                            92-28871
                                             CIP

Manufactured in the United States of America
Fourth Edition/First Printing

Contents

Indexes

The West is . . . a state of mind: the idea still of El Dorado, of getting away from it all, of leading a new and luckier life . . .

—Alistair Cooke, *Alistair Cooke's America*

A Few Words about
Visiting Western Inns

On the West Coast, at least, no one is certain what you mean when you talk about an inn. Inns snuggle uncertainly in a lodging land bordered by small hotels, motels, cabins, resorts, and homestays. We have only a few that serve meals beyond breakfast, and the emergence of urban inns rules out the strictly "country" definition. There are Old Guard innkeepers who insist that their profession is nothing less than the full-service nurturing of wayfaring strangers and who scoff at the explosion of bed and breakfast establishments calling themselves inns but offering little more than a bed and a croissant.

Let the innkeepers sort out the labels. My task is to acquaint you with a variety of hostelries up and down the West Coast that offer a level of individual decor not found at motels, an ambience cozier and more intimate than that found at a resort, innkeepers who treat you like their very special house guest, and homemade meals or knowledgeable pointers to the best food nearby.

These choices differ vastly from one another, from sleek urban digs to solitary island retreats. Each one has its own individual flavor. None is stamped out of a corporate room plan. There probably won't be a paper strip across the toilet or a chain lock for the door. You're more likely to find a basket of fruit, a bouquet, a plate of freshly baked cookies, or a carafe of wine to greet you.

Not all of these lodgings will be your cup of tea. Even the best can disappoint, but keep a sour note in perspective. It does not signal the decline of civilization as we know it; it is simply the risk we take when we search for the noncommercial.

Unique lodgings are one of the last frontiers to explore. Dare a little! It can be exciting to check into a place where you don't know the floor plan and where someone may actually talk to you at breakfast!

At the best inns, when you bid an innkeeper goodbye, you leave feeling that you've made a friend whom you really must have to *your* place.

About This Inn Guide

The inns are arranged by states in the following order: California, Oregon, and Washington. California inns are subdivided into six areas: Southern California, The Central Coast, The San Francisco Bay Area, The North Coast, The Wine Country, and The Mother Lode and Sierras.

Before each state and area is a map and index to the inns in that section, listed alphabetically by town. At the back of the guide is a complete index to all the inns in the book listed alphabetically by name. Additional indexes list inns by category.

"J:" following an inn description means a personal comment from Julianne.

You may not need a passport or shots, but inns can be foreign territory if you've not tried them, and a few ground rules are in order.

Rates: They can change almost as fast as the sheets. I list the high–low range for two people *at the time I visited.* Many innkeepers have unadvertised off-season and midweek rates, but you sometimes have to ask.

Reservations/Deposits: These are almost always a necessity. But even the most popular places have cancellations, and a last-minute telephone call or your name on a backup list can bring results. Policies vary, but you will likely be charged if you're a no-show or a last-minute cancellation.

Minimum Stay: A two- or three-night stay is commonly required over weekends and holidays. *Sometimes* you can negotiate this, if the traffic is slow.

Children/Pets: Most inns are not set up to deal with either. I specifically note it when the little nippers are welcome, and I have put these inns into a special index in the back of the book.

Credit Cards: Unless otherwise specified, most inns accept MasterCard and Visa. Other cards may also be accepted.

Television/Air Conditioning/Telephone: Most inns do not have these facilities in the bedrooms, but I have noted when they do. You're supposed to be getting away from it all—remember?

Food: Small inns that serve meals usually have a limited menu.

If you have a dietary request, inquire when you reserve.

Smoking: A majority of West Coast innkeepers prefer that their guests not smoke. I mention it when they are adamant.

Wheelchair Access: I have noted when inns have rooms with wheelchair access, and I have included them in the special index in the back of the book.

Space: Pack lightly. The inn room with a place for long garment bags or a matched luggage set has eluded me.

Manners: At an inn, you're often a paying guest at someone's home. It is frowned upon to plop your bag down on Grandmother's prize quilt, monopolize the shared bathroom while you leisurely floss between your teeth, inhale all the sherry, or act silently superior at a common breakfast table.

No inn was charged to be in this guide. I visited all the inns included, as well as hundreds of others that I did not choose. Obviously, things can change between my visit and the time you use the guide. But if you feel that I have steered you wrong or if you have a comment, please write to Julianne Belote, The Globe Pequot Press, P.O. Box 833, Old Saybrook, Connecticut 06475.

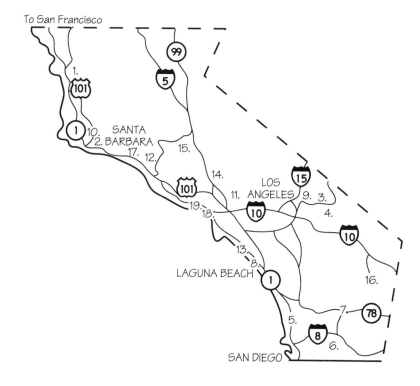

To San Francisco

1.

101

1

10.

SANTA
2. BARBARA

17. 12.

15.

14.

101

19. 18.

99

5

LOS
ANGELES

11.

10

15

9. 3.

4.

10

16.

13.

8.

LAGUNA BEACH

1

5.

7.

78

8

6.

SAN DIEGO

WA

OR

CA

Southern California

Numbers on map refer to towns numbered below.

Olive Metcalf

Rose Victorian Inn
Arroyo Grande, California
93420

Innkeepers: Diana and Ross Cox
Address/Telephone: 789 Valley Road; (805) 481–5566
Rooms: 11; 7 with private bath. Wheelchair access. No smoking inn.
Rates: $130 to $175, double occupancy, full breakfast and five-course dinner.
Open: All year, Thursday, Friday, Saturday, Sunday.
Facilities and activities: Restaurant, full bar, facilities for garden weddings, banquets. Nearby: winding back roads to wineries, 55 miles to Hearst Castle, San Luis Obispo Mission, Mozart Festival in summer, Spring Fiesta.

When a four-story gingerbread Victorian house sits alone, surrounded by acres of flat farmland, you notice it. When it's painted four shades of rose (please, don't call it pink!)—you can't miss it. The Rose Victorian is that rare California phenomenon, a country inn with breakfast and dinner included in the rate. It's a pleasant break in the long drive on Highway 101 between Los Angeles and San Francisco: a beautiful 1885 house surrounded by 200 rose bushes, with authentic period furniture, good beds, and a first-rate restaurant.

The intensely rose exterior tended to have me guessing that the inside would be doilies and kitsch. Wrong. The rooms are tastefully decorated, blending some outstanding antique pieces with comfortable traditional sofas and chairs. Bouquets of fresh roses, as

2

well as good reading lights, are in every room.

At dinner we had two view choices: one to the green lawn with rose arbor and white gazebo (it's a wedding setting about as romantic as one could ask); the other to a large window looking into the kitchen where you can watch Chef Stephen Schultz and a talented kitchen staff do their thing. We chose the kitchen view. (Tell me, Dr. Ruth, is this an indication of complacency, or merely hunger?)

Smug San Franciscans and Angelinos who think only *their* cities have sophisticated cooking have a surprise in store. It was fun to watch the cooks in full-speed dinner-hour action . . . and the results were outstanding. My baked halibut was moist and dressed with zippy, fresh salsa and sliced avocado. The traveler's companion had fork-tender veal, sautéed with wine and fresh thyme and finished with cream. They also do fresh local salmon and an elegant abalone-scallop combination sautéed and finished with lemon, wine, and almonds. A mostly California wine list, much of it from the surrounding Central Coast wineries, was very fairly priced. A house specialty, peanut butter pie in a chocolate crumb crust, is so good, I regretted our decision to order one piece, two forks.

Breakfast is done elegantly. Inn guests gather around the dining room table for orange juice with champagne, sliced melons, hot orange muffins, and superior eggs Benedict, all served on delicate china.

How to get there: 200 miles north of Los Angeles, exit Highway 101 at Traffic Way. Turn left at stop sign (Fair Oaks). Go ¹/₄ mile and turn left on Valley Road. Drive ¹/₄ mile to the inn on your left.

J: *A splendidly ornate piano that belonged to General John Fremont sits in one of the parlors.*

Olive Metcalf

The Ballard Inn
Ballard, California
93463

Innkeeper: Steve Hyslop
Address/Telephone: 2436 Baseline Avenue; (805) 688–7770
Rooms: 15; all with private bath and air conditioning, some with fireplace.
Wheelchair access.
Rates: $155 to $185, double occupancy, full breakfast and afternoon wine
tasting and hors d'oeuvres.
Open: All year.
Facilities and activities: Accommodates business meetings, private parties; picnic baskets packed and excursion arrangements made by request.
Nearby: many horse ranches and wineries in the valley; good biking
and hiking; small towns in the valley (Buelton, Los Olivos, Santa Ynez,
Solvang) with shops, restaurants, galleries, and little theater; fishing,
boating, horseback riding at Lake Cachuma; Gaviota State Park.

Beautiful Santa Ynez Valley is one of those treasured places
you don't just happen by; you have to want to get there. Its history
goes back to the Chumash Indians. The Ballard Inn's nineteenth-
century decor fits right in, but it is actually sparkling new with all
contemporary comforts. When you drive into Ballard, don't think
you've missed downtown—this is it. Eighty-one families make up
the township, and the two-story gray-and-white inn is city center.
Rocking chairs and white wicker furniture decorate a broad porch
that wraps around the inn. Roses and a white picket fence encircle
it further.

The generous size and elegance of the common rooms tell you this is an inn prepared for big parties and important business to take place. In this sleepy valley? Oh, yes. Wine makers, country-estate owners, farmers, and horse breeders have made this seemingly quiet countryside a productive (and wealthy) part of California. Owner/innkeeper Steve Hyslop would have you know that a very classy guest list of business people and celebrities have found their way to Ballard—but he's much too discreet to give any names.

Guest rooms are large, bandbox neat, and mint fresh. (That's the payoff when you have a new inn that merely pretends to look old.) The appointments are all one could ask: soundprooof walls, individually controlled heating and air conditioning, and a large, well-stocked bath. Each room celebrates a person or quality in the valley's history. There's not a dreary one among them, but I was particularly taken with the Mountain Room decorated in rich dark green and earth tones, with a brass-and-iron headboard, comfortable chairs before a fireplace, and a private balcony providing you a closer look at the magnificent mountains.

Try to make the time to explore some valley towns just minutes away. Solvang, the pseudo-Danish village, is quite a tourist lure, but Los Olivos is my favorite and still in the early adolescence of cuteness. Its small shops and art galleries are fun to explore, and there are some delightful places to eat.

The inn has a good working relationship with all the valley wineries and can arrange special tours and tastings for their guests. This is a chance to sample some world-class chardonnays and pinot noirs being produced by Au Bon Climat, Sanford, and others.

How to get there: For a beautiful winding drive from Santa Barbara, take Highway 154 north about 25 miles to the Edison/Baseline exit; turn left, then right onto Baseline Avenue and proceed to the inn. Driving south on Highway 101, exit at Highway 154, proceed to Edison/Baseline Avenue, and turn right, then right again onto Baseline Avenue.

J: *In case you're wondering . . . yes, this is the area where Michael Jackson has an estate. And the Reagans are just a mountaintop or two away.*

Olive Metcalf

Gold Mountain Manor
Big Bear City, California
92314

Innkeepers: Conny and John Ridgway
Address/Telephone: 1117 Anita (mailing address: P.O. Box 2027); (714)
  585–6997
Rooms: 7; 1 with private bath, 2 with half-bath, 6 with wood-burning fireplace. No smoking indoors.
Rates: $75 to $180, weekends, double occupancy, full breakfast and evening
  hors d'oeuvres and beverages. Ask about ski packages.
Open: All year.
Facilities and activities: Pool table; computerized player piano; will cater small
  weddings, business seminars; woodsy setting to walk. Nearby: restaurants, skiing, fishing, boating, riding stables.

In the 1930s and 1940s, the kind of good-time players that are
in *People* magazine today used to journey up the twisting mountain
roads to this log mansion. Set 6,750 feet high in a grove of tall pine
trees, rustic but comfortable, it was a favorite hideaway for the
pre–jet set crowd from L.A.

World War II gas rationing, waning popularity, and neglect
inevitably took a toll, but new young owners with a creative flair
began a restoration in 1985. I liked the looks of it as soon as I saw
the broad green lawn in front dotted with Adirondack-style chairs
and tubs of flowers. School principal Conny and her husband,
John, appreciated the 1930s atmosphere and have enhanced it with
their decor and furniture choices. They may or may not be period

pieces, but it all *looks* right for the house. There are big sofas and wingback chairs around a huge rock fireplace in the parlor. A wonderful-looking red-pine stairway goes from the parlor up to most of the bedrooms. A large playroom has a pool table, more comfortable seating, and a great selection of magazines.

The picturesque house and setting are frequently used for professional photo layouts. Photographers for Spiegel and Eddie Bauer catalogs and for Olivia Newton John's company have worked here. You may find it interesting to hang around and watch the activity, or you may care seriously about avoiding the distraction. Ask about what's happening when you reserve.

There are nostalgic touches, too, like the Franklin stove that kept Clark Gable and his bride Carole Lombard cozy when they honeymooned at Big Bear. These are snuggly, colorful bedrooms, each with a wood-burning fireplace, a puffy down comforter, a hodgepodge of antiques, lacy curtains, and painted stencil designs on ceilings and walls. One room is named for Clark Gable and one for that scamp, con man, and mining baron, Lucky Baldwin. The Ted Ducey Room, named for one of the mountain's earliest settlers and a friend of the former innkeepers, has its own Jacuzzi.

Breakfast the morning I visited began with juice and baked apples. Then came blueberry muffins and an excellent crab quiche.

After all that it was time to move, and there are plenty of things to do around Big Bear. My breakfast companions were off to the stables for a ride in the woods. Winter skiing is a big attraction.

How to get there: From San Bernardino take Highway 215 north to 30 east until it ends. Follow BIG BEAR signs to Highway 330 and continue 33 miles to Big Bear Dam. Stay left around dam 7 miles past Fawnskin. Turn left at Anita. Inn is on the left. Fly-in: Big Bear Airport.

Olive Metcalf

The Knickerbocker Mansion
Big Bear Lake, California
92315

Innkeeper: Phyllis Knight
Address/Telephone: 869 South Knickerbocker Road (mailing address: P.O. Box 3661); (714) 866–8221
Rooms: 9 in main house and Carriage House, including 1 suite with lake view, spa tub, refrigerator, microwave, VCR; 4 with private bath, all with television, 4 with balcony. No smoking inn.
Rates: $95 to $165, double occupancy, breakfast, afternoon refreshments, and Grandma's Kitchen privileges. $10 each additional person. Two-night minimum on weekends.
Facilities and activities: Outdoor Jacuzzi, woodsy grounds, wedding and small seminar facilities. Nearby: restaurants, cross-country and downhill skiing, boating, fishing, riding stables, mountain biking.

This is my idea of a perfect mountain retreat—a wonderful-looking log mansion sitting on two and a half acres of fir trees. It is a comfortable house for unwinding, where you can always find a quiet spot to be alone: in the large sitting room with upholstered chairs and sofas, a fireplace, music, books . . . on one of the long covered porches extending from each floor of the house . . . in Grandma's Kitchen, where you're invited to help yourself to tea, coffee, and some baked treat . . . in the sunny old-fashioned dining room with individual tables and morning newspapers . . . on the back deck with a Jacuzzi . . . or on the lawn and wooded area surrounding the house.

The bedrooms are cozy retreats, too, with patchwork quilts and comforters, thick towels, guest toiletries, and television. From my Calico Room in the main house I sat out on the second-floor porch to watch a spectacular sunset. The Carriage House above the back lawn has a higher vantage over the lake. The rooms are slightly smaller here—but each has a private bath and a little balcony.

The rambling three-story house is only a quarter of a mile from the village of Big Bear Lake, so you can stroll down for the usual resort-community restaurants and shops or stay here quietly in the trees above it all. Jacuzzis work a therapeutic magic, it's true, but try a few hours in a big hammock looking out at the woods and breathing the scent of pine trees. I did, and it has my unqualified recommendation.

Owner Phyllis Knight can use her life experiences in real estate, family counseling, mothering, and entertaining to offer unusually interesting inn events. The "Lovers Only" weekends may sound terribly "California," but people love them. A certified body therapist instructs couples in how to help each other reduce stress. With the advantage of a 7,000-foot altitude and clean skies, the Knickerbocker's star parties are always booked ahead. An astronomer shows guests how to track the heavens with several telescopes set up outside. Mystery weekends, too, are popular but held irregularly, so ask to be on the list.

An excellent breakfast with a variety of fresh fruits, hot muffins, and an egg dish is served buffet style. You can eat in the dining room or take it to a sunny spot outdoors.

How to get there: Going east on Highway 10, pass San Bernardino Freeway to the Alabama cutoff and turn left. Continue to Highland and turn right; it becomes Highway 330. Proceed to Running Springs, where it becomes Highway 18. Continue into Big Bear Lake Village. When Highway 18 turns left, continue straight for 2 blocks to Knickerbocker. Turn right and proceed to the inn on the left.

olive Metcalf

Rock Haus
Del Mar, California
92014

Innkeeper: Doris Holmes
Address/Telephone: 410 15th Street; (619) 481-3764
Rooms: 10; 4 with private bath, all with telephone. No smoking inn.
Rates: $75 to $135, double occupancy, continental breakfast and late-afternoon refreshment.
Open: All year.
Facilities and activities: Available for weddings and small parties. Short walk to Del Mar shops, restaurants, beach. Nearby: Del Mar Race Track, Torrey Pines Golf Course/State Reserve.

This is one of those absolutely captivating inns you visit with enormous pleasure and contentment, then grumble on the way home, "Why can't we make *our* house look like that?"

You can, of course. Just start with an early California bungalow that's a historic landmark and overlooks the Pacific Ocean. Make sure it has a colorful past, as this one has: stately home of a land company executive; a dining room used for Catholic Mass by beach parishioners in 1910; gambling house in the roaring '20s; a boardinghouse and hippie pad. Then do the extensive renovation houses with "colorful pasts" always require, and you'll be close, but not there.

You'll still need a decorator with a feel for old houses. Today, the sprawling house on a hill looks just the way a 1910 summer house should look. There's wicker and rattan, floral cotton comforters, and fresh flowers everywhere. It all looks light, cheerful, and clean.

First-floor bedrooms are especially comfortable with private baths and private entrances, and one has a fireplace. But upstairs you get the splendid ocean views.

We gave our room the tough Mother-Daughter Bunk-Together Test: Choose the smallest, least expensive room in the house to share, and see if somebody is snapping at somebody by morning. The Wren's Nest room was a total success—as serene to stay in as it is to look at. Its twin beds are dressed in crisp pastel linens and big fluffy pillows; there's a *bright* reading light over each bed and a wall of windows looking out at the ocean. Bathrooms are modern and so conveniently appointed that sharing was never a problem.

The broad glassed-in sun porch is an inviting place to start your day with its clear view of the Pacific. Individual tables are set with teapots of fresh flowers, and newspapers, coffee, and tea wait on a sideboard along with a buffet of fruit, breads, granola, and juices. The staff enhances an already appealing breakfast atmosphere by scorning the easy jeans routine and wearing fresh, pretty outfits. It adds to a very pleasant breakfast. Just a block from the inn is a street of colorful restaurants, from small bistros and outdoor cafes to elegant eateries with ocean views.

How to get there: From Los Angeles on the San Diego Freeway, take Via de la Valle exit and head southwest along Jimmy Durante Boulevard to Del Mar Village. Turn left on 15th Street to inn on the left at number 410. From San Diego, take Del Mar Heights exit off San Diego Freeway and go west to Camino Del Mar. Turn right, and at 15th Street, turn right again.

Olive Metcalf

Brookside Farm
Dulzura, California
92017

Innkeepers: Edd and Sally Guishard
Address/Telephone: 1373 Marron Valley Road; (619) 468–3043
Rooms: 8; 6 with private bath; 2 cottages with private bath; 3 wood-burning
  stoves. No smoking inn.
Rates: $60 to $80, double occupancy, full breakfast. Weekend rates available
  with dinners.
Open: All year.
Facilities and activities: Eat, sleep, sit by the stream; hot tub under grape
  arbor, for the hyperactive.

The first time I visited Brookside Farm, the innkeeper led us
into an old barn and indicated a large unfinished room they used as
a game room and where local meetings were sometimes held. "And
this," I was told, "is the Dulzura Convention Center." It was good
for a laugh then, but never underestimate the perseverance of a
good innkeeper. Today the old barn has been converted into several
new guest rooms.

Edd Guishard has an innkeeper's salvation—a sense of humor,
plus vision. He can have you laughing with him over the tribula-
tions of renovation. But do look at his album of "before-and-after"
shots to appreciate the hard work it takes to renovate a dilapidated
building into the charming country inn so many of us *think* we'd
love to have. Even his real estate broker was doubtful about selling

him this 1928 farmhouse, fearing it might ruin their friendship.

Hard work has resulted in an unpretentious, rambling house where it's easy to feel utterly at home. A dining room and sunny living room have oversized Mexican bricks as flooring, covered with oriental rugs. A comfortable sofa and chairs, taped music, books, and a fireplace are inviting. Guest rooms are simply done in a fresh country style using handmade quilts.

Dulzura is a mountain community about 10 miles from the Mexican border and 30 miles southeast of San Diego. Things got pretty exciting once about fifty years ago when big gun Adolph Spreckles considered running his railroad through the town. But after his engineers decided it was too mountainous, the town returned to its natural pace.

When you have an urge to "get away from it all" and do nothing, this is the place: four rolling acres to stroll, fresh country air, a tree-shaded patio, and the only sound a bubbling stream. Tell your troubles to Emily, the current resident goat, or one of the pigs; they'll never disagree with you.

But my kind of quiet contemplation goes better with food, so it was good to learn that your stomach is not stranded in Dulzura. Edd is a chef, and besides serving a full breakfast, he'll do dinners for guests on weekends by request. A succulently sauced loin of pork is typical, accompanied by a selection of Southern California's abundant fresh vegetables and fruits. Brookside does not have a wine license, but guests are welcome to bring their own. The rest of the house is country charm, but Edd's kitchen is strictly high-tech. There's first-rate equipment and space for the hands-on cooking-class weekends Edd likes to host. Given his talent and easy humor, it sounds like fun.

How to get there: From San Diego, take Highway 94 1½ miles past the Dulzura Cafe. Turn right on Marron Valley Road. Inn is on the left.

J: *Prices here aren't in the range of other inns with comparable pleasures simply because the world has not yet discovered Dulzura. Meanwhile, enjoy.*

olive Metcalf

Julian Gold Rush Hotel
Julian, California
92036

Innkeepers: Steve and Gig Ballinger
Address/Telephone: P.O. Box 1856; (619) 765–0201
Rooms: 18; 5 with private bath, 13 share 4 baths.
Rates: $64 to $145, double occupancy, full breakfast and afternoon tea.
  Children especially welcome.
Open: All year.
Facilities and activities: Walk to shopping, restaurants in historic Julian. Horse
  and carriage tours of town available. Nearby: still-producing Eagle
  Mine, Anza-Borrego Desert State Park, Fall Banjo and Fiddle Festival,
  Apple Days, cider press locations for fresh-squeezed juice, Spring Wild-
  flower Festival. Unique day trips arranged by innkeepers.

Come to Julian for a scenic drive, for the flavor of a gold-rush
town, and for a stay in the oldest continuously operating hotel in
Southern California. You're 4,000 feet high in this back country
east of San Diego, and the air is pure and clear. In the fall there's
brisk weather that brings changing colors and an abundant apple
harvest.

The entire town is a historic California landmark, but the
Julian Gold Rush Hotel is the sole survivor of the fifteen hotels it
had in its heyday at the turn of the century. This hotel was known
then as "Queen of the Back Country," a luxury hostelry boasting
two bathtubs and the "most modern mountain accommodations."

It was the remarkable achievement of a former slave, Albert

Robinson, and his wife, Margaret, who built it in 1897. Albert planted the cedar and locust trees that encircle the hotel today. When the Butterfield Stage stopped here after its two-day journey from San Diego, Mrs. Robinson's cooking, especially her hot apple pie and bread, welcomed miners and travelers to the Southern Mother Lode.

The Ballingers are carrying on the Robinson tradition of hospitality and adding their personal country inn touches. They've decorated the lobby sitting room with big chairs, games and books, and an old Silvertone radio (masking a stereo) that will look familiar to anyone of a certain age. Some evenings they play tapes of old-time radio shows.

The rooms all have a genuine American West feeling, simple and airy. If you arrive early enough in the afternoon, you're encouraged to peek into unoccupied rooms and choose the one that appeals to you most. Plaques on the doors bear the names of entries in the old guest register; U. S. Grant for one. Each room is decorated with authentic American antique pieces, without gimmicks or reproductions (except for a few light fixtures). Separate from the hotel are the Honeymoon Cottage, with a dressing room and fireplace, and a recently renovated Patio Cottage, with chairs on a veranda-style porch.

Guests are served a full, hearty breakfast on the patio in the summer: juice and fresh fruit, eggs Florentine, breads from Dudley's Bakery, and coffee and tea.

How to get there: From San Diego, take I–8 east to Highway 79. Turn north to Julian; about 1³/₄ hours from San Diego.

✻

J: *My advice is to eat every bite of breakfast and then embark on one of Steve's well-researched day trips. This country is rich in Indian and gold-rush history. Rolling hills and streams are at one turn, mountains at another, and . . . no smog, no freeways.*

Olive Metcalf

The Carriage House
Laguna Beach, California
92651

Innkeepers: Tom, Dee, and Vern Taylor
Address/Telephone: 1322 Catalina Street; (714) 494–8945
Rooms: 6 suites; all with private bath, sitting room, and separate bedroom.
Rates: $95 to $150, double occupancy, breakfast. $20 each additional person. No credit cards.
Open: All year.
Facilities and activities: Two blocks from the ocean, steps down to beach. Nearby: walk to Pottery Shack; visit Laguna's art galleries, shops, restaurants; bus stop on corner.

Instead of one of the large modern hotels on the waterfront, this might be just the secluded, pretty spot you're looking for from which to enjoy Laguna Beach. Cecil B. deMille thought it was sweet enough to buy back in the '20s when Laguna was Hollywood's Riviera. It's now one of the town's designated historic landmarks, a charming old New Orleans–style house.

Every room here is a suite with a sitting room and separate bedroom. Several have two bedrooms and a fully equipped kitchen. That kind of convenience and space is scarce anywhere; in a beach town it's rare; and done with antique charm and in a lush setting, it's almost unheard of.

Each room is decorated distinctively with antiques and memorabilia. There's Mandalay with a tropical, oriental theme in shades of coral and pink and with an ocean view. Primrose Lane has an English country feeling in yellow and deep blue. Green Palms is elegantly cool with white wicker furniture against emerald green carpet, and a bay window opens onto the courtyard. Whichever suite you have, you'll be welcomed with a bottle of California wine and fresh fruit.

All the rooms surround the quiet brick courtyard filled with tropical plants. There's a tiered fountain, chairs, and plenty of room to relax. If you don't take breakfast in the dining room, it's delightful to eat here beneath the hanging moss of a carrotwood tree. In addition to juice, fresh fruit, and cereals, there's always something hot from the oven—such as a coffee cake or muffins.

It's an easy walk to the beach from here, but for exploring more of Laguna Beach you'll appreciate the convenient bus stop on the corner.

How to get there: From the Pacific Coast Highway going through Laguna Beach, take Cress Street up the hill away from the ocean. Driving south, Cress is the first stoplight past the Pottery Shack. Inn is 2 blocks up on the corner of Catalina Street, number 1322.

olive Metcalf

Casa Laguna Inn
Laguna Beach, California
92651

Innkeeper: Kevin A. Henry
Address/Telephone: 2510 South Coast Highway; (714) 494–2996 or (800) 233–0449
Rooms: 20, including 1- and 2-bedroom suites and the Cottage; all with private bath, television, and ceiling fan.
Rates: $105 to $225, double occupancy, breakfast and afternoon refreshment. $20 for each additional person. Special winter rates.
Open: All year.
Facilities and activities: Pool, patios, and gardens with views of the Pacific; in-house library, television. Nearby: walk to Victoria Beach; Moss Point; Laguna shops, galleries, restaurants.

Even local "Lagunatics" have reserved rooms at Casa Laguna in order to see what's happened to their old landmark. It's always had a Southern California Spanish glamour, but its recent facelift has made it a more magical place than ever.

The original Mission House and Cottage were built in the 1930s as guest facilities for historic Villa Rockledge, the Frank Miller (owner of the Riverside Mission Inn) estate across the street. The Casitas, nineteen courtyard and balcony rooms and suites, were added in the 1940s as the Laguna Beach art colony grew and more visitors began coming.

This is a romantic inn of meandering brick paths, courtyards, and fountains. Colorful tiles, rock walls, even a bell tower, provide a fantasy retreat. In the complex of balconies and decks, plants, and flowers, there are many private little spots to relax, away from the bustle of Laguna at the height of the tourist season. There's also a cozy library for guests to use.

Every room is decorated with a blend of antiques and contemporary furnishings and has color television; many have refrigerators. Some rooms open onto the flower-filled Spanish patio and pool; some have superb views of the ocean. Suites have well-equipped kitchens and deluxe space, especially the Cottage.

But charming facilities don't make an inn; it takes the fine old innkeeping tradition of pampering guests to do that, and you're on safe ground here. "We just try to make people feel right at home here at the Casa," says Kevin. "It's one of the things that make it such a unique place."

Attention to detail in every area keeps guests returning. The gardens especially are a labor of love. Breakfast includes freshly squeezed juices, fresh fruits, cereals, a variety of nut breads and muffins, bagels and cream cheese, hard-boiled eggs, cinnamon Kona coffee, and many teas. Afternoon snacks include wine, lemonade, hors d'oeuvres, and cheeses.

How to get there: On the east side of the Pacific Coast Highway, just south of downtown Laguna Beach, number 2510. It's white with a red-tile roof.

J: To send an East Coast chum a color photograph of you on this patio some February—flowers, palms, pool, and blue Pacific in the background—would be cruelly insensitive. Do not do it.

Olive Metcalf

Eiler's Inn
Laguna Beach, California
92651

Innkeepers: Annette and Henk Wirtz
Address/Telephone: 741 South Coast Highway; (714) 494–3004
Rooms: 12, including 1 suite; all with private bath.
Rates: $100 to $165, double occupancy; $10 for each additional person; $5
less for single; extended continental breakfast, afternoon refreshments.
Open: All year.
Facilities and activities: Swimming, sunning on Laguna Beach. Nearby:
restaurants, art galleries, shops.

You can lose your heart when you walk through the cozy entry
lobby at Eiler's Inn into a central brick courtyard. It's a beguiling,
airy scene of plants and flowers around a tiered fountain. Balcony
rooms look down on round tables covered with blue-and-white
print tablecloths. At one end is a brick counter where the breakfast
buffet is set out: baskets of fresh fruit and hot breads, juices, cereals,
and boiled eggs.

Laguna Beach may be the essence of Southern California
beach towns, but Eiler's has a Country French feeling. You'll notice
it at once in the two inviting parlors on either side of the entry. One
is a small library/den with books and a television. The other is a
pretty sitting room with a small blue-and-white patterned wallpaper and a comfortable fat sofa and chairs. Afternoon wine and
cheeses are served here or in the courtyard.

Some bedrooms are relatively small, but opening onto the courtyard or balcony above, as they do, gives them a pleasant openness. They're each furnished differently with antiques and especially colorful linens and comforters. You'll find fresh flowers, fruit, and candy in each room.

A suite upstairs has a fireplace. It's off a sun deck that is available to all guests. The ocean views are superb (you're right on the beach), and you can enjoy both sunning and sunsets without so much as a grain of sand between your toes.

You couldn't find a more secluded, romantic setting in Laguna Beach on a Saturday night than the courtyard. Aperitifs and classical guitar music are the perfect additions to this Southern California inn.

How to get there: On the South Coast Highway in the center of Laguna Beach, the inn is at number 741 on the ocean side.

J: *I'm one who appreciates their complimentary tea and coffee available all day long, but the bottle of champagne you're presented at check-in is truly a sparkling extra.*

21

olive Metcalf

Bluebelle House
Lake Arrowhead, California
92352

Innkeepers: Rick and Lila Peiffer
Address/Telephone: 263 South State Highway 173 (mailing address: Box 2177); (714) 336–3292 or (800) 429–BLUE
Rooms: 5; 3 with private bath. No smoking inn.
Rates: $75 to $110, double occupancy, hot breakfast. Seasonal and senior citizen weekday discounts; two-night minimum weekends.
Open: All year.
Facilities and activities: Short walk to mountain village shops, restaurants, entertainment. Nearby: Lake Arrowhead beach, excursion boats. Winter sports within thirty minutes.

Nestled in fir trees on the edge of a bustling mountain village, Bluebelle House has a Swiss-Alpine feeling. Fresh air and recreation on Lake Arrowhead are attractions in summer; in winter, skiing is less than thirty minutes away.

Rick and Lila Peiffer's innkeeping style is to lavish hospitality and personal attention on their guests. The warmth of their welcome says unmistakably that they're sincerely glad to see you. And if you arrive after sundown, you'll be grateful for their well-lighted parking area.

After your drive up the mountain, relax with late-afternoon refreshments on a large deck with the smell of fresh pine all around, or indoors beside a warm fire on crisp winter days. This is a good time to look at the Peiffers' menu collection from village restaurants and their "Things to Do in Lake Arrowhead" scrapbook. Rick and Lila have helpful suggestions and will make any reservations you need.

Bluebelle House reflects the talents and interests of both its innkeepers. Rick is a skilled carpenter and has redesigned or improved many details of the inn. Lila specializes in silk floral arrangements that she has designed for each room. Guests often comment there is so much to see they feel as though they're in a boutique. Objects the Peiffers have collected from their European holidays are everywhere. There is antique crystal, an interesting egg collection, and, in the parlor, a Swiss cuckoo clock. There are posters, prints, art objects, lace, and crocheted items. Those who are collectors themselves will find it a cheerful assembly, and the housekeeping is impeccable.

While the Fleur de Lis and Blue Bavarian rooms on the main floor share one bathroom, each room has a lighted makeup vanity (more inns should think of this!). The largest room, the Edelweiss, has two queen-sized beds and a spacious private bath with double sinks. Lila has decorated each of the five rooms individually using comforters and ruffled spreads, print and lace curtains, lots of pillows in velvet and eyelet, and romantic wallpapers.

Breakfast appointments are as colorful as the decor: pretty china, linen, and crystal. Typical of the fare is fresh fruit and juice, soft-boiled eggs, homemade muffins or cinnamon rolls or croissants and jam, and hot beverages.

How to get there: From San Bernardino, take Highway 18 to Lake Arrowhead turnoff, which is Highway 173. Follow signs to Lake Arrowhead. At the village, turn right at the only stoplight. Continue $1/5$ mile to the inn on the right.

Olive Metcalf

Union Hotel
& The Victorian Mansion
Los Alamos, California
93440

Innkeeper: Dick (Dick *only,* in all matters)
Address/Telephone: 362 Bell Street (mailing address: Box 616); (805) 344–2744
Rooms: 20; 14 in hotel, 3 with private bath, others with shared bath with sink in room; 6 in Mansion, all with private bath.
Rates: $80 to $100, double occupancy; $200, Victorian Mansion rooms; full breakfast.
Open: Hotel and restaurant open Friday, Saturday, Sunday all year; Victorian Mansion open every day.
Facilities and activities: Restaurant, saloon (available for private parties), swimming pool, Jacuzzi, pool table, table tennis, shuffleboard, rides around Los Alamos in 1918 White touring car. Nearby: historic Los Alamos, antiques shops, wineries. Fourteen miles to Solvang, largest Danish community in America.

Make no mistake about it, when you visit the Union Hotel you're in for a happening, not a quiet reverie. Owner Dick (he eschews a last name) keeps an entertaining place that one guest was heard describing as part inn and part theme park.

The hotel is his home, hobby, and occupation. Knowing this, you might feel it possibly rude to laugh when you walk in, but he's obviously decorated to get just that reaction. In the lobby you'll see red-flowered wallpaper, stuffed life-size fabric figures, and a copper bathtub in front of the fireplace, together with an astonishing collection of wonderful antique objects, like two-hundred-year-old Egyptian burial urns and funky furniture. The saloon has a great Old West feeling, with doors that came from a bordello and a bar Dick says is about 150 years old. After 9:00 P.M. it's closed to everyone except hotel guests.

Upstairs is a parlor for overnight guests with a pool table and an extensive library. Each bedroom is restored and furnished with brass fixtures, pedestal sinks, and a variety of china washbowls and pitchers and handmade quilts. In Union Hotel lingo, a room with a shared bath is a dry room; a wet room has a private bath.

And then for a completely different experience in lodging, you walk past the 1930s gas station (he'll be restoring it next) to Dick's Victorian Mansion. In this renovated Victorian house, you can choose a room and private bath designed for fantasy. Each theme room has appropriate background music, games, robes, and films for the VCR. If you're a fan of the '50s, here's your chance to sleep in a bed that's a '56 Cadillac convertible, listen to '50s rock 'n' roll, and run *Rebel Without a Cause*. Other fantasy themes available are Gypsy (the bed is a Gypsy wagon); Roman (a chariot bed, of course); Egyptian; Pirate; and French. Dick says the rooms are not decorated to shock. "I am the architect of my life as well as my eyes and what you see is the way I enjoy life."

Overnight guests can eat dinner together in the hotel's large dining room. Soup, salad, corn bread, chips, and salsa are served family style, followed by a main course such as Santa Maria–style barbecue boneless breast of chicken or shrimp.

The town of Los Alamos (it means "The Cottonwoods" in Spanish) is just a jog off Highway 101 and well worth a stop for a look back at the West of the 1880s. The way to see it in style is from one of Dick's original 1918 White touring cars.

How to get there: From Highway 101, exit at Los Alamos. Follow the road into town. Inn is on the right.

ప

J: *What has been missing at this wildly different inn? Why, a labyrinth, of course. So Dick now has a maze on the grounds (one of only three living adult mazes in the United States, he claims).*

Eastlake Inn
Los Angeles, California
90026

Innkeepers: Murray Burns and Planaria Price
Address/Telephone: 1442 Kellam Avenue; (213) 250–1620
Rooms: 9, including 2 suites; 6 with private bath and sitting area. No smoking inn.
Rates: $65 to $150, double occupancy; $49, single; breakfast. Special packages available.
Open: All year.
Facilities and activities: Special weekend celebrations planned by innkeepers. Nearby: walk to restaurants, Dodger Stadium, Music Center, Olvera Street, the Old Plaza, Echo Park Lake; minutes from central Los Angeles business district.

There is a Los Angeles lots of people don't know about: gracious old neighborhoods, houses that have survived since the 1800s, and tree-shaded streets where you actually *walk* places. Angelino Heights, the city's oldest suburb, is one of those areas making a comeback. The Eastlake Inn, built in 1887 as a duplex, sits on a hill in this first L.A. Historic Preservation zone.

Both innkeepers have years of historic preservation experience and have combined talents to restore the Victorian. From the spacious living and dining room, two stairways lead to the bedrooms upstairs. Two guest rooms are large, one with white wicker and a fireplace, the other with a romantic queen canopy bed and a pink velvet "fainting couch." Two tiny rooms fine for a solo traveler are

Tom Thumb and Thumbelina. The latter features an amazing trompe l'oeil painting (I love to write this phrase because I don't have the nerve to say it) creating the impression of an open door to a balcony overlooking a sea view. The two recently added suites are especially spacious and sunny. One, The Hummingbird, has a private entrance to the landscaped garden. This pretty area features a Greek Revival temple (remember, this is L.A.) and is a lovely wedding or party site.

Amenities for the business traveler are thoughtful ones. Besides fresh flowers, fruit, and a robe in my room, I appreciated being asked how early I'd like my coffee and morning paper. When I said I'd be working at the inn a few hours before going out, Murray showed me to a small library with a desk. The sitting room would be just as quiet and pleasant for work, but you could easily be distracted with the stereopticon, jigsaw puzzles, old and new books, and the Victorian costumes from Planaria's collection. All the rooms have antiques and curiosities of the period.

After a day of business or touring, afternoon wine and cheese in this setting is a change that refreshes. Maybe you'll want to take in a night game at Dodger Stadium. No need to get out the car—just walk over.

Don't miss Carroll Avenue, just behind the inn. The contrast between its row of restored Victorian homes and the sight of modern downtown Los Angeles beyond is a pleasing one, especially at dusk when the lights are coming on.

How to get there: Drive north on the Hollywood Freeway; exit at Echo Park/Glendale Boulevard. Make hard right on Bellevue to first stop sign, left onto Edgeware, left at Carroll (to see the Victorian houses). Turn right on Douglas and go 1 block to Kellam. Turn left; inn is last house on left at 1442 Kellam.

J: *When you call for reservations, be sure to ask if any special packages are available. These innkeepers are always coming up with some new adventure—like last year's St. Patrick's Day celebration, a chauffeured pub crawl of L.A.'s finest watering holes. Their latest brainstorm is a "Frequent Sleeper Club."*

Salisbury House
Los Angeles, California
90018

Innkeepers: Sue and Jay German

Address/Telephone: 2273 West 20th Street; (213) 737–7817 or (800) 373–1778

Rooms: 5, including an attic loft; 3 with private bath, some with air conditioning, all with fan. No smoking inn.

Rates: $75 to $100, double occupancy, full breakfast.

Open: All year.

Facilities and activities: Nearby: restaurants, downtown Los Angeles, Convention Center, freeways.

There's good news for travelers to downtown Los Angeles. Business people who never considered an inn are likely to reappraise their usual lodgings if they sample the comforts of Salisbury House. Not many hotel suites provide the ambience of leaded-glass windows, beamed ceilings, wood paneling, and a sitting room filled with antique pieces and cushy sofas and chairs.

This spacious 1909 California Craftsman house is in Arlington Heights, a quiet residential neighborhood regaining its former elegance. It's an oasis after a day of city bustle, yet it's only minutes from the Convention Center and downtown businesses. Actually, this is a good central location as a base camp for all of the Los Angeles basin.

Since our last visit, new innkeepers are ruling the roost. Without making any drastic changes, the Germans have been gradually doing what all innkeepers must—putting their own stamp on the house. The exterior has been freshly painted, and a baby grand piano has been added to the furnishings. The cozy common room is even more relaxing now with classical music on the stereo and a collection of books on art, museums, and music.

Each of the five guest rooms has a different feeling. They're comfortable rooms, with good beds and reading lights, as well as having pretty linens, lace curtains, and ceiling fans. There's the Victorian Rose room and a sunny garden room with a collection of garden books. The paneled attic suite is 600 square feet of privacy and charm with an antique claw-footed tub, game table, king-sized bed, and pine walls and floors. On the landing at the top of the stairway are a desk and a telephone for guests to use.

In the morning, Sue or Jay opens sliding wood-paneled doors and reveals the blue-and-white dining room with the table set for breakfast. At the sight of sparkling crystal and silver, fresh flowers, and pastel linen napkins on white lace, you're likely to wonder why you ever put up with a plastic hotel coffee shop.

Sue varies the breakfast buffet (as she does the table settings), but at our visit it held a bounty of mixed fresh fruits with praline cream, crepes Normandy, sausage, corn pudding, and boiled eggs in pretty blue-and-white egg cups.

How to get there: Take the Santa Monica Freeway (10) east to downtown. Go north on Western Avenue. Turn left onto West 20th Street; it's the first street. Inn is on your right at 2273 West 20th.

❀

J: *Early-morning jamoca almond coffee or herb tea and the newspapers is a pretty civilized way to start the day while you await breakfast. And you said you were dreading L.A.?*

olive Metcalf

Terrace Manor
Los Angeles, California
90006

Innkeepers: John and Joyce Elder
Address/Telephone: 1353 Alvarado Terrace; (213) 381–1478
Rooms: 5, including 1 suite; all with private bath, some with air conditioning. No smoking inn.
Rates: $70 to $100, double occupancy, full or continental breakfast. $20 for each additional person.
Open: All year.
Facilities and activities: Available for small parties and meetings, ample off-street parking. Nearby: Convention Center, Sports Arena, Coliseum, USC, Dodger Stadium, Chinatown, and the Music Center.

Alvarado Terrace is a Los Angeles surprise. Nestled between Pico and Hoover streets, it is one curved block of splendid turn-of-the-century houses, all registered as national historic landmarks. This is an L.A. few visitors even know exists, surrounded as it is by typical inner city streets. But Terrace Manor, along with its neighbors, is a beautiful house and enjoys great convenience to freeways and downtown.

It shakes a lot of preconceived notions about gaudy L.A. to step into this refined 1902 mansion with its original stained- and lead-glass windows, paneled walls, and gracious atmosphere. Each of the guest rooms is decorated in a fresh, tasteful style in deep, rich colors. Some antiques, brass beds, Victorian settees, and collections are used, but none of it is overdone. Our room was the Sun Room Suite, especially comfortable with an attached porch and a trundle bed making an airy sitting room.

The common rooms are fascinating (there's an Ionic-columned fireplace with a built-in clock that still chimes on cue) and handsomely furnished with period pieces. I was particularly drawn to an inviting paneled library off the living room with stunning windows of lead glass.

In addition to the pleasure of exploring this unique period house, you're going to be captivated by the innkeepers. John and Joyce are both from Scotland and have accents that leave no doubt. After years of working in large hotels, they're thrilled with this more personal style of innkeeping. Their enthusiasm for the house and their genuine delight in their guests are refreshingly apparent.

The Elders are thoughtful hosts who know L.A. well. They're ready to tell you what's going on in town that's new and make any reservations you may need. They can also make arrangements for business luncheons at the inn. A very special perk they can arrange is an entree to Hollywood's famed Magic Castle. This stylish private club offers both a glamorous place to dine in the Hollywood hills and an opportunity to see outstanding magic acts.

John (who is also the chef at Culver Studios) and Joyce offer guests a choice between a light continental breakfast—fresh fruits, juice and pastries—or a full cooked meal. The menu changes daily, but some of their specialties are stuffed French toast, banana/strawberry pancakes, and the Terrace Manor Breakfast of eggs, sausages, and toast.

How to get there: From LAX Airport take Century Boulevard east about 8 miles to Harbor Freeway (10) west. Immediately get into left-hand lane for Pico off-ramp. On Pico, turn left (west) to Alvarado Terrace; turn left to the inn.

J: *In case you should get a bit lost in the Scottish brogue, John says not to worry. He says, when needed, he can sound more American as easily as "swapping change."*

olive Metcalf

San Ysidro Ranch
Montecito, California
93108

Innkeeper: William Shoaf, general manager
Address/Telephone: 900 San Ysidro Lane; (805) 969–5046, fax (805) 565–1995
Rooms: 44; all with private bath, television, telephone, fireplace, porch, and stocked refrigerator.
Rates: $195 to $375 for cottage rooms; $425 to $625 for cottages with private Jacuzzi; double occupancy, breakfast included with Sunday-through-Thursday night stays. Two-night minimum on weekends.
Open: All year.
Facilities and activities: Breakfast, lunch, dinner, Sunday brunch. Horses, guided rides, swimming pool, tennis courts, golf.

Meanwhile, back at the ranch, things are changing. The San Ysidro has been around since 1893, always a premier hideaway and favorite of celebrities and writers. I admit being worried when I heard about its new corporate ownership, but the blue business suits have wisely not changed the unique feeling at this gorgeously situated inn. There are more elegant room appointments now—televisions, telephones, and fresh decor—but I was relieved to see the ranch has not gone California chic. Those infamous cheery signs announcing "I am a Catalpa Tree," or "late check-outs will be charged an arm and a leg" have disappeared, but the special low-key ambience, elegant but not slick, still prevails.

Admittedly, the San Ysidro is not inexpensive, but I think

you'd have the curiosity of a turnip if you didn't want to see the place where John and Jacqueline Kennedy honeymooned, where Laurence Olivier and Vivien Leigh married, and where Winston Churchill and John Galsworthy relaxed and wrote.

Privacy, in a setting of great natural beauty, was and still is the story of the ranch's appeal. The soft foothills of the Santa Ynez Mountains offer miles of riding trails with breathtaking views. You can disappear into one of the cottages and not see another soul for days, though the innkeepers claim if a guest doesn't come out for twenty-four hours, they do force-feeding.

There is no typical room in the buildings scattered around the lush grounds. Some are parlor suites with patio or deck; some are individual cottages nestled here and there. They're not all equally spiffy, it must be admitted. There's the odd piece of antique plumbing or worn upholstery, but luxury appointments aren't what has attracted people here for so long.

A kind of "we're all country gentlemen here" atmosphere is also part of the charm. Take the stocked refrigerators in every room that serve as honor bars. Mix your own and keep tabs. Very upper class, don't you think?

One other major lure is the outstanding food at the Stonehouse Restaurant. From alfresco breakfasts on the deck to candlelit continental dinners in the beautiful white-stuccoed dining room, the cuisine ranges from Western to sophisticated. The manager calls it "American Regional." The important thing is that its reputation attracts even diners who aren't ranch guests.

How to get there: From Highway 101, take San Ysidro Road exit in Montecito, 4 miles south of Santa Barbara. Follow signs to San Ysidro Ranch, 2 miles toward the mountains.

J: *John Galsworthy wrote, of San Ysidro Ranch, "The loveliness of these evenings moves the heart; and of the mornings, shining, cool fragrant."*

Olive Metcalf

Doryman's Inn
Newport Beach, California
92663

Innkeeper: Michael Palitz
Address/Telephone: 2102 West Ocean Front; (714) 675–7300
Rooms: 10; all with private bath, fireplace, television, and air conditioning.
Rates: $135 to $275, double occupancy, extended continental breakfast.
Open: All year.
Facilities and activities: Directly across from Newport Pier, swimming, sail-
boarding, deep-sea fishing, largest pleasure craft harbor in the world.
Bicycle rentals, off-street parking available. Nearby: restaurants, water-
front shops, cabarets.

If you get up very early here, you'll see traditional small boats
of the commercial Dory Fishing Fleet returning from the sea with
their catch. For nearly one hundred years they've supplied fresh
fish for sale in the open-air market at McFadden Wharf, Newport
Pier area. It's now one of California's designated historic landmarks.

Such a humble basis for Newport's origins contrasts sharply
with the opulence of Doryman's Inn. The bed and breakfast is on
the second floor of a modest red brick building that dates from the
1920s. The Rex restaurant occupies the first floor (inn guests can
order meals sent to their rooms), but a private elevator whisks you
to the inn's lobby upstairs.

Victorian is the motif and resoundingly elegant is the atmosphere. But elegance is not surprising when you consider that it

took five years and a couple of million dollars to renovate and decorate the ten rooms. There's ample use of polished oak and brass for staircases and doors, hand-stenciled trim on ceiling borders, luxurious carpets, and etched-glass light globes.

The romantically decorated bedrooms are furnished with antiques and elaborate beds. Some are brass; others have carved headboards or canopied four-posters. There are matching floral draperies and quilted bedspreads, lace curtains, ruffled pillow shams, gilt-edged beveled mirrors, and plants. Each room has a gas fireplace turned on with the flick of a wall switch, and perhaps a porcelain animal sits on the hearth.

Should this setting sound too austere for your taste, I recommend you proceed to the bathroom, where you'll find a taste of extravagant luxury. Tubs are sunken Italian marble—two with Jacuzzis—highlighted by sun streaming in from fern-filled skylights.

Guests can see each other in the parlor for breakfast, but it's not hard to see why many opt for enjoying it in the privacy of their rooms. Or you might prefer the blue-tiled roof deck with its unobstructed views of the pier and the Pacific. International coffees and teas are served along with fresh pastries, seasonal fresh fruits, brown eggs, and juice.

How to get there: From Highway 405 (San Diego Freeway), take Highway 55 to Newport Boulevard. Continue to 32nd Street, and turn right. Turn left on Balboa Boulevard; bear right at signs to Newport Pier. Inn is on right at 2102 West Ocean Front.

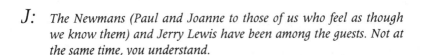

J: *The Newmans (Paul and Joanne to those of us who feel as though we know them) and Jerry Lewis have been among the guests. Not at the same time, you understand.*

olive Metcalf

La Maida House
North Hollywood, California
91601

Innkeeper: Megan Timothy

Address/Telephone: 11159 La Maida Street; (818) 769–3857

Rooms: 11, 4 in main house, 7 in bungalows; all with private bath and some spa baths; telephones. No smoking, no fur clothing on premises.

Rates: $80 to $210, double occupancy, continental breakfast and evening aperitif. Two-night minimum stay; one-night reservations accepted depending on availability.

Open: All year.

Facilities and activities: Dinner and pretheater supper available by prior arrangement. Pool, gym, masseuse by appointment. Nearby: Universal Studios, Beverly Hills, downtown Los Angeles, shopping, Hollywood/Burbank Airport, restaurants.

No matter how splendid a stay you have at La Maida House—and I don't see how you could avoid it—you're going to leave feeling like an underachiever after meeting Megan Timothy. She's turned a derelict 1920s Italianate mansion into a luxury inn that rises above the valley bungalows and exudes elegance, inside and out. The two black swans that used to cruise over a pond outside the drawing room proved to be too noisy and have been replaced with lilies, but the tone is the same: old-style Hollywood glamour.

The formidable talents Ms. Timothy brings to innkeeping start with her design skills. The stunning decor in every room and the ninety-seven original stained-glass windows (and an exquisite shower door) throughout the house are remarkable.

Then there are her professional-caliber cooking skills. Megan grows all the herbs and much of the fruit and vegetables she serves. Timothy standards are high, even for the continental breakfasts she serves her guests. "Every innkeeper should invest in a first-rate juice machine," she declares. Hers is one that can make juice out of everything but the *Los Angeles Times.*

No other meals are served regularly, but everything is possible. Megan will prepare an intimate dinner for two to four, served in a second-floor balcony overlooking the garden or an alfresco meal on an outside patio off the main dining room. She'll do an elegant dinner for eight around a glass-topped table in a solarium dining room, or a formal affair in the candlelit, chandeliered dining room with seating for thirty-two at round tables covered with peach linen. This is a Limoges and crystal affair, you understand, not California pottery. The food, custom planned to your wishes, is as beautiful as the surroundings, and *everything* is made from scratch.

From the entryway with its graceful staircase to the handsome drawing room with grand piano, Carrara marble fireplace, and polished oak floors, this flower-filled house is a pleasure. Every bedroom is a knockout and has all the comforts you might need: robes, bath toiletries, even crocheted lap throws made by Megan's mother. Bungalow accommodations are as comfortable and glamorous as those in the mansion. Several suites have fireplaces and private patios with fountains, a perfect place to hide out and write your screenplay. Release the tension between creative bouts with a stroll to the pool area with its plant-filled cabana.

How to get there: The inn is close to a cross section of freeways, and directions depend upon where you're coming from. Megan advises it is much less confusing to call the inn and let them give you specific directions.

J: *It's no wonder the guest list includes movers and shakers; this is a class act in personalized Hollywood digs.*

olive Metcalf

Ojai Manor Hotel
Ojai, California
93023

Innkeeper: Mary Nelson
Address/Telephone: 210 East Matilija Street; (805) 646–0961
Rooms: 6 share 3 baths.
Rates: $80 to $90, double occupancy, continental breakfast and complimentary wine.
Open: All year.
Facilities and activities: Walk to Ojai shops, galleries, restaurants. Nearby: golf, tennis, Wheeler Hot Springs Mineral Baths, music festivals, Shakespeare Festival, hiking, camping in surrounding mountains, fishing in Lake Casitas, bike path from Ojai to Foster Park.

Travelers on the California coast who dash between San Francisco and Los Angeles and fail to explore some of the more obscure places in between are missing copious treasures. The beautiful Ojai Valley is one of the jewels.

Imagine a small-town version of Santa Barbara's Spanish architecture, Carmel's artists and galleries, and San Francisco's smart shops. Bless it with Los Angeles weather (but with sparkling clean air), and you have the lovely little town of Ojai, population 6,325.

Comfortably settled into Mary Nelson's inn, you'll have no need for a car to get anywhere in town. But you should take some of the scenic drives around the area: up Dennison Grade for memorable vistas of the abundant valley; up Sulphur Mountain Road for spectacular views of the Pacific Ocean on one side, the Ojai Valley on the other. Other big attractions close to town are the hot mineral baths at Wheeler Hot Springs and their highly recommended restaurant.

Mary and her late partner, artist Boyd Wright, restored the oldest building in town as a fresh, inviting inn. In 1874 it was a school in the heart of this agricultural community. Now the polished oak floors and the pale lavender–gray-white walls are an intriguing background for Wright's contemporary art pieces—many of them large and dramatic. Guests get to enjoy a fascinating home gallery.

The colorful living room has a beautiful oriental rug and an Art Deco–looking blue plush sofa and club chair by the fireplace. Adjoining it is a sunny dining room with a long table where Mary serves a generous continental breakfast. This day it was juice, fresh raspberries, and a variety of her freshly baked breads and muffins with preserves and cream cheese.

The six fresh bedrooms upstairs feature the best-looking beds you'll find anywhere. It must be those oversized down pillows and fine linens! What a luxury for people who like to prop up in bed and read—and there are good lights on both sides of the bed, too.

Mary cautions guests to be sure to call ahead for reservations. This is a one-person show and a drop-by during the week could miss Mary.

How to get there: About one hour south of Santa Barbara on Highway 101, take Lake Casitas exit, Highway 150, east to Ojai—a beautiful drive. At Libby Park in town center, turn left 1 block to East Matilija.

J: *Be sure you walk to Bart's Corner, a unique tree-shaded outdoor meeting place, garden, and used-book store. Books are everywhere, even outside the fence. A plaque at the gate sets the tone: "When closed please throw coins in slot in door for the amount marked on the book. Thank you."*

Olive Metcalf

Villa Royale
Palm Springs, California
92264

Innkeepers: Monika and Stephen Maitland-Lewis
Address/Telephone: 1620 Indian Trail; (619) 327–2314, fax (619) 322–4151
Rooms: 31 suites and rooms; all with private bath, television, telephone, and
   some with fireplace, kitchenette, and private spa. Limited wheelchair
   access.
Rates: $75 to $300, double occupancy, continental breakfast. Lower sum-
   mer rates and for longer stays.
Open: All year.
Facilities and activities: Restaurant serves lunch and dinner; full bar and piano
   lounge. Two swimming pools, bicycles, spas, courtyards with fountains, outdoor fireplaces. Nearby: golf, tennis, horseback riding, Palm
   Springs shops, restaurants, aerial tramway ride up Mt. San Jacinto.

Only a few blocks from slick downtown Palm Springs with
glamorous big hotels lining the main drag, a heartwarming alternative lies low on the desert plain just waiting to beguile you. Everything conspires at Villa Royale to make you think you're in an old
European resort. Winding brick paths connect a series of courtyards
with ancient-looking pillars under the red-tile roofs of surrounding
rooms. Everywhere there are shade trees and pots of flowers, exotic
vines and palms, small gardens and fountains. And on my March
visit, the cascading bougainvillea was dazzling.

From the blazing Palm Springs sun, you step into a lobby/sit-
ting room with a cool brick floor and squashy sofa and chairs. Just

outside the door in the courtyard are bicycles ready for guests to borrow for sightseeing around the quiet residential streets or touring the shopping plazas. The kitchen will pack you a picnic basket to take along on request. Owners Monika and Stephen, along with a well-trained staff, are always ready to help. There aren't just *two* bikes; there are lots of them. You don't get just *one* extra towel for the pool; you get big thick ones, as many as you need.

The variety of accommodations at Villa Royale is only one of its attractions. Whether you take a standard guest room or splurge on a deluxe studio with kitchenette, private patio, and spa, all the colorful ambience of flowers, fountains, and dramatic views of the San Jacinto Mountains is available to everyone. Every room, large or small, is decorated in an individual international style, the result of the former owners' frequent buying trips to Europe. Each one has interesting treasures: woven hangings and table covers, wall carvings, bright pottery, sculpture, pillows, and antique furniture. The inn's facilities are not well suited to children.

Across the first courtyard is the dining room with a glass-enclosed casual area where breakfast is served looking out at the pool. The brick floor extends into a more formal interior room with a wonderful feeling. Armchairs with rush seats and cushions surround tables skirted with dark floral cloths to the floor and topped with lighter color linen. The walls are a rosy adobe, and the soft lighting, beautiful china, and glassware create an atmosphere I would like to get used to. Our dinner was an attractively presented, relaxing experience: tortellini soup, green salad, scampi, and a marvelous fresh mango sherbet with fresh peaches and raspberries.

Visually rich as days are here relaxing in the sunshine surrounded with colorful flowers, wait 'til you see it at night! Dozens of small ornate brass lanterns hanging from trees and vines gleam with tiny lights and cast light and shadows throughout the courtyards. If you aren't enchanted, check your pulse.

How to get there: Proceed through downtown Palm Springs on its main street, North Palm Canyon. When it becomes East Palm Canyon, look for Indian Trail, just past Indian Avenue. Turn left to the inn on your right.

The Cheshire Cat
Santa Barbara, California
93101

Innkeepers: Chris Dunstan, owner; Midge Goeden, manager
Address/Telephone: 36 West Valerio Street; (805) 569–1610
Rooms: 12; all with private bath, telephone, and some with fireplace, patio, or spa. No smoking inn.
Rates: $89 to $195, double occupancy, generous continental breakfast and wine and cheese hour Saturday evenings. No credit cards.
Open: All year.
Facilities and activities: Bicycles, spa, meeting room with fireplace for groups of up to twenty. Nearby: walk only 4 blocks to Santa Barbara restaurants, shops, theaters.

Chris Dunstan knew exactly what she wanted to accomplish when she began restoring two elegant Victorian houses: simply to create a showplace among Santa Barbara inns. By George, I think she's done it! Inside and out, The Cheshire Cat looks as pretty as if a Victorian set designer had put it all together.

Ms. Dunstan's theme, beginning with the inn's name, is "Alice in Wonderland." A set of porcelain figurines representing characters from the story sits on an antique desk in the living room, and most of the rooms are named for the characters. If all this sounds too cute for words, let me tell you it's gorgeously done.

The finest Laura Ashley prints in fabric and wallpaper are used throughout the house as the background for beautiful English antique furniture. How can you resist an atmosphere of high ceilings and fresh flowers, where the glow of polished wood vies with the sparkle of beveled glass? How genteel.

Every room is a stunner with Ashley print bed linens and coordinated drapes and wall coverings. Color schemes have to be described as delicious: the Caterpillar Suite in rose, moss green, and stone; Mad Hatter in plum and cream; Alice's Suite in ivory and pink, which has a private patio overlooking an oak tree, gardens, and mountains.

A flower-filled brick patio with a white gazebo separates the two houses. White chairs and round tables are dressed for breakfast in pink cloths. Add Wedgwood china in the "Wild Strawberry" pattern and you have a scene as engaging as a stage setting. A beautiful continental breakfast is set out around a palm tree in the center of the courtyard: fresh fruits, fresh croissants, homemade jams and granola, yogurt, tea, and just-ground coffee.

Take a look at the professionally equipped kitchen. Cooking classes with notable chefs were offered here for a time. (They're not at present. Too bad. Maybe they'll start again.) Arriving guests will find another kind of treat—Bailey's Irish Cream liqueur and fresh chocolates from a local chocolatier waiting in their room.

How to get there: From Highway 101 going through Santa Barbara, take Mission Street toward the mountains, turning south onto State Street for 3 blocks, then right on Valerio to number 36.

Olive Metcalf

Harbour Carriage House
Santa Barbara, California
93103

Innkeeper: Kimberly Pegram

Address/Telephone: 420 West Montecito Street; (805) 962–8447 or (800) 594–4633

Rooms: 9; all with private bath, most with fireplace, some with telephone. Wheelchair access. Smoking on outdoor patios and balconies only.

Rates: $85 to $185, double occupancy, full breakfast and early evening refreshment. $10 each additional person. Two-night minimum weekends and holidays.

Open: All year.

Facilities and activities: Television in main house living room, gardens of two historic homes. Nearby: 3 blocks to beach; short drive to shopping, art galleries, restaurants, Mission Santa Barbara.

The Santa Barbara you see in your mind probably has sun shining on sparkling blue water, red-tile roofs capping white stucco buildings, and flowers blooming everywhere. That's an accurate picture of this lovely city much of the time, but not the raw March afternoon we checked into Harbour Carriage House. We were shown upstairs to an attractive, spacious room, where my eyes went directly to the laid fire ready to be lit and plenty of extra logs on the hearth.

An hour later I was ready to take in the other comforts the room offered. Sitting in one of a pair of wingback chairs by the fireplace, sipping a restorative sherry and listening to the room radio (already tuned to a "good music" station), I saw I was in a delightful spot indeed. The feeling was Country French, with an antique pine dresser and queen-sized bed and French doors opening to a small balcony. There were good reading lights on either side of the bed and a selection of current magazines. Even on a chilly winter day, Santa Barbara can still charm you with its flowers. A fresh bouquet in the room was outshone by a jasmine vine that wrapped the outside stairway leading to the room. Just opening the door let in its intoxicating aroma.

The Harbour Carriage House has four accommodations in the main house and five in the newer Carriage House, each one more appealing than the last. A garret room called Lily of the Valley overlooks the gardens and is especially large. It has a pair of settees and a daybed in addition to a king-sized bed. The Magnolia Blossom has a grand mountain view and a spa tub for two. And if you want it all, the Forget-Me-Not has a mountain view from the canopied bed and a private balcony, fireplace, and spa for two.

Breakfast is served in a setting bound to please even a morning grouch: a solarium with tall windows looking out at the garden. Tables set for two or four are covered with crisp white linen cloths and colorful pottery. That morning's menu was fresh fruit with a yogurt topping, piping hot muffins, and a hot entree of baked eggs, cheese, and vegetables. And for a sweet finish, a crumble cake with raspberry sauce. Coffee, tea, and juices, of course.

How to get there: On Highway 101 northbound take Cabrillo Boulevard/Beach exit. Go left on Cabrillo about 3 miles; right on Castillo Street for 2 blocks; left on West Montecito Street for half a block to number 420 on the right. Southbound on 101, take Castillo Street exit; go right on Castillo 1 block, right on West Montecito to number 420.

olive Metcalf

The Old Yacht Club Inn
and The Hitchcock House
Santa Barbara, California
93103

Innkeepers: Lucille Caruso, Nancy Donaldson, and Sandy Hunt
Address/Telephone: 431 Corona Del Mar; (805) 962–1277 or (800) 549–1676
   in California, (800) 676–1676 outside California; fax (805) 962–3989
Rooms: 5 in Old Yacht Club, 4 in Hitchcock House; all with private bath and
   telephone. No smoking inn.
Rates: $75 to $120 at Old Yacht Club; $95 to $135 at Hitchcock House; double occupancy, full breakfast. Extra person $25.
Open: All year.
Facilities and activities: Dinner by reservation, usually weekends. Bicycles
   provided. Nearby: half a block to beach; restaurants, swimming, fishing, sailing, tennis, golf.

After the first clubhouse of Santa Barbara's Yacht Club was
swept out to sea during a terrible storm in the 1920s, this house
served as the headquarters. The name seemed a perfect choice
when it became Santa Barbara's first bed and breakfast inn. It does
sit a mere half a block from the waterfront, but there's nothing
nautical about it.

It's a 1912 Craftsman-style house, which means it has the period charm of a wide, covered front porch and balconies and dormers
that provide charming, light-filled rooms. One of the upstairs bed-

rooms at the Old Yacht Club has a built-in window seat—surely one of the most appealing details a room can have; another has a whirlpool tub. They're decorated with an old-fashioned, personal touch and accented with fresh flowers and decanters of sherry. It always makes me particularly happy to find good lights over every bed (and these, as Nancy says, have "real bulbs") and extra pillows and blankets.

Hitchcock House is just next door, a good choice for privacy. Its four large rooms have the advantages of sitting areas plus private baths *and* private entrances. These are especially personal rooms, since each of the three innkeepers decorated a room to reflect her heritage. The Italian Room, for instance, has the trunks that came with the immigrants from Europe, family photographs, and other treasures.

Downstairs at the Old Yacht Club, guests of both houses are welcome to enjoy the warm atmosphere of antiques and oriental rugs and to join in sherry or tea by the fire. An exceptional breakfast is served here in the dining room: freshly ground coffee, juice, fresh fruit, home-baked breads, and interesting omelets (maybe spinach or zucchini). These innkeepers maintain their Santa Barbara omelet is the best.

Check the dinner schedule with the innkeepers when booking your room. Most weekends (and for special events) Nancy Donaldson does a five-course candlelit dinner, by reservation, that could be the highlight of your visit. She's a professional member of the American Wine and Food Institute and loves to cook. Home-made fettuccine, Artichokes Athena, halibut Florentine, and Chocolate Decadence are some of her specialties. *Bon Appetit* says, "Her five course meals . . . rival the finest the city has to offer."

How to get there: From Highway 101, exit on Cabrillo Boulevard, follow 1 mile west toward the ocean. Pass bird refuge to Corona Del Mar, the street between Sheraton Hotel and Cabrillo Inn Motel. Turn right to 431.

J: *It's great to see even longtime innkeepers, as these three are, not getting blasé but still looking for ways to make their guests comfortable. One of them is always on duty to provide the warmest possible hospitality.*

Olive Metcalf

The Parsonage
Santa Barbara, California
93101

Innkeeper: Hilde Michelmore
Address/Telephone: 1600 Olive Street; (805) 962–9336
Rooms: 6, including 1 suite; all with private bath. Wheelchair access. Smoking discouraged.
Rates: $85 to $160 for suite, double occupancy, full breakfast. Two-night minimum on weekends.
Open: All year.
Facilities and activities: Sun deck. Nearby: restaurants, shopping, theaters, walk to Mission Santa Barbara.

If ever the talk about splitting California into northern and southern states is seriously considered, you can bet that the custody battle over Santa Barbara will be ferocious. Both sides would fight to keep this lush, distinctly Mediterranean city.

From The Parsonage, one of Santa Barbara's many notable Victorian houses, you can explore a host of the city's attractions on foot. The inn is nestled between the mountains and the downtown area in a quiet residential neighborhood. This splendid Queen Anne was built in 1892 as a parsonage for the Trinity Episcopal Church. It's now home and business to Hilde Michelmore, who has restored and decorated it with her impressive collection of antiques and rugs.

The minister's library on the first floor is now the Rosebud

Room in pinks and mauves and furnished with antiques. The Versailles, with Louis XIV decor, is another main-floor room. You might appreciate having immediate access to an attractive living room with a fireplace and oversize sofa. A large iron baker's rack filled with books and plants decorates one wall, and there's a small television. I wonder what the long-ago cleric would think of the unusual lilac-and-green Chinese rug that now decorates his Victorian sitting room. It's memorable!

At the top of the redwood staircase are four uniquely decorated rooms. There's the Peacock Room, with exotic blues and greens in comforter and oriental rug; the Lavender and Lace Room; and Las Flores, with a bay window looking out at the ocean. The Honeymoon Suite runs the entire length of the house. It comprises a bedroom, a solarium (old-fashioned sun porch), and an enormous bathroom with a handsome pedestal sink and footed tub. It has a king-sized canopied bed and an antique armoire. The views from here of mountains, ocean, and city are quite spectacular.

A formal dining room with a graceful bay window, or a sunny deck and gazebo with more outstanding views are equally pleasant spots for breakfast. Hilde serves a large one, with favorites like scrambled eggs, quiche, or French toast.

How to get there: Driving south on Highway 101, exit at Mission Street east toward The Mission. Turn right on Laguna Street; turn left to Olive Street. Driving north on 101, exit at Milpas Street; cross town to Olive Street. Turn right.

olive Metcalf

Simpson House Inn
Santa Barbara, California
93101

Innkeepers: Glyn and Linda Davies; Gillean Wilson
Address/Telephone: 121 East Arrellaga Street; (805) 963–7067 or (800) 676–1280
Rooms: 6 in main house, plus 4 suites in barn; all with private bath. No smoking inn.
Rates: $75 to $185, double occupancy, full breakfast and afternoon tea or wine. Ask about business and winter rates.
Open: All year.
Facilities and activities: Croquet on lawns, gardens, bicycles, attractive neighborhood to walk. Nearby: Santa Barbara attractions: beach, Santa Barbara Mission, shopping plazas, restaurants, museums, theaters, and galleries.

Now that B&B inns have become commonplace to U.S. travelers, Victoriana may be a style genre you've had quite enough of, thank you. What you may not know is that "Victorian charm" does not necessarily mean a suffocating hodgepodge of dark furniture and knickknacks. There are also distinguished houses like Simpson House—spacious, airy, handsomely decorated, and meticulously maintained.

Simpson House sits in a beautiful neighborhood close to downtown Santa Barbara on an acre of fine old trees, with an English garden as background. It has received a Structure of Merit award for its unique 1874 architecture (Eastlake-style Victorian) and is considered by many to be one of Southern California's finest Victorian homes. That it survived the developers and thrives as an inn today is a testament to the perseverance of Glyn and Linda Davies. "We just couldn't bear the thought of this place being torn down," Linda says.

Instead of restoring and decorating the historic home as an inn in one bold stroke, the Davieses had years of research and work ahead after buying the house in 1976. Then there was a wrenching battle over zoning restrictions. But what a difference it makes when a house is loved like one of the family rather than just a business. Every corner tells the tale of careful, well-planned work and a dedication to quality. The result is the kind of mellow look that is only achieved when treasures are acquired gradually. Much of the furniture was brought back from trips to England.

The guest rooms are all different in mood, but each is elegantly appointed with European goosedown comforters, fine linen, and fresh bouquets. Several rooms open to a large private deck overlooking the gardens. Even here, there are large tubs of blooming flowers. By this reading, four deluxe suites will have been completed in the restored barn. Downstairs, the sitting room with its fireplace and book-lined walls and the large formal dining room have French doors opening to the garden verandas. Teak floors, white wicker furniture, and the aromas of wisteria and orange blossoms create a nostalgic atmosphere.

Our breakfast served out here was a pleasure we extended as long as possible. A help-yourself buffet offered big glass containers of terrific homemade granola and other cereals, plus yogurt, milk, and raisins. Then came just-squeezed juice and a fruit compote. I was halfway through the crossword puzzle and feeling quite well fed when thick French toast topped with fresh, chunky applesauce appeared, accompanied by a basket of hot blueberry bran muffins and yet another pot of coffee.

Admittedly, it was an idyllic March morning in Santa Barbara, but it will be a long time before I'll forget breakfast on this wisteria-draped veranda.

How to get there: From Highway 101 as it rounds Santa Barbara, turn right on East Arrellaga Street if heading north; turn left if heading south, off Mission Street. Follow it east 1 block past State Street. Turn right on Anacapa Street 4 blocks, then left on Arrellaga ½ block.

Olive Metcalf

The Tiffany Inn
Santa Barbara, California
93101

Innkeepers: Carol and Larry MacDonald
Address/Telephone: 1323 De La Vina Street; (805) 963–2283
Rooms: 7; 5 with private bath and fireplace, 2 with Jacuzzi. No smoking inn.
Rates: $75 to $175, double occupancy, full breakfast and evening refreshments. Reduced rates in winter season; two-night minimum on weekends.
Open: All year.
Facilities and activities: Walking distance to many restaurants, shops. Nearby: Santa Barbara Mission, Stearn's Wharf, mountains, beach, museums, galleries, theaters, local wineries.

Some inns are just so outlandishly pretty that the good breakfast they serve, their convenient location, the way they pamper you with style are all lagniappes—wonderful extras. The Tiffany Inn scores high on all those counts, but the first thing you're going to notice is what a beautiful, enchantingly decorated house it is.

This stately 1898 Victorian that Carol and Larry have restored so lovingly and authentically is a picture-perfect setting for the collection of fine furniture and antiques that they've acquired over the years. The ambience begins with the genuine articles—glowing dark wood, colonial diamond-paned bay windows, a century-old wood staircase, and a bathroom with all the original fixtures.

What Carol MacDonald has done is make the antique background stunning by lavishly decorating with the finest colorful fabrics, artfully arranging her splendid furniture, and then maintaining it all immaculately.

I couldn't choose a favorite among the upstairs bedrooms. They each have a romantic feeling and delicious appointments: rockers placed to look out at mountains or garden, lace curtains at French windows, elegant bed linens, and a wood-burning fireplace in several.

The impeccable garden is as Victorian in atmosphere as is the house. It's a lovely place to relax, or you might enjoy the wicker chaise on the old-fashioned lattice-covered porch.

I would love to see the house when the MacDonalds and son David decorate it for Christmas. They offer a low holiday rate then to encourage guests to come and stay while doing their Christmas shopping in Santa Barbara—where there's some of the greatest shopping anywhere. The idea sounds appealing to me. Shop all day, have dinner at one of Santa Barbara's outstanding restaurants, and return to the richly decorated inn for wine or a grog in the elegant parlor around the fire. Retire for the night to your beautiful cozy room and dream of no-limit Visa Land. Next morning, after breakfasting, perhaps on the veranda overlooking the garden, on fresh fruits, muffins, and an entree of artichoke quiche or strawberry crepes or maybe banana bacon waffles, you'll be ready to hit the shops again.

How to get there: From Highway 101 through Santa Barbara, exit at Mission Street. Drive east to De La Vina Street and turn right. Inn is on the right at number 1323.

The Seal Beach Inn and Gardens
Seal Beach, California
90740

Innkeeper: Marjorie Bettenhausen

Address/Telephone: 212 Fifth Street; (213) 493–2416, or fax (213) 799–0483

Rooms: 24, including 14 suites; all with private bath and television, many with small kitchen. Smoking only on patios.

Rates: $98 to $155, double occupancy, breakfast. $10 each additional guest. Ask about weekend package rates off season.

Open: All year.

Facilities and activities: Gardens, pool, wedding or small business facilities; special picnic baskets and package getaways by reservation. Nearby: short walk to beach; Old Town restaurants, boutiques, bistros; easy freeway access to L.A., airports, Disneyland, Convention Center.

If ambience could be packaged, I would like to market the kind of feeling Seal Beach Inn and Gardens exudes. Potential guests might doubt my claims that you can find a gentle, old-world atmosphere of wrought-iron balconies and flower-filled patios just a jog off several major freeways, but it's true. Not a hint of plastic or slick California chic touches this quiet, utterly charming hideaway.

Seal Beach enjoys an enviable low profile; it's even missing from many maps of the area. The quaint old town with its clean beach and pier are a surprise to Southern California visitors expecting the usual commercial sprawl. I took an early morning walk past tile-roofed bungalows to the beach and shared the waves for a time with only two windsurfers and the sea gulls.

The inn was built in the 1920s. The Bettenhausens found it and began a restoration in 1977. They imported crates of antiques from Europe—a 2,000-pound iron fountain from Paris, old murals, seventeenth-century iron gates—and put the inn together with a light touch. The look is mostly French-Mediterranean, but there is no "decorated" look, and nothing is predictable. Rooms and baths range from tiny to large. In my Royal Villa room I slept in a bed from the John Barrymore estate surrounded by lace curtains, big easy chairs, and oriental carpets. Like many of the rooms, this one had a sitting area, kitchenette, and eating area.

But it's the color of brilliant flowers that you'll remember. They bloom in profusion around the brick courtyard and in pots lining the steps, and exotic vines spill over the railings and balconies. Little wonder that this romantic setting makes the inn a favorite choice for weddings. The inn does an outstanding job of catering parties and has seven lavishly decorated bridal suites.

I ate breakfast in a sunny tea room adjoining a downstairs library/sitting room. Both rooms open to a snug patio. Platters of ripe fruit, cereals, breads, and pastries seemed just right with the never-ending supply of excellent coffee, but an egg casserole dish was also fresh from the oven and too good to pass up.

How to get there: Exit the San Diego Freeway (405) at Seal Beach Boulevard going south. Turn right on Pacific Coast Highway and left on Fifth Street to the inn on the left.

J: *I chatted at breakfast with a couple from Texas in town for business appointments. We all felt pretty smug about making Los Angeles business travel this pleasant.*

olive Metcalf

Venice Beach House
Venice, California
90291

Innkeeper: Betty Lou Weiner
Address/Telephone: 15 Thirtieth Avenue; (310) 823–1966
Rooms: 9; 5 with private bath, all with cable television. No smoking inn.
Rates: $85 to $165, double occupancy, hearty continental breakfast.
Open: All year.
Facilities and activities: Nearby: walk to swimming beach, Venice Pier; close
  to Los Angeles Airport, restaurants, shops.

Abbot Kinney bought this stretch of California coast at the
turn of the century with a slightly wacky but grandiose vision of re-
creating Venice, Italy: canals, elegant hotels, boardwalks, piers, and
cultural events—and he did it. "Kinney's Folly" was a success for
more than thirty years before it fell out of fashion.

This gray-shingled beach house was built a half-block from the
beach in 1911, the heyday of Venice, by Warren Wilson, a wealthy
newspaper publisher. Two of his eight daughters married Kinney
sons, and the house was filled with family for many years. It's that
kind of house still—big and friendly.

Now that the '60s hippie encampment is past, Venice is having
a revival of popularity. The beach is clean for swimming, property
values have skyrocketed, and the boardwalk is lively with shops,
tourists, and roller skaters.

Once you're over the age of sixteen, it's probably best to dip into the exotic scenes of Los Angeles beach life from a base that is utterly sane, even conventional. This house is a quiet, tasteful retreat that will welcome you back when you've had enough "colorful sights."

The living room is restful in shades of rose and mauve with a beautiful antique oriental rug in those shades, comfortable furniture, and a fireplace. Bedrooms are romantically decorated with fabric over padded walls, and there are fine bathrooms. One has a deep tiled shower with dueling shower heads at either side of the shower, one has a Jacuzzi tub for two, and another has two gilded claw-footed tubs.

A sheltered veranda or the cheerful sun room adjoining the living room are the breakfast spots. Fruits, cereals, hot breads, home-baked coffee cakes, tea, and coffee are set out to help yourself. You sit at small, round tables covered with flowered skirts. Outside the bay window are pink hibiscus and a bit of ocean view.

How to get there: From San Diego Freeway (405), go west on Washington, one street past Pacific to Speedway. Turn right, and go 1 block to Twenty-ninth Place. Turn right; park immediately at gray board fence.

J: *Among the performers on the boardwalk recently were a one-man blues band, the "Texas Chainsaw Juggler," and a man who swallows dipsticks. Just your everyday, homespun entertainment—Venice style.*

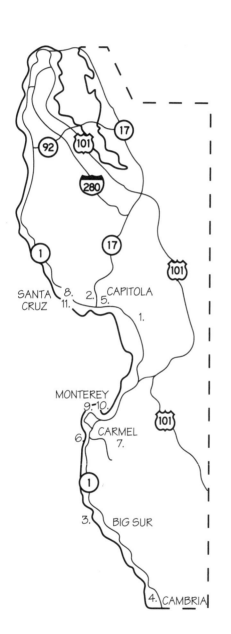

92

101

17

280

1

17

101

SANTA
CRUZ   8.   2.   CAPITOLA
       11.   5.
                    1.

MONTEREY
9-10.

101

6.   CARMEL
      7.

1

3.   BIG SUR

4. CAMBRIA

WA

OR

CA

California: The Central Coast

Numbers on map refer to towns numbered below.

olive Metcalf

Apple Lane Inn
Aptos, California
95003

Innkeepers: Douglas and Diana Groom
Address/Telephone: 6265 Soquel Drive; (408) 475–6868
Rooms: 5; 3 with private bath. No smoking inn.
Rates: $70 to $125, double occupancy, full country breakfast.
Open: All year.
Facilities and activities: Wedding site, Victorian gazebo and gardens, croquet, badminton, horseshoes, barn and farm animals. Nearby: beaches within walking distance; Santa Cruz mountain wineries, antiquing, good restaurants, Cabrillo Music Festival in August, U.C. Santa Cruz, Capitola Begonia Festival in September.

Apple Lane Inn has all the ingredients that first made people fall in love with B&Bs. It's a sweet Victorian farmhouse set amid vineyards and apple orchards on three country acres. There's an old-fashioned parlor with comfortable old-fashioned furniture, sweetly decorated bedrooms, and a bountiful breakfast served at one big table. This is vintage B&B stuff.

And the indispensable ingredient that makes the mixture work is a warm-hearted, interested-in-you, helpful-about-the-area innkeeper. In this case, it is the new owners/innkeepers, Douglas and Diana Groom. Both teachers, both history buffs, they love sharing stories of the house and grounds, recently designated a historic landmark.

This rural charmer of an inn is well off the highway on a hill that used to contain an apple orchard. Now the driveway up to the house is lined with apple trees. A brick patio at the front is sheltered by grape and wisteria vines, hanging begonias, roses, and hydrangeas.

Three bedrooms on the second floor are not large but comfortable and charmingly decorated. One has white wicker furniture, hearts-and-flowers wallpaper, and a claw-footed tub with hand-held shower; one has antique pine furniture and a four-poster queen-sized bed. A small sitting room on this floor has a view of Santa Cruz and is the kind of bonus room that makes inn lodging especially pleasant. Furnished with an heirloom love seat, a teak desk from which you have a view of Santa Cruz, a television, and a tea cart, here you can read and relax and help yourself to afternoon tea. Diana has coffee waiting here, also, for early risers.

On the third floor are two beguiling attic rooms with exposed rafters painted white. One has two double beds; the other has a queen. They share a bath, but each has a basin in the room.

An easy atmosphere around the breakfast table usually brings on an exchange of travel tales and recipes. Diana has a background in catering and is willing to share the "how to" secrets behind some of her dishes. Her breakfasts always include fresh fruit and juice, two or more homemade pastries and breads, and a hearty main dish made with eggs from Apple Lane's own flock of chickens.

While nearby Santa Cruz is filled with interesting restaurants, I found a place down the road called The Farm that was well worth a visit. The 5-acre complex of gardens, bakery, and shops includes the attractive Greenhouse Restaurant. And now there is The Veranda, the beautiful restaurant in the old Bayview Hotel.

How to get there: From Highway One, south of Santa Cruz, take Park Avenue exit east. Turn right on Soquel Drive. The inn is on the left, just before you reach Cabrillo College.

olive Metcalf

Bayview Hotel
Aptos, California
95003

Innkeepers: James and Katya Duncan
Address/Telephone: 8041 Soquel Drive; (408) 688–8654
Rooms: 7, including a bridal suite and a 2-room family suite; all with private
bath. No smoking inn.
Rates: $80 to $145, double occupancy, full buffet-style breakfast. Extra per-
son, $10.
Open: All year.
Facilities and activities: The Veranda Restaurant, bar. Small-conference facili-
ties. Nearby: Entrance to 10,000-acre Forest of Nisene Marks State
Park with miles of hiking trails; golf, tennis, antiques shops, restau-
rants.

It was news of a fine new restaurant in the historic Bayview
Hotel that brought me back after many years to this area south of
San Francisco. The impressive old building hiding behind a cluster
of shrubbery and a giant magnolia tree is in the ascendancy once
again, looking fresh and downright smart.

At one time, a sign at the Aptos rail station next door read SAN
FRANCISCO 87 MILES; NEW ORLEANS 2,478 MILES. The connection was the
hotel's first proprietor, Joseph Arano, a Frenchman who had lived
in New Orleans before coming West to build the Bayview in 1878.
His hotel became a gathering place for a mixture of social classes
unlikely to occur anywhere but in a small Western town. Million-

aire entrepreneurs socialized with lumbermen and railroad workers, and the guest list included names from high society and politics to Lillian Russell and actor John Drew.

After barely getting started in its new incarnation, the Bayview suffered considerable damage in the October 1989 earthquake. Interior renovations have been extensive—new walls and sprinkler system—but in excellent taste. The building's graceful exterior now encloses a light, sturdy, and very fresh interior. Seven rooms are now available for guests, including a bridal suite and a 2-room family suite with a queen bed and one double bed. Plans proceed to continue renovation of the third floor also. The rooms are simple but uncluttered, with a few antiques; all have private baths.

The Veranda Restaurant is garnering rave reviews from all who have tried it. Chef/proprietor Jeff Huff has a lovely setting to work with, but to please the educated palates of Northern Californians, you have to deliver the goods—and he does. Some of his appetizers alone are taste experiences you could make a meal on. Mostaccioli with chicken fennel sausage, sweet peppers, and mushrooms with raclette cheese, or corn fritters and Smithfield ham on bitter greens with chives and sour cream, or smoked prawns and hopping John served with tomato and scallions are a sampling. He also makes a Kentucky burgoo filé gumbo. This attractive dining room, a handsome Victorian bar, and the veranda are impressive additions to the Bayview.

James and Katya Duncan, the new innkeepers, have recently moved here from England, a country that produces innkeepers than whom there are no better. James, in fact, comes from a family of British innkeepers. What is it about British innkeepers? They not only charm you with impeccable manners and a wonderful sense of fun, but their confident accent seems to say you're going to be well looked after.

How to get there: From Highway One, take the Seacliff Beach exit to Soquel Drive. Follow to the inn on your right.

❋

J: *To be perfectly aboveboard, the name "Bayview" is really a misnomer. You're close, but you don't actually see the bay.*

olive Metcalf

Mangels House
Aptos, California
95001

Innkeepers: Jacqueline and Ron Fisher
Address/Telephone: 570 Aptos Creek Road (mailing address: P.O. Box 302); (408) 688–7982
Rooms: 5; all with private bath. Smoking only in the sitting room.
Rates: $96 to $130, double occupancy, full breakfast and afternoon refreshment.
Open: All year except Christmas.
Facilities and activities: Darts and table tennis. Nearby: restaurants; excellent hiking and biking in Forest of Nisene Marks; minutes from New Brighton Beach, ³/₄ mile from Monterey Bay; November to March winter whale watch, elephant seal watch, summer Cabrillo Music Festival and theatrical events.

Driving down the lane through dense trees, your heart lifts at the sight of this handsome white house glimpsed through the gateposts. Looking somewhat like a white Southern mansion, it sits on four acres of lawn and orchard bordered by the Forest of Nisene Marks. It was built in the 1880s as the country home of Claus Mangels, who, together with his brother-in-law Claus Spreckels, founded the sugar beet industry in California.

Remarkably, the house remained in the same family until 1979 when the Fishers bought it. Perhaps its stable history accounts for the peaceful feeling the house exudes. I certainly felt contented in the long sitting room with tall ceilings, polished wood floors, and oriental rugs. Chintz-covered sofas face a large stone fireplace; a grand piano sits at one end of the room. A huge back porch is another pleasant sitting area where you can pursue the gentle sports of table tennis and darts.

Upstairs are five spacious guest rooms, airy and decorated in delicate colors, except for Nicolas's Room, which has brown walls and an African motif. (The Fishers spent two years in Zaire.) The Mauve Room has a marble fireplace, and one room has a deck with garden views.

Coffee is ready and set in the hall by 7:00 A.M. for the early risers. Later, Jackie serves an attractive breakfast in the big family kitchen—homey things like scones or oatmeal, fresh egg dishes, or puffed apple pancakes along with fruits and juice. And when they're in season, fresh-picked berries with yogurt are a treat.

Berry picking in the area is first-rate, and Mangels would be a lovely spot to rest up from your labors. But this Northern Monterey area offers so much to do. The Forest of Nisene Marks was a new discovery for me. Not as well known as many recreation areas, its 10,000 acres of redwoods, creeks, and trails offer wonderful hiking and biking. A variety of summer music and drama festivals are becoming more popular every year, and Jackie will advise you about what's coming up. But the natural attractions of winter are even more seductive. This quieter, less crowded time means whale watching and beach walks to see the elephant seals and monarch butterflies.

Plenty of good dinner options are nearby. If you can try only one, check out The Veranda, a beautiful new restaurant in the old Bayview Hotel in the village.

How to get there: From Highway One, exit at Seacliff-Aptos State Park Drive. Turn right on Soquel Drive to Aptos Creek Road. Turn left and continue ¹/₂ mile to the inn.

J: *If you collect inn brochures while anticipating future visits, this one is especially appealing. Black-and-white photos of some of the inn's rooms and exterior capture its quiet feeling.*

Olive Metcalf

Fairview Manor
Ben Lomond, California
95005

Innkeepers: Nancy Glasson and Frank Feely
Address/Telephone: 245 Fairview Avenue; (408) 336–3355
Rooms: 5; all with private bath.
Rates: $89 to $99, double or single, breakfast and complimentary wine.
Open: All year.
Facilities and activities: Wedding facilities, mini-conferences; fishing the San Lorenzo River. Nearby: walk to Ben Lomond restaurants, shops; Henry Cowell Park, Roaring Camp Narrow-Gauge Railroad rides from Felton, twenty-minute bus ride to Santa Cruz Boardwalk, many local wineries.

If you ever want to hide out for a while but can't go far from San Francisco, you might head for Ben Lomond. Once at this remote little town in the Santa Cruz Mountains, follow a country road to a tree-shaded driveway and a sign saying FAIRVIEW MANOR.

The house you see is deceptive—just a well-maintained 1920s vintage attractive country house. But open the front door and you look straight through a large living room/dining room to a deck, and beyond that to a green forest of redwoods, madrone, and live oak trees. Walk through those trees down a short path and you're on the San Lorenzo River. Here's your hideaway.

It's the idyllic kind of shaded, sandy riverbank with smooth round rocks and see-through water that some of us could spend whole days playing on. Others are much more interested in the steelhead and salmon fishing. The season is mid-December to the end of February, no nets allowed. A local fishing columnist reports not a lot of catches but big sizes when you get one.

The house sits on three acres of total privacy, but it's just a short walk to central Ben Lomond, where there are restaurants and antiques shops. Landscaped grounds around the house have winding paths, a fish pond, and shady areas to sit in. The whole feeling here is of an earlier, quieter time.

Inside are five simple, immaculate guest rooms. The wood-paneled living room is cheerful, with a rich green carpet, a floral-covered sofa, and comfortable chairs grouped before a rock fireplace. Magazines, books, a refrigerator stocked with cold beverages, and an electric organ make a warm, inviting atmosphere. You won't need days to unwind here—you'll feel at home right away.

Being a retired fireman, Frank is as proficient in the kitchen as Nancy. Together they turn out a full breakfast that ought to light your fire for a full day of activity: juice, fresh fruit, home-baked muffins, and a variety of hot main dishes like crab quiche or frittata with Canadian bacon.

It's all served at a long dining table in front of a big window looking out at the trees or, in good weather, out on the deck.

How to get there: From San Jose on Highway 17, turn right on Highway 9 north to Ben Lomond. Turn right on Main Street at the Bank of America, left at Central, and right on Fairview. Inn is on the left.

◆

J: *Frank has recently cleared a meadow area by the house and added a gazebo and rose garden. One look will have you thinking wedding . . . dancing . . . party.*

Olive Metcalf

Deetjen's Big Sur Inn
Big Sur, California
93920

Innkeeper: Bettie Walters; restaurant manager, Doris Jolicoeur
Address/Telephone: Highway One; (408) 667–2377
Rooms: 19; 14 with private bath. Limited wheelchair access.
Rates: $60 to $110 midweek, $75 to $125 weekends, double occupancy,
    breakfast extra. No credit cards; cash or traveler's checks preferred.
    Reservation hours: noon to 4 P.M. daily.
Open: All year.
Facilities and activities: Breakfast (no smoking), dinner daily (one room for
    smoking); wine/beer bar. Nearby: high meadowlands, beaches, red-
    wood canyons; several restaurants, shops along 6-mile section of High-
    way One.

"When I have to begin *explaining* Big Sur Inn to people, I know
it's probably not for them," says one of the staff. In other words, if
you like the manicured luxury of The Lodge at Pebble Beach, Big
Sur Inn may not be your style. But for many people, Deetjen's Big
Sur Inn reflects the character of the area better than any other
place.

You can't compete with the heart-stopping beauty of the Big
Sur coast stretching 80 miles from Carmel to San Simeon, and the
inn does not try. It is a rustic lodge with an add-on tumble of cottages that simply blend into the mountains and trees. Helmuth
Deetjen, a Norwegian immigrant, built the homestead in the '30s.

Today, the inn is owned by Deetjen's Big Sur Inn Preservation Foundation, a nonprofit corporation, with all profits used to preserve, restore, and maintain the inn. It is now on the National Register of Historic Places.

The atmosphere is California casual, a nonpolyester, natural-fabric feeling, with a few traces of hippie life remaining. You're as likely to meet a San Francisco stockbroker as you are a breakfast companion who'll discuss the meaning of Zen. Accommodations are unabashedly simple, still very much the way Grandpa Deetjen built them. Some bathrooms are shared, and heating is provided by fireplace, wood-burning stove, or heaters. The old hand-hewn doors have no keys but may be secured from within. Recent improvements are new beds, down comforters, and new rag rugs.

Fresh food, thoughtfully prepared, is the premise behind a menu that ranges from old counterculture favorites like crisp vegetable stir-fry with brown rice, to duckling with fresh peach sauce, or pasta with fresh basil. A good wine list is frequently revised. A comfortable, family feeling among the staff extends over to guests, and the atmosphere is enhanced by hearth fires always burning, candles lit, and classical music playing on tape. Breakfasts are popular here, too.

Ask the innkeeper for directions to Pfeiffer Beach. A hidden one-lane road leads to a very private, special beach. And don't miss having a drink or lunch down the road at Nepenthe. Originally an adobe and redwood house that Orson Welles bought for Rita Hayworth, and at one time a refuge for Henry Miller, it's become a California equivalent of the Via Veneto: Eventually *everyone* makes the scene on its terrace perched 800 feet above a dramatic surf.

How to get there: The inn is on the east side of Highway One, about 26 miles south of Carmel.

ও

J: *If that fine word* funky *did not exist, it would have to be invented for Deetjen's Big Sur Inn.*

Clive Metcalf

Ventana Inn
Big Sur, California
93920

Innkeeper: Robert E. Bussinger

Address/Telephone: Big Sur; (408) 667–2331 or in California, (800) 628–6500

Rooms: 60; all with private bath and television, most with fireplace, some with private hot tub on deck.

Rates: $155 to $775, double occupancy, continental breakfast and afternoon wine-and-cheese buffet.

Open: All year.

Facilities and activities: Restaurant serves lunch, dinner; cocktail lounge. Hot tubs, saunas, swimming pool. Nearby: hike, picnic, Ventana general store.

The Big Sur Coast has always welcomed the offbeat, and even this sybaritic paradise was designed as a "different" kind of place: no tennis, no golf, no conventions, no Muzak, no disco delights.

What it does offer is a window (*ventana* means "window" in Spanish) toward both the Santa Lucia Mountains and the Pacific Ocean from a redwood and cedar lodge on a magnificent slope. This is the ultimate hideaway, a tasteful, expensive world of its own harmonizing with the wilderness surrounding it. For activity there are two 75-foot pools (heated all year) and two separate bathhouses with luxurious Japanese hot tubs, one of them with saunas. And there are walks over grassy slopes, through the woods, or on the beach. From every point your eyes go to the spectacular Big Sur Coast, where boulders send white foam spraying into the air.

Some rooms in the cottages clustered around the lodge look down into a canyon of trees; others face the ocean. Their uncluttered blend of natural fabric and design makes each room seem to be the best one. Every detail—folk baskets holding kindling, window seats, quilts handmade in Nova Scotia, private terraces—has been carefully conceived.

A gravel path leads to the restaurant, with the opportunity of seeing native wildflowers and an occasional deer or bobcat on the way. The food is colorful California cuisine: fresh fish, veal, chicken, creative pastas, and a good wine list. The place to be at lunch is the expansive terrace with a 50-mile view of the coast. Dinner inside is a candlelight and pink linen affair. If you've walked the hills enough, indulge in a chocolate torte the *Washington Post* called "celestial."

At breakfast, a continental buffet, accompanied by baroque music, is spread in the lodge lobby by the rock fireplace: platters of melons, papayas, strawberries—whatever is fresh—pastries and breads baked in the Ventana kitchen, honey and preserves, yogurt and homemade granola. An afternoon wine and cheese buffet has an incredible array of domestic and imported cheeses.

The Store by the restaurant (books, baskets, mountain clothing, handmade knives, bird whistles) is as intriguing as its staff—all of whom seemed to be bilingual and have fascinating histories.

How to get there: On State Highway One, Ventana is 311 miles (about a six-and-a-half-hour drive) north of Los Angeles. The inn's sign is on the right. From San Francisco, the inn is 152 miles, 28 miles south of Carmel.

J: *I've heard that the best substitute for a rich father is a rich father-in-law. Short of that, a few days at Ventana will do.*

olive Metcalf

The J. Patrick House
Cambria, California
93428

Innkeeper: Molly Lynch

Address/Telephone: 2990 Burton Drive; (805) 927–3812

Rooms: 8; all with private bath, 7 with wood-burning fireplace, 1 with wood stove. Room and bath facilities for wheelchairs. No smoking inn.

Rates: $100 to $120, double occupancy, breakfast, beverages, and appetizers.

Open: All year.

Facilities and activities: Nearby: Cambria beaches, shops, restaurants; 6 miles to Hearst Castle; vineyards.

It wasn't too long ago that this warm early American–style inn wasn't here, only the log house in front. Guests gather there in the living room for wine and cheese in the early evening. With its rosy rug and wingback chairs flanking the fireplace, it's especially inviting on those damp, cool days that come winter and summer along the Central Coast.

The log house also has the dining room, office, and one large bedroom upstairs. It has log walls and a big brick fireplace, a spacious bath, and windows galore that look out into the garden.

Passion vine is growing up an arbor that connects the main house to a fine, two-story cedar building with seven bedrooms. I liked the feeling of the guest house the moment I walked in, partly because of the wonderful aroma. The cedar gives it a light fresh look, besides smelling good. All the bedrooms are spacious and have great tile baths. Another pleasant sitting room is on the first floor.

The early American decor is not the fussy, uncomfortable kind. It's appealing but uncluttered, with cushioned window seats framed by pretty curtains, some beautiful hand-crocheted bed coverings, and a few special pieces. A huge California-willow rocker and headboard in one room are wonderful. (A smaller version of the rocker is in the living room.) They're the work of a local craftsman, says Molly.

Across the back of the log house is a sunny breakfast room that looks out on the garden. Molly's idea of continental breakfast is first-rate: coffee from freshly ground beans, freshly squeezed juice, cinnamon rolls or another baked treat just made, as well as granola, yogurt, and fresh fruit to layer and mix as you choose.

Running an inn is a business, but it's an intensely personal one for this innkeeper. The inn bears her father's name, and every room is named for a county in southern Ireland: Tipperary, Kerry, Kilkenny, and the like. Says Molly, "My whole point is that people are comfortable and that they feel they've been treated well. After that, this business is all fluff."

How to get there: From the south, exit Highway One right on Burton Drive and follow ¹/₂ mile to the inn on the right.

❀

J: *There's not a shred of truth to the rumor that you have to be Irish to get a reservation here.*

Olive Metcalf

The Inn at Depot Hill
Capitola-by-the-Sea, California
95010

Innkeeper: Suzanne Lankes
Address/Telephone: 250 Monterey Avenue; (408) 462–3376, fax (408) 458–0989
Rooms: 8 suites; all with private bath, fireplace, television, VCR stereo system, telephone, modem; some with private patio and outdoor Jacuzzi. Smoking on outside patios only. Wheelchair access.
Rates: $145 to $225, double occupancy (cannot accommodate third person in a room), full breakfast, afternoon tea or wine, after-dinner dessert.
Open: All year.
Facilities and activities: Railroad memorabilia. Concierge services. Garden. Nearby: Capitola galleries, shops, restaurants; sunset cruises and sea otter excursions; nineteen wineries in county association, many offering daily tours and tastings.

Consider this for a romantic getaway. You drive through the Santa Cruz Mountains or else along the coast on Highway One to a seaside resort called Capitola-by-the-Sea. Now imagine checking into an entire turn-of-the-century railway station with a Doric-columned facade—set on a bluff 2 blocks above the village and Monterey Bay—transformed into a designer-created vision of a classic bed and breakfast inn. It all exists at The Inn at Depot Hill.

So elegant is this inn, the fact that the building actually *was* a railroad station serving thousands of visitors to Capitola for years dating back to the early 1900s may be lost on a guest today. Owner

Suzie Lankes says maps gave her the idea to design the bedrooms around grand destinations, some from the old *Orient Express*. Each of the eight suites is a world of its own, decorated to evoke a singular time and place, from Paris to Portofino to the Côte d'Azur.

Every room is simply sensational. The Delft, to pick one, is the most elegant taste of Holland that you're likely to find outside the queen's own palace. This enchanting suite has a blue-and-white sitting room with every possible appointment for your comfort. An overstuffed sofa faces a fireplace framed in blue-and-white tiles. There is a chaise and a desk holding a stationary, multiline telephone with fax and modem connections. In the bedroom is a huge featherbed draped in linen and hand-worked lace. As do several other suites, the Delft has a private patio and theme garden, this one planted with tulips and irises. By day sunlight floods the room; at night the lighting is soft, recessed into the ceiling, and controlled by a dimmer.

Every room has an artfully concealed television and VCR, and the sound system (AM/FM radio and tape player) is of the highest quality. Bathrooms are large and luxurious . . . marble floors, countertops, walls, and double shower, many with two oversize shower heads at both ends, even a small television on the counter.

Common areas include a parlor, with library and a grand piano, and a lovely tree-shaded patio with tables and chairs, a formal pond, and a fountain.

In the dining room, guests enjoy a suitably international breakfast menu at a glass-top table on a three-legged lion-and-paw pedestal from the Philippines: croissants and sweet rolls, juice and fruit, and a hot entree like quiche, frittata, or crepes. Service is elegant with silver, beautiful linen, and gold-rimmed china displaying the inn's logo. During the evening wine hour, a buffet is set up here, usually something like canapes, meatballs in a chafing dish, and fresh vegetables. And when you return from dinner, a dessert buffet is spread.

Despite the lovely common areas, you're not likely to see many other guests. Probably because the suites are so grand, many guests choose to have all food service delivered to their room. Privacy seems to be a valued part of a stay at Depot Hill. And this inn's style is "whatever you want."

How to get there: From Highway One, take the Capitola-Soquel exit to Bay Avenue toward the ocean. Bay becomes Monterey Avenue. Or take the Park Avenue exit to Monterey Avenue. One-and-a-half-hour drive from San Francisco.

olive Metcalf

The Cobblestone Inn
Carmel-by-the-Sea, California
93921

Innkeeper: Janet Miller
Address/Telephone: Junipero Street between Seventh and Eighth (mailing
  address: Box 3185); (408) 625–5222
Rooms: 24; all with private bath; fireplace, color television, small refrigerator
  in most rooms. No smoking inside.
Rates: $95 to $175, double occupancy, breakfast buffet and afternoon hors
  d'oeuvres and wine. $15 each additional person.
Open: All year.
Facilities and activities: Short walk to Carmel Beach, shops, restaurants, art
  galleries. Nearby: picnicking at Point Lobos State Reserve, Pebble
  Beach, Big Sur; tennis, golf facilities.

The Cobblestone is one of five inns owned by the same management. Having visited all their inns, I'm ready to suggest that this
group write a text on the art of personalized innkeeping. Each of
their inns, from the Cobblestone here in Carmel to the Petite
Auberge in San Francisco, is a classic example of exquisite decorating, first-class comforts, and exceptionally high standards of service
and personal attention.

An on-duty innkeeper keeps it all working—in this case, Janet.
She thoroughly oversees all the basics, like impeccable housekeeping and a friendly staff, but it's those deftly done little extras that
are so winning: flowers, fruit, and a handwritten card in your room

welcoming you by name; champagne, if she knows it's a special occasion; a morning newspaper outside your door, and your shined shoes or golf clubs, too, if you put them out the night before.

Bedrooms have a French country feeling, with pretty wallpapers, fresh quilts and pillows, and handsome antiques. It's a pleasure to relax in a room with a comfortable sitting area, good reading lights, and a cobblestone fireplace.

When you cross the courtyard to the living room lounge, you'll discover still another area where the Cobblestone shines. The lavish breakfast buffet is beautifully presented and is the essence of fresh California eating. There are fresh juices and colorful platters of fresh fruit, homemade hot muffins and breads, a daily-changing hot baked egg dish, homemade granola, yogurt, cider, hot chocolate, teas, and coffee.

From 5:00 to 7:00 P.M. guests are invited to gather by the big stone fireplace and enjoy complimentary tea, sherry, wine, and a variety of hors d'oeuvres. The tempting platters of fine cheeses alone make it mandatory that you *walk* to dinner. The innkeeper is happy to make dinner suggestions and reservations for you. When you return, your bed will be turned down, and a fresh rose and a piece of candy will be on the pillow.

Given this kind of comfort and attention, it's not surprising that a weekend reservation is needed almost three months in advance. Weekdays and winter are easier.

How to get there: Exit State Highway One on Ocean Avenue. Proceed down Ocean to Junipero; turn left. The inn is 2 blocks farther on the right, at the corner of Eighth Street.

olive Metcalf

The Happy Landing
Carmel-by-the-Sea, California
93921

Innkeepers: Carol and Robert Ballard
Address/Telephone: Monte Verde Street between Fifth and Sixth (mailing
   address: Box 2619); (408) 624–7917
Rooms: 7, including 2 suites; all with private bath and television, 3 with fire
   place. 1 nonsmoking room.
Rates: $90 to $145, double occupancy, breakfast delivered to your room.
   $15 each additional person.
Open: All year.
Facilities and activities: Wedding facilities; some designated parking spaces off
   street. Nearby: short walk to Carmel Beach, unusual shops, art gal-
   leries, restaurants.

I'm not the first to describe the architecture of this inn as pink
Hansel and Gretel. It has a picturesque, fairy tale cottage-in-the-
woods look, and Carmel is exactly the right setting. To be perfectly
accurate, however, it's really not a cottage, but rather a cluster of
accommodations all connected by rambling flagstone paths.

Each room opens onto a colorful central courtyard with a
gazebo and a small pond. As I arrived, a young couple were making
arrangements to have their wedding there. The poor kids didn't
realize that a veteran mother-of-the-bride was standing right there
ready to approve their choice . . . if only they'd asked. This was late
November, but the abundant plants, flowers, and bright hanging
baskets of fuchsias were dazzling. Ah, California.

The rooms are delightfully decorated with antiques and a romantic flair. Their steep roofs are especially inviting, and high cathedral ceilings make even the smallest room seem light and open. A television and a decanter of sherry in every room are pleasant to come back to after a day of shopping at Carmel's unusual stores or walking the beach.

A warm, attractive common room is also available for guests to use. You might enjoy afternoon coffee or a steaming cup of English tea here by the fireplace.

Breakfast is delivered to guest rooms on wicker trays, but given the pleasant courtyard, many people elect to take theirs outside. A hot baked item is always fresh every morning in addition to juice and fresh fruit. This fall day it was warm gingerbread with a lemon sauce.

The innkeepers are professionals, but better still, they have the knack of making each guest feel special and comfortable. You can't beat the personal touch.

How to get there: From State Highway One at Carmel, turn off at Ocean Avenue. Continue to center of town; turn right at Monte Verde Street. Inn is 2 blocks on the right.

J: *Part of experiencing Carmel is walking everywhere! This is a good location, just off the crowded main street and only 4 blocks from the beach.*

Olive Metcalf

The Sandpiper Inn At The Beach
Carmel-by-the-Sea, California
93923

Innkeepers: Irene and Graeme Mackenzie
Address/Telephone: 2408 Bay View Avenue; (408) 624–6433
Rooms: 16, including 3 cottages; all with private bath.
Rates: $90 to $167, double occupancy, continental breakfast and afternoon
   sherry. Two-day minimum on weekends.
Open: All year.
Facilities and activities: In-house library, color television in lounge. Nearby:
   restaurants, golf, tennis, Carmel Beach for walking.

"We're different from those B&Bs," Graeme Mackenzie says emphatically. "No miniature rooms here; no cold croissant and call it breakfast; no rules and regulations saying you must do this or you can't do that. *We're an inn!"*

The declaration is delivered in an unreconstructed Scottish burr, and with a smile, but the message is clear: The Mackenzies are professional innkeepers, and not to be confused with those other birds. Graeme has a wealth of experience in Europe, Hong Kong, Bermuda, and Dallas, where he became president of a hotel company.

Mackenzie's blue eyes are scornful as he relates the unbelievable behavior of some hosts who call themselves innkeepers. "Why,

I know of one place that demands you take off your shoes in the house! Is that any way to treat a guest?"

Since returning to the Monterey Peninsula in 1975 and acquiring The Sandpiper Inn, Graeme and Irene have remodeled and redecorated the thirteen guest rooms and three cottages. They all have private baths, queen- and king-sized beds (Graeme recalls his unhappy encounters with small beds in other inns), and quilted comforters. They're furnished with country English and French antiques, and he's particularly proud of some recently acquired antique headboards. Freshly picked nosegays add to an impeccable, tranquil atmosphere, with no television or telephone to intrude.

Some rooms have wood-burning fireplaces, and others are situated to take full advantage of the inn's sweeping views across Carmel Bay and out to the Pacific. The house is set only 70 yards from the beach in a quiet, private neighborhood. Just a quirk of luck—it was an inn before the strict zoning laws went into effect— accounts for its being there. The result is that you feel like a house guest at someone's exclusive seaside home.

That's precisely the mood Irene and Graeme promote. They invite you to help yourself to glasses, ice, coffee, or tea in the kitchen; take a rental mountain bike down the cypress-dotted streets along Carmel's beach; enjoy the warm English-feeling library, or relax by the fireside in the gracious living room ("lounge," to the Mackenzies) with sherry at 5:00 P.M.

How to get there: Take Ocean Avenue through Carmel to Scenic Avenue; turn left and proceed along the beach to the end. Just past the stop sign in the middle of the road, turn left at Martin Way. Inn is 1 block on the right at the corner of Bay View Avenue.

J: *The Scottish motto hanging above the door reads* Ceud Mile Failte—*"A Hundred Thousand Welcomes."*

Olive Metcalf

The Stonehouse Inn
Carmel-by-the-Sea, California
93921

Innkeeper: Barbara Cooke
Address/Telephone: Eighth below Monte Verde (mailing address: Box 2517);
(408) 624–4569
Rooms: 6 share 3 baths. No smoking inn.
Rates: $90 to $125, double occupancy, breakfast and afternoon refreshments.
Open: All year.
Facilities and activities: Nearby: restaurants; Carmel Beach; unique shops and art galleries 2 blocks away; Point Lobos State Park 2 miles south; Seventeen Mile Drive at Pebble Beach.

Writers have always been attracted to the Monterey Peninsula. It's an atmosphere that seems conducive to creativity—dramatic surfs, the misty cool weather, towering pines and evergreen oaks, and the famous Monterey cypresses with their twisted, gnarled shapes. It's inspiring even if you're only writing postcards.

The original owner of The Stonehouse, Mrs. "Nana" Foster, often invited notable artists and writers to stay in her Carmel home. Sinclair Lewis, Jack London, Lotta Crabtree, and George Sterling were among her guests. The inn still seems to reflect the old, quieter Carmel, when this area first became an artists' colony. When you gather around the fireplace for wine and hors d'oeuvres, you're likely to meet people who have been returning to The Stonehouse for years.

This is just the kind of sprawling, old-fashioned vacation house many of us would choose—if a staff came with it. It's large and luxurious, with a completely stone exterior, hand-shaped by local Indians when it was built in 1906. It's surrounded by wonderful gardens and a big, broad, partially glassed-in front porch, with pots of flowers and comfortable chairs and sofas.

There's a warm, colorful living room with a large stone fireplace. Fine furniture and white wicker with bright cushions are all put together so tastefully with vivid rugs, plants, flowers, books, and *things*, you tend to think it just happened. On consideration, you realize it's been done artfully, that it's invitingly clean and fresh.

Two bedrooms on the main floor and four upstairs have board-and-batten walls painted white that are typical of early Carmel houses. They're beautifully decorated in soft colors (peach, ivory, mossy green, pale blue), with quilts and antiques. Each room is reminiscent of the artist or writer for whom it was named. The Jack London has dramatic gabled ceilings, a bed and a daybed set in brass, with a ceiling fan and a glorious ocean view. The Lola Montez has a four-poster bed, a gabled ceiling, and a view of the garden.

You eat well here, too. Breakfast is the only meal served, but it's a full and proper one. There are always juices, fresh fruits, a selection of homemade breads or muffins, and homemade granola. A hot entree often follows and is served with plenty of fresh coffee and tea.

How to get there: Exit State Highway One on Ocean Avenue; continue into town to Monte Verde. Turn left 2 blocks to 8th Street; turn right. The inn is in the center of the block.

J: *"We have absolutely the best guests ever," says Barbara. "I think it's because they share the bathrooms. It means they're all good sports, and they seem to have a wonderful time sitting in the living room and talking to each other."*

olive Metcalf

Vagabond House Inn
Carmel-by-the-Sea, California
93921

Innkeeper: Honey Jones
Address/Telephone: Fourth and Dolores streets (mailing address: Box 2747);
 (408) 624–7738; outside California, (800) 262–1262
Rooms: 11; all with private bath, most with fireplace, kitchen, or small
 refrigerator. Television; telephone.
Rates: $79 to $135, double occupancy, continental breakfast. Lower winter
 rates.
Open: All year.
Facilities and activities: Nearby: walk to Carmel shops, art galleries, restau-
 rants, beach; short drives to Pebble Beach golf courses, Big Sur, Point
 Lobos.

It's hard to believe that this romantic inn ever had a military
connection, but it did. It was built during World War II to provide
lodging when nearby Fort Ord was bursting at the seams.

A more poetic part of its history is that the poet Don Blanding
lived here in the '40s, but no one seems to know if the house was
named for his poem "Vagabond House," or if he named his poem
for the house.

The shake-roofed, oak-shaded Vagabond has heart-robbing
qualities that have won it a loyal following through the years. Its
half-timbered look is English Tudor, perfectly appropriate for the
picture-book village of Carmel. The flagstone courtyard dominated

by old and very large oak trees is the focal point for each of the rooms. Its lush scene of camellias, rhododendrons, hanging plants, ferns, and flowers is really quite magical. Dutch-style half-doors to the rooms open onto this courtyard garden.

The bright, airy, and especially spacious rooms are constructed of knotty pine, brick, and barn board. Decorating themes range from nautical to early American to English Hunt. "We want our rooms to look wonderful," says innkeeper Honey Jones, "but it's even more important that you get comfort . . . be able to put up your feet and relax." One example of the thoughtful attention you get here is that each room is supplied with its own coffeepot, freshly ground coffee, and a decanter of cream sherry.

Continental breakfast is delivered to your room or served on the patio. It's most pleasant to fix a tray from the selection of juices, fruits, muffins and rolls, boiled eggs, and cheeses, and then take the newspaper and repair to the courtyard. The news goes down better this way. And, what better place to plan a day than under a hanging pot of brilliant fuchsias listening to the waterfall?

The management here at Vagabond House also owns Lincoln Green, a cluster of four spacious English country-style cottages. They're in a quiet residential neighborhood near the ocean and the Carmel River. Each beautifully decorated unit has a living room with fireplace, separate bedroom, and kitchen. There is no food service here, but guests are invited to come up to Vagabond House for breakfast, if they wish.

How to get there: From State Highway One, take Ocean Avenue turnoff to downtown Carmel. At Dolores Street, turn right to Fourth Street. The inn is on the right.

J: *It is worth remembering that winter visits to Carmel have some distinct advantages: fewer people, lower rates, and, while reservations are still needed for weekends, you can often find appealing lodgings on the spur of the moment.*

olive Metcalf

Robles Del Rio Lodge
Carmel Valley, California
93924

Innkeeper: Glen Gurries
Address/Telephone: 200 Punta Del Monte; (408) 659–3705
Rooms: 31, including some cottages; all with private bath and cable television, some with fireplace and kitchenette. Wheelchair access.
Rates: $80 to $250, double occupancy, generous continental breakfast.
Open: All year.
Facilities and activities: Exceptional restaurant, The Ridge, serves lunch and dinner; Cantina serves wine and beer. Swimming pool, tile hot tub with Jacuzzi, sauna, tennis. Nearby: golf, horseback riding, 12 miles to ocean beaches, surrounding woodlands to hike, ten minutes to Carmel attractions.

Driving the twisting road up to Robles Del Rio gives you a feeling that you're deep in the heart of California countryside, though it's only a ten-minute drive from Carmel. The lodge looks just right for its rustic setting. Surrounded by live oak trees and perched on the mountaintop (well, high hill) surveying the valley below, this is true country-inn feeling. A tree-shaded flagstone terrace extends from the lodge with flowers in profusion and a pool, Jacuzzi, and an outdoor fireplace to be enjoyed night and day.

It was built in the 1920s, the oldest resort still operating in the Carmel Valley. The lodge is now owned by the Ron Gurries family with son Glen and his wife Adreena as resident managers. Former longtime owner Bill Wood lives just across the road. He ran the place for over forty years and approvingly watches the renovations and improvements going on. He can reminisce about the early days of the lodge, when Arthur Murray would check in for a month or so, when Alistair Cooke visited after the war, and how the swimming pool was dug with horse and plow because they couldn't get a tractor up the crooked road.

Six rooms are in the main lodge; the others are in separate buildings scattered over nine acres. These rooms are unpretentious but entirely comfortable, and the views are wonderful. Some have a rustic board-and-batten decor, and others have a more contemporary country look using Laura Ashley fabric. The cottages with outfitted kitchens and fireplaces are convenient for longer stays.

Beginning with a bountiful breakfast buffet set in the main lodge living room, good food is a big part of the Lodge's appeal. With a crackling fire going to chase away the morning chill, much of the original 1920s furniture still in place, and wide views of the valley, this room has a good feeling.

Lunch or dinner in The Ridge restaurant, also in the main lodge building, is a dining experience equal to the best available in Carmel or Monterey. Chef David Allen has extensive credentials from the East Coast, but he's now a California specialist. He relies on Monterey agriculture for daily deliveries of whatever is freshest and best.

His wine list, too, has a deliberate regional focus. (Did you know more grapes are grown in the Monterey region now than in Napa?) Notice the hand-painted china, the fresh flowers, the broad deck overlooking the valley. What a seat to watch a fog bank form over Carmel and quietly roll in. A fresh rockfish soup and a chicken breast stir-fry with ginger, bell pepper, and tomatoes were pretty impressive, too.

How to get there: From Highway One at Carmel, drive east on Carmel Valley Road about 13 miles to Esquiline Road. Turn right and follow the signs up the hill to the lodge, about 1 mile.

olive Metcalf

Stonepine
Carmel Valley, California
93924

Innkeepers: Gordon Hentschel and Noel Irwin-Hentschel, owners; Dirk Oldenburg, managing director

Address/Telephone: 150 East Carmel Valley Road; (408) 659–2245

Rooms: 13 suites; all with private bath with Jacuzzi and cable television, most with wood-burning fireplace.

Rates: $195 to $575, double occupancy, continental breakfast. Exclusive use of the chateau (up to 16 people) $4,000 per night; Paddock House exclusive (up to 8 people) $1,200. Children welcome in Paddock suites.

Open: All year.

Facilities and activities: Dinner by reservation, swimming pool, tennis court, croquet, archery range, soccer field, health club, steam bath; Equestrian Center, instruction, moonlight hayrides; acres of riding and running trails; horse-drawn Victorian carriage rides; facilities for small to large parties, business gatherings. Nearby: Carmel, Monterey, Big Sur.

If F. Scott Fitzgerald had wanted Gatsby to make his splash in California's Carmel Valley instead of West Egg, the once-private estate of Stonepine would have been the perfect background. Fitzgerald missed it, but you need not. The splendid Mediterranean-style house is now a remarkable country inn.

When you press the button that opens an electric gate guarding a mile-long road to the main house, you enter a world of quiet luxury and 330 acres of natural beauty. After four years of restoration and redecoration, the Chateau Noel has eight magnificent suites, and five less formal suites are in the Paddock House.

The common rooms include an elegant foyer, living room, dining room, and handsome library paneled with burnished nineteenth-century French oak. Every detail is first-class, even to the library shelves stocked with hardback copies of current titles and classics. Across the back of the estate is the loggia with stone arches supported by centuries-old columns from Rome. In daylight, you look out to gnarled olive trees and gardens that frame a rolling meadow. At night, it's a romantic place to watch the sunset or dine by a blazing fire.

In the early 1930s, the estate was the foremost thoroughbred horse–breeding farm in California. (The owner was the daughter of the Crocker banking family of San Francisco, and the social set motored over from Pebble Beach to play polo and ride.) Today, the Equestrian Center is the primary atttraction at Stonepine with the finest examples of classic breeds in residence. Debby and Tommy Harris run the center. They give English and Western riding lessons and two-day equestrian clinics—beginners welcome. Tommy's drives around the estate and moonlight hayrides are popular with guests.

To dine here is to feast on superb food and drink served on Limoges, Waterford, and Baccarat with sterling silver at a prix fixe of $50 (plus tax and gratuities) per person. If you want to entertain, a creative staff will produce a unique party with music, food, and entertainment. A recent Civil War extravaganza even had hairdressers and costumes for the guests—everything but live bullets in the battle reenactment that took place off the loggia.

How to get there: From Highway One proceed east on Carmel Valley Road past a 13.0 mile marker; Stonepine will be on your right. Pick up telephone at the gate for entry. Complimentary airport pickups available in a Phantom V Rolls Royce. Monterey airport 30 minutes from Stonepine.

olive Metcalf

New Davenport Bed and Breakfast Inn
Davenport, California
95017

Innkeepers: Marcia and Bruce McDougal
Address/Telephone: 31 Davenport Avenue; (408) 425–1818 or 426–4122
Rooms: 12; all with private bath. No smoking inn.
Rates: $65 to $110, single or double occupancy, expanded continental
  breakfast with champagne. $10 for each additional guest.
Open: All year.
Facilities and activities: Lunch and dinner. Folk art, textiles, pottery, other
  crafts in the Cash Store. Nearby: Ano Nuevo State Elephant Seal tours
  8 miles north, beach walking, whale watching; state parks, University
  of California, Santa Cruz campus; Cabrillo Music Festival each summer.

You can talk to native Californians who have never heard of
Davenport—and that's just fine with most of the citizens of this
town. But there it is, halfway between San Francisco and Carmel,
smack dab on one of the most spectacular coastlines anywhere.

The McDougals saw it as the perfect site for their pottery
gallery (Bruce once taught pottery) and decided to build a new
Davenport Cash Store. The original Cash Store occupied the same
corner for many years during the first half of the century when
Davenport was a thriving town with a cement plant, hotels, and
businesses. When Marcia and Bruce rebuilt, they added delightful

accommodations and a restaurant.

The Cash Store is a gathering place for local artisans. It sells their wares in pottery, textiles, wood, and glass. The original jewelry, especially, caught my eye.

Some of these arts and crafts articles also decorate the eight bedrooms above the store. Each one has a cheerful mixture of antiques, ethnic treasures, and local arts. The pleasant rooms all open onto the balcony that wraps around the building.

Beside the Cash Store is the oldest remaining original building in Davenport. The McDougals have renovated it to provide a warm sitting room and four bedrooms. These rooms are smaller than the new ones over the store, but they're fresh and pretty, with quilts and an old-fashioned appeal. The quiet garden patio here is another attraction. In the sitting room are books, a comfortable sofa and chairs, coffee makings, and an ocean view. Breakfast for weekend guests is served here, including champagne, fresh juice, coffee, teas, and homemade pastry. Weekday guests breakfast in the restaurant.

In the restaurant your eyes go from one interesting display to another: costumes from Yugoslavia, Mexican rugs, African masks, and handcrafts from around the world. The menu seems to offer as wide a variety of dishes as the decor is varied—and the bakery is outstanding. My luncheon choice of shredded cooked chicken on a fresh tortilla topped with spicy salsa, cilantro, avocado, and lettuce was a winner.

After lunch, walk across the highway and down a short path to savor the discovery of a secluded stretch of sandy beach. It could be awfully pleasant to take a blanket and a book, maybe some provisions from the restaurant, and spend a few hours here listening to the surf.

How to get there: On California Highway One, 9 miles north of Santa Cruz.

The Jabberwock
Monterey, California
93940

Innkeepers: Jim and Barbara Allen
Address/Telephone: 598 Laine Street; (408) 372–4777
Rooms: 7; 3 with private bath.
Rates: $95 to $170, double occupancy, full breakfast and evening aperitifs
  and hors d'oeuvres. No credit cards.
Open: All year.
Facilities and activities: Nearby: a walking/jogging/biking path along the Bay
  to Cannery Row, Monterey Bay Aquarium, restaurants; short drive to
  Carmel, Pebble Beach.

Have you ever breakfasted on Snarkleberry Flumptious? How
about Burndt Flambjous? You'll recognize the inspiration of Lewis
Carroll nonsense as the theme of The Jabberwock, with originally
named breakfast dishes, decor, and room names. There's also a Bur-
bling Room (a telephone nook), and The Tum Tum Tree (a refrigerator stocked with complimentary soft drinks).

Now I'm the first to admit that a little whimsy oozes like
chocolate on a hot day—and can be just as sticky—but the innkeepers use this bit of fancy with a winning sense of fun. It seems only
to enhance the charm of a well-run, solidly comfortable inn. As a
kid, Jim Allen loved the poem "Jabberwocky" from *Through the
Looking Glass* (he says it was the only one he ever learned), and he
and Barbara thought it was the perfect name for their inn.

The towered and turreted 1911 house sits on a hill in a neighborhood 4 blocks above Cannery Row. A glassed-in veranda wraps around two sides of the building and overlooks their colorful English garden and beyond to Monterey Bay. A chalkboard on the wall lists each room name, and beside it, the first names of the occupants. Barbara says she wants everyone to be on a first-name basis when a five o'clock bell summons guests to the veranda for aperitifs and hors d'oeuvres.

Every room is engagingly decorated with elegant antique beds, beautiful linens, and down pillows and comforters. Robes and every toiletry you might have forgotten are thoughtfully provided. The third floor has an arrangement two couples will enjoy—two bedrooms, The Mimsy and The Wabe, share a bath and a private sitting room that has views all the way to Santa Cruz.

When you breakfast by the fireside in the dining room, the name of the day's special dish is etched in reverse on a glass sign. You have to hold it up to a mirror to read it. Notice the clock on the mantel, too. It's backwards!

Steady yourself, and have a brillig day. Retire with one of the house volumes of Lewis Carroll, and the homemade cookies and milk Barbara sets out.

How to get there: Exit State Highway One at Munras Avenue. Take an immediate left at Soledad Drive; then turn right at Pacific Street. Continue as name changes to Lighthouse. Turn left at Hoffman; proceed 2 blocks to Laine Street. Inn is on the left corner, number 598.

J: *The Allens will prepurchase your Aquarium tickets so you can go when you please and not stand in line.*

Olive Metcalf

Old Monterey Inn
Monterey, California
93940

Innkeepers: Ann and Gene Swett
Address/Telephone: 500 Martin Avenue; (408) 375–8284
Rooms: 10; all with private bath, most with fireplace. Smoking in garden only.
Rates: $160 to $220, double occupancy, full breakfast and afternoon tea with homemade cookies. No credit cards.
Open: All year.
Facilities and activities: Accepts small executive retreats winter weekdays. Nearby: short walk to historic district of Monterey, Fisherman's Wharf, shops, restaurants; Monterey Bay Aquarium; short drives to Carmel, Pebble Beach, Point Lobos State Reserve, Big Sur coastline.

Let's discuss lodgings for particular people. Does the word *rustic* give you a headache? When the phrase "Victorian charm" is mentioned, do you have an acute attack of nausea? Do you feel that anything built after World War II is faintly tacky? Have I got an inn for you!

The Old Monterey Inn is an elegant architectural gem built in 1929 and until recently had always been a private residence. It's a half-timbered, Tudor-style house sitting on an oak-studded hillside in a quiet residential neighborhood. More than an acre of astonishingly beautiful gardens surround it and give each room a view of begonias, fuchsias, hydrangeas, and wooded banks of ferns and rhododendrons.

Ann and Gene Swett are the proprietors of this paradise, the family home where they raised their six children. Their hospitality and these beautifully appointed rooms are all the most discriminating guest could want. Choose any room and you can't go wrong, but the Library captured my heart with book-lined walls, a stone fireplace, and a private sun deck overlooking the garden. Everyone who stays in the Ashford Suite plots a return to this triumph of refined chic: a sitting room, separate dressing room, and large bedroom in antique pine and Ralph Lauren fabrics.

Eight of the ten rooms have wood-burning fireplaces. All of them have luxuries like elegant linens, goosedown comforters, the gleaming wood of period furniture, family antiques, and bathroom items you might have forgotten. Other personal touches include soft challis robes in each room, a refrigerator stocked with complimentary juices and soft drinks, and the loan of an outfitted picnic basket for a day's outing. The Swetts include a list of the best delis, the most interesting picnic sites, and directions for getting there.

Another fireplace is in the elegant step-down dining room where breakfast is served. You can have breakfast sent to your room, but it's awfully grand to sit around the long antique table with your hosts and meet the other lucky people who are here. Fresh fruit compotes and things like strata soufflé, Belgian waffles, or Orange Blossom French Toast are featured.

In the evening, a fire burns in the living room and the Swetts join their guests for wine and cheese. It's another lovely room, with oriental rugs and fine furniture. The ultimate standard of good taste runs throughout the house: comfort and quality, without pretension.

How to get there: Take Munras Avenue exit from Highway One; make an immediate left on Soledad Drive, then right on Pacific. Continue ³/₅ of a mile to Martin Street on the left. Inn is on your right at number 500.

J: *If checking into an inn is buying a bit of magic for your life, get ready to be enchanted.*

olive Metcalf

The Centrella
Pacific Grove, California
93950

Innkeeper: Gayle Kaiser
Address/Telephone: 612 Central Avenue; (408) 372–3372 or (800) 233–3372
Rooms: 26, including suites and cottages for 2 and 4; 24 with private bath, 1 with wheelchair access.
Rates: $85 to $180, double occupancy, breakfast and wine and hors d'oeuvres. Two-night minimum on weekends.
Open: All year.
Facilities and activities: Nearby: bayside walking and bicycling path; walk to Cannery Row, Monterey Bay Aquarium; Seventeen Mile Drive, Carmel, restaurants, shops.

Time your journey down Highway One to arrive at The Centrella in time for the social hour, 5:30 to 6:30 P.M. inviting living/dining area offers just what a weary traveler needs: decanters of wine and sherry and a substantial cocktail buffet: rye bread sliced thin, pâté, cheese spreads, hard cheese, crackers, guacamole and tortilla chips, marinated artichoke hearts, and dieter's delight—crudités.

It's difficult, but use some moderation at this repast, or you'll tend to tune out the good information that the staff have about the excellent choice of restaurants you can walk to in the area or that are just a short drive away. It's tempting to just relax by the fire in this pleasant room and read. There are books and magazines about, good reading lights, even an in-progress stitchery project set up with an invitation to contribute a few stitches.

Unlike so many inns of this vintage, The Centrella was never a private home. Built in 1889, it was described by the Monterey newspaper as "The largest, most commodious and pleasantly located private boarding house in 'The Grove.'" It's now listed in the National Register of Historic Places and has survived restoration beautifully, earning several design awards.

Guest rooms are decorated and appointed for comfort, but old touches remain. I liked the big claw-footed bathtub, the high ceilings, and the quilt in my room. But the good firm bed, a telephone, and an ice machine down the hall were appreciated, too.

Cottages in the back garden are a good arrangement for family vacations. One that sleeps four has an attractive sitting area, fireplace, television, small refrigerator, and wet bar.

Breakfast in the dining room is an easy introduction to a day of touring. A morning paper is at the door of your room, and the full breakfast buffet has all you require. A friendly staff going in and out of the adjoining kitchen might even pop your Danish into the oven for a few minutes, if you ask.

How to get there: From Highway One, take Del Monte/Pacific Grove exit. Continue on as street name changes to Lighthouse, then to Central. Inn is on the right.

J: *I had an early-morning walk along the Bay Shore—just me, the scuba divers, and the seals.*

Olive Metcalf

The Gosby House
Pacific Grove, California
93950

Innkeeper: Suzi Russo
Address/Telephone: 643 Lighthouse Avenue; (408) 375–1287
Rooms: 22, including 16 in main house; 20 with private bath, 7 with private entrance. Smoking in newer rooms only.
Rates: $85 to $130, double occupancy, full breakfast and afternoon wines and hors d'oeuvres.
Open: All year.
Facilities and activities: Nearby: restaurants; bicycling and walking paths along shoreline; Victorian architecture in Pacific Grove; watch seals, otters, and migrating whales; golfing, tennis; deep-sea sportfishing, charter boats, tours available.

The Gosby House is a showcase Victorian, vintage 1887, the kind you turn around to look at again as you drive by. Though it was built as a private residence, it's not a newcomer to the proliferation of elegant inns in this area. It's been providing accommodations to Monterey Peninsula visitors for nearly one hundred years.

The inn's current brochure includes the Oscar Wilde quotation, "I have the simplest of taste. I am satisfied with only the best." Oscar would not be disappointed were he to magically check into Gosby House. He'd be captivated right at the front door with the brimming pots of bright flowers clustered on the steps, and with the rich, colorful interior. And he'd appreciate the quiet, private places to relax throughout the house and along the brick garden paths.

You've seen dark, serious Victoriana? This is cheerful, playful Victoriana. (One does hope Herself would have been amused.) In the elegant parlor are polished woods, fine antiques, and comfortable English and French furniture around the fireplace. There's also a carousel horse, old teddy bears, a set of *Winnie the Pooh* volumes in the bookcase, and a grand glass-door cabinet filled with antique dolls. Guests gather here for afternoon tea or sherry, fresh fruits, and hors d'oeuvres.

In the handsome dining room, a large buffet is covered in the morning with an array of fresh fruits, cereals, hot breads, a hot dish like a frittata or quiche, and granola and yogurt—for yogurt parfaits.

The charm doesn't fall off when you go upstairs. Bedrooms are a special delight in a house of this style. With turrets and dormers you get window seats to be decorated with fat cushions in bright prints, and cozy slanted ceilings with delicately colored wallpapers. Fluffy comforters, and a handwritten card welcoming you by name are nice touches.

Oscar surely would have appreciated the teddy bear waiting on the bed.

How to get there: From San Francisco, take Highway One south past Monterey; exit at Highway 68 west to Pacific Grove. In town, follow Forest Avenue to Lighthouse Avenue; turn left, and go 3 blocks to the inn.

✳

J: *A wistful comment written by one guest in the register reads: "I wish home was just like this!"*

olive Metcalf

The Green Gables Inn
Pacific Grove, California
93950

Innkeeper: Jillian Brewer
Address/Telephone: 104 Fifth Street; (408) 375–2095
Rooms: 11, including 1 suite and separate Carriage House accommodations;
7 with private bath.
Rates: $100 to $160, double occupancy, breakfast and afternoon tea.
Open: All year.
Facilities and activities: Nearby: restaurants; shoreline paths for bicycling and
jogging; public beach, scuba diving, swimming, picnicking; short walk
to Cannery Row, Monterey Bay Aquarium; golf and tennis.

Green Gables is a romantic gem of a Queen Anne–style mansion with a fairy-tale look about it, half-timbered and gabled, sitting
above the shoreline of Monterey Bay. It was once the family home
of Roger and Sally Post and their four daughters, all grown now
and running the family's flock of elegant inns under the banner
Four Sisters Inns. This is one of them, and it is a beauty.

Looking at the dormers and peaks of the roofline, you just
know that the upstairs ceilings will be entertaining—and they are.
One cozy accommodation tucked under the eaves is The Garret
Room, an enchanting hideaway with dark beams against bright-
flowered wallpaper. The Chapel Room is larger, also with a steep
slanting ceiling, and tiny diamond-paned windows. The Gable
Room, once the bedroom of the Posts' youngest daughter,

Stephanie, has a sitting area, a loft, and superb views. Adjoining the Balcony Room is a glassed-in porch fitted with tall camp chairs to enjoy the Bay view.

In the adjacent Carriage House accommodations, every room has a fireplace and bath, but the most romantic rooms are those in the main house. A suite off the living room is quite grand, with a fireplace, sitting room, and a large private bath. All the rooms are furnished with antique pieces, and beautiful fabrics cover the quilts and pillows. Fresh flowers and fruit, those gracious extras, are in every room.

The large living room and dining room are elegant, yet completely inviting. An ornate ceiling with delicate plaster designs painted in blue and apricot is impressive. Low tables and chairs are in bay-window alcoves facing the bay. A unique fireplace framed by stained-glass panels is flanked by matching, dark blue sofas. Flowered draperies are at the tall windows, polished wood gleams, and tasteful accessories are everywhere. You'll feel terribly civilized having a nip of sherry and an hors d'oeuvre here in the afternoon.

The staff serves breakfast in a style appropriate to the surroundings—sitting down in the dining room. Juices and a wide offering of fresh fruits are followed by muffins, cereals, granola, and a substantial hot dish, perhaps a frittata or quiche.

How to get there: From San Francisco, take Highway One past Monterey and exit at Highway 68 west to Pacific Grove. Once in town, continue on Forest Avenue to the beach. Turn right on Ocean View to Fifth Street.

J: *Green Gables proves you can have Victorian charm without a trace of cloying quaintness.*

Olive Metcalf

The House of Seven Gables Inn
Pacific Grove, California
93950

Innkeepers: The Flatley family (John, Nora, Susan, Ed, and Fred)
Address/Telephone: 555 Ocean View Boulevard; (408) 372–4341
Rooms: 14; all with private bath. No smoking inn.
Rates: $95 to $185, double occupancy, sit-down full breakfast and afternoon
"high tea." Two-day minimum on weekends.
Open: All year.
Facilities and activities: Four patios for sunning. Nearby: shoreline paths for
bicycling, walking; short walk to Cannery Row, beaches, restaurants;
close to all attractions of Monterey Peninsula.

It was surprising to walk into this big, showy Victorian and
find, not the Victoriana I expected, but an extraordinary collection
of fine American, Asian, and European antiques. The Flatley family
has collected so much that visitors who have been coming to the
inn for years still find things they hadn't noticed before.

Guests here can enjoy the best of both times. While the house
and the antiques collection are old, the quality of the linens, bed-
ding, and the plumbing is fresh and new. This is an especially well-
maintained inn.

The house was completed in 1886 and still has the same unobstructed view of Monterey Bay it had then. At the end of the centu-

ry, Lucie Chase, a well-to-do widow and civic leader, added sun porches and gables, giving the house its amazing configuration.

Every room has excellent beds, good reading lights, a private bath, and elegant appointments. All have beautiful ocean views and sitting areas. Some of the newer bungalows behind the house are every bit as grand. No rustic country style here.

This is a fine house for relaxing, and the Flatleys think of every comfort. Tea is served in the afternoon on the sun porch or outdoors on the patio. There's always something homemade—shortbread, mini-muffins, and often Nora's homemade fudge. A television is on the sun porch, and an antique (working) telephone booth is in the hallway.

Breakfast is an elegant sit-down affair. Beautiful blue-and-white china is used on white linen at the dining room table. Silver platters of every available fresh fruit are always served along with fine teas and coffee, yogurt, a hot egg dish, and a variety of home-made breads and cakes, or Nora's apple cobbler.

How to get there: From Highway One, take Pebble Beach/Pacific Grove exit. Follow signs to Pacific Grove. Once in Pacific Grove, the road becomes Forest Avenue. Turn right on Ocean View Boulevard and continue 2 blocks to the inn at the corner of Fountain and Ocean View.

J: *With a name like The House of Seven Gables, I felt there must surely be a Hawthorne Room—and there is—but the theme isn't labored. In all those nooks and crannies, alcoves and bays, I couldn't possibly have avoided naming at least a little closet "Hester," or perhaps putting a simple scarlet "A" on a door.*

Olive Metcalf

The Martine Inn
Pacific Grove, California
93950

Innkeepers: Marion and Don Martine
Address/Telephone: 255 Oceanview Boulevard; (408) 373–3388
Rooms: 20; all with private bath and telephone. Smoking only in rooms
   with fireplace.
Rates: $115 to $225, double occupancy, breakfast buffet and afternoon wine
   and hors d'oeuvres.
Open: All year.
Facilities and activities: Wedding, conference facilities; Jacuzzi, oceanfront
   views. Nearby: paths for bicycling, walking; short walk to Cannery
   Row, Monterey Bay Aquarium, restaurants; tennis, golf.

Don't lose heart when you pull into the parking area of this
big pink palace and see how far above you the house is. As befitting
a palace, you merely step to the handy house telephone, tell them
you've arrived, and help will come.

The mansion looms high on the cliffs of Oceanview Boulevard
overlooking the shore of Monterey Bay. It was built in 1899 and
purchased by the Parke-Davis Pharmaceuticals family. Looking at
the distinctly Mediterranean style it is today, it's hard to imagine
that it was originally a true Victorian with cupola and dormers, all
changed over the years.

Mr. Parke was especially fond of exotic woods and employed
one craftsman to create Siamese teak gates, Honduras mahogany

trim in the living and dining rooms, and a Spanish cedar staircase.

A huge parlor with one wall of windows looking to the ocean is the setting for afternoon wine and hors d'oeuvres while a baby grand player piano provides the background music. An extravagant breakfast is also served here. Lace-covered tables by the windows are set with juices and fruit. Then guests help themselves from a buffet in the formal dining room. The Martines' special collection of Old Sheffield and Victorian silver is used to display and serve the rest of the menu, perhaps omelets, pancakes, or eggs Benedict.

As you might suppose in a house this large, the bedrooms are spacious, almost regal. Many have a fireplace, and all are furnished in Victorian style with authentic antiques. Telephones in all the rooms are another convenience. A pleasant sitting room is also upstairs with a spectacular ocean view.

A courtyard, protected by the carriage house and a 14-foot wall, is at the back of the house. With a pond and an elaborate oriental fountain, the courtyard makes a lovely setting for a wedding. The Martines chose it for theirs.

One of the joys of staying in a grand house is all the special places in it to discover. Besides upstairs and downstairs sitting rooms, there's also a spa, a game room, and a marvelous library. It looks just the way a Victorian library ought to look—beautiful wood paneling, shelves of books and magazines, a fireplace, oriental rugs, and oversize dark furniture.

A display area shows two cars from the Martines' vintage-auto collection.

How to get there: From Highway One, exit on Highway 68 west to Pacific Grove. Once in town, continue on Forest Avenue to the beach. Turn right and continue to inn on the right, between Fifth and Third streets.

Olive Metcalf

The Old St. Angela Inn
Pacific Grove, California
93950

Innkeepers: Barbara and Don Foster
Address/Telephone: 321 Central Avenue; (408) 372–3246
Rooms: 9; 6 with private bath. No smoking inn.
Rates: $90 to $150, double occupancy, full breakfast and afternoon wine
and hors d'oeuvres. $20 each additional person.
Open: All year.
Facilities and activities: Backyard garden and gazebo suitable for small wed-
dings. Nearby: 1 block to ocean beaches, parks; short walk to Mon-
terey Bay Aquarium on Cannery Row; many excellent restaurants.

The Old St. Angela is a refreshing change in the midst of so
many Victorian inns. It was designed by a Boston architect, so it's
not surprising to find true Cape Cod details. It was built in 1910 and
was the first Roman Catholic church in Pacific Grove, then a recto-
ry, later a convent.

The house has an Americana theme, with mellow pine
antiques and country wallpaper. A large country-stone fireplace is
in the living room; also an antique game table, beveled windows in
Dutch doors, and comfortable furniture in warm, earthy colors.
Among the handsome accents are duck prints, decoys, and a collection of Currier and Ives prints.

The afternoon light in this attractive room, a glass of port,
music, and a crackling fire add up to the perfect way to dispel the

winter of your discontent. Books all over the house are the best accent of all.

The bedrooms have a well-decorated country ambience—upscale country, that is, with tile bathrooms, fine linens, and down comforters. The Newport Room has a nautical feeling with a smart navy and brick color scheme. Ocean views are best from the Bay View Room. The Carriage House over the garage is the largest and grandest of the rooms. Out in the pretty back yard, The Cottage and The Nook are good choices for two couples traveling together or for a family. The rooms are completely separate accommodations, each with a private bath, but can be connected when the double doors between them are opened. And you can't beat fresh flowers, little bouquets here and there, to give a room appeal.

Outside attractions are an English garden and a white, latticed gazebo for dreaming under. For a broader look at the area try the new walking trail beginning at Lovers Point at Asilomar and going to the Monterey Wharf. If you would rather bike it, the innkeepers will arrange for bike rentals if you haven't brought your own.

Breakfast in a solarium of glass, redwood, and tile is a memorable part of your visit. It is ready by 8:30, but, in this inn's relaxed atmosphere, you can wander in when you're ready over the next hour and a half. Don cooks and Barbara serves their repertoire of breakfast specialties. It might be Pumpkin Cornmeal Pancakes or frittata or an elegant French toast concoction, accompanied by sausage or peppered bacon, fresh fruit and juice, and the best of coffees and teas.

The variety of outstanding restaurants nearby, some of them within walking distance of the inn, is almost overwhelming. The innkeepers are ready to suggest, report the latest, and make any reservations you require.

How to get there: From San Francisco, take Highway One south; exit at Del Monte/Pacific Grove. Follow Del Monte Street. The name changes to Lighthouse, then to Central. Inn is on the left at 321 Central.

olive Metcalf

The Babbling Brook Inn
Santa Cruz, California
95060

Innkeeper: Helen King
Address/Telephone: 1025 Laurel Street; (408) 427–2437 or (800) 866–1131;
   fax (408) 427–2457
Rooms: 12; all with private bath, telephone, and television. Wheelchair
   access. No smoking inn.
Rates: $85 to $135, double occupancy, full breakfast. Seasonal discounts.
Open: All year.
Facilities and activities: Wedding facilities. Nearby: walk to restaurants,
   Municipal Wharf, beach, boardwalk, specialty shops; picnics, golf, ten-
   nis, whale watching, fishing, wine tasting at local wineries arranged.

Babbling Brook Inn couldn't be named better. It's built right
over the sight and sounds of Laurel Creek, a bubbling natural brook
that cascades at this point into a pond. Lush landscaping is around
the pond and follows the creek through winding garden pathways
and patios, complete with a covered footbridge and a gazebo.

The Ohlone Indians lived on the cliffs surrounding Laurel
Creek and fished where the waterfall is now. A touring acting couple built a log cabin on the site in 1909, and some silent motion pictures were filmed here. Later owners included the flamboyant
Countess (so she claimed) Florenza de Chandler, who added the
upstairs and balcony.

Resident innkeeper Helen King brings plenty of travel know-how to running her inn. Twenty years in the airline industry took her to unusual lodgings the world over. What she aims to offer at this oldest and largest B&B in the area is comfort in a relaxed, friendly atmosphere. Most of us claim we love the simple country style, but we *do* like our conveniences. You'll lack nothing here, from private baths, telephones, fireplaces, and outdoor decks, to fresh flowers and a hidden-away television in every room.

The twelve guest rooms are divided among four buildings in the one-acre garden setting. Every room has been designed to provide maximum privacy and views of the lovely gardens. Each room is different, but the Country French motif carries throughout. Most are named for impressionist painters, and the colors—delft blues, rich burgundies, and beiges—originate with the artists' works.

Breakfast here gives you options instead of enforced camaraderie. Help yourself from an attractive buffet presentation and join others in the dining area adjacent to the parlor, or take a tray to the deck for the morning sun or back to your room and your own private deck. Morning papers, even the *Wall Street Journal*, will be there along with selections from Helen's breakfast repertoire. At my last visit there were pitchers of ice water (innkeepers seldom think of this), fruit juice, croissants and jams, zucchini tart, hot "Pookie" muffins, fresh fruit Southern style (with flaked coconut), and red grapes in a fluffy fruit dressing.

Helen also sets out an early-evening wine and cheese selection to graze over while you check the local restaurant menus. Santa Cruz has so many outstanding places, it's good to have an innkeeper and staff who are up to date with what's new and good.

How to get there: From Highway 17 take Highway One toward Half Moon Bay and continue on Mission Street. Turn left on Laurel toward the ocean. The inn is on your right.

৯

J: *A word must be said about "Pookie" muffins—it's a Texas term of endearment. Helen doesn't serve them every day, but if you're lucky enough to be there when she does, I predict a day filled with life force!*

Chateau Victorian
Santa Cruz, California
95060

Innkeepers: Franz and Alice-June Benjamin
Address/Telephone: 118 First Street; (408) 458–9458
Rooms: 7; all with private bath and fireplace. No smoking inn.
Rates: $99 to $131, double occupancy, expanded continental breakfast and afternoon wine and cheese.
Open: All year.
Facilities and activities: Nearby: walk to beach, boardwalk, restaurants, shops; winter spectaculars include arrival of the monarch butterflies (October–March), elephant seals (October–February), whale migration (November–April).

It is amazing what people will do in the name of improving a house. Chateau Victorian was constructed around the turn of the century, a perfectly typical and lovable Victorian house. Then came the 1950s with architectural philistines who decided that graceful lines were old-fashioned and unfunctional. With righteous fervor, bay windows and dormers were removed; thus, a charming period house became a typical '50s tract house, with a "picture" window.

Hooray for the arrival of Franz and Alice-June Benjamin. They set about turning the lamentable hybrid back into a cozy Victorian home with modern comforts. Back came a graceful bay window, and fine tile baths for each bedroom were added. Franz landscaped a sheltered patio garden and renovated a cottage that opens onto it.

Then the Benjamins individually decorated each room in beautiful colors to suit the era of the house—mauves, burgundies, and blues. They've chosen fine fabrics for bedcovers, draperies, pillows, and appealing window seats. The expected antique furniture pieces were added, including some particularly handsome armoires. Now we're talking about a pretty house!

The house sits high enough on a hill to offer a splendid ocean view from one of the rooms. Its location makes it an easy walk to restaurants, shops, and Santa Cruz's claim to fame, the last of the real boardwalks with its amusement park.

Breakfast, with the morning papers, is an expanded continental, meaning there's plenty of variety. Fine coffee and teas, juices and fruits, cream cheese, and croissants or other pastries are served from the dining-room buffet. You can eat there, or enjoy a sunny morning in the patio or on the decks.

How to get there: Driving south on Highway One, exit on Bay. At West Cliff, turn left, then right on Beach to Main. Turn left at Main, and at First Street, turn right. Inn is on left. Off-street parking available.

J: *This boardwalk has a major attraction: the oldest surviving roller coaster in California—tested by my daughter many times and rated a four-star screamer in all the books.*

olive Metcalf

Cliff Crest
Santa Cruz, California
95060

Innkeepers: Sharon and Bruce Taylor
Address/Telephone: 407 Cliff Street; (408) 427–2609
Rooms: 5; all with private bath. No smoking inn.
Rates: $80 to $125, double occupancy, full breakfast and afternoon wine and cheese.
Open: All year.
Facilities and activities: Nearby: restaurants, boardwalk attractions of Santa Cruz; Monterey Bay.

What a pleasure to stay in this well-maintained Queen Anne Victorian. If you don't "ooh" and "ahh" the minute you walk in, you're just not a fan of Victorian style. Everything sparkles, from the beveled stained-glass front door, to the sitting room that opens onto a glassed-in bay solarium that looks out on the garden and patio.

This was the home of William Jeter. You do remember, don't you, that he established Henry Cowell Redwoods State Park, was interested in ecology, and was lieutenant governor of California in 1890? Of course you do. Jeter also had the good luck to have as a personal friend John McLaren, the designer of Golden Gate Park in San Francisco. McLaren planned the beautiful grounds around this mansion.

Each of the bedrooms looks freshly decorated and offers special attractions. The smallest, the cozy Pineapple Room, is on the main floor and has pineapples carved on the four-poster queen-sized bed. The Rose Room is the largest and has an extra-long claw-footed tub in its bathroom across the hall and a sitting area with a view of Monterey Bay. All the bathrooms are a particular pleasure with their thick towels and terry cloth robes, shampoo, and lotions.

The sitting room is deliciously pretty: white wicker furniture against soft blue-gray woodwork and blue rugs. A white latticed archway opens to the solarium with two round tables and chairs. Across the top of the large bay window is a stained-glass border, and under the sills is an inside window box spilling over with Boston ferns. Can you imagine a cozier setting for breakfast?

Coffee is ready at 8:00 A.M., and the morning paper is there for a quiet beginning to the day. At nine you're served fresh juice and fruit. The entree might be French toast and sausages, or egg puffs with fresh muffins, or cinnamon–sour cream coffee cake. Sharon also makes some interesting phyllo creations that she arbitrarily names "Chef's Surprise Number 5" or "Number 8," or whatever she decides at the moment. In the afternoon, wine, mineral water, or iced tea and snacks magically arrive, accompanied by taped music.

How to get there: From Highway 17, exit on Ocean Street. Follow to the end of the street. Turn right on San Lorenzo Boulevard. Go to stop light, and turn left on Riverside. Go over bridge, turn right on Third Street; go up the hill to Cliff Street and turn left. Inn is on the left.

❀

J: *The Taylors lost two of their big cypress trees during the October '89 earthquake, but it only spurred them on to new beginnings outside—a new cutting garden and a fresh exterior paint job.*

Olive Metcalf

The Darling House
Santa Cruz, California
95060

Innkeepers: Karen and Darrell Darling
Address/Telephone: 314 West Cliff Drive; (408) 458–1958 or (800) 458–1958
Rooms: 7 rooms in house, 1 self-contained cottage sleeping 4 to 5; with private and shared baths. Smoking only in cottage.
Rates: $50 to $95, garden-view rooms; $125 to $225, ocean-view rooms; double occupancy; includes continental breakfast and complimentary gourmet dinner for two on weeknights except holidays and high season (June, July, August).
Open: All year.
Facilities and activities: Complimentary dinners available on weeknight package September through May. Hot-tub spa, wedding and small-party facilities. Nearby: walk to secluded beach, sailing; good place to see wintering monarch butterflies and elephant seals; Santa Cruz Boardwalk.

If you guess from its name that this inn is a gabled Victorian, you would be way off the track. It's a 1910 Mission Revival masterpiece sitting on the cliffs high above Monterey Bay. The owners and innkeepers, Karen and Darrell Darling, are simply calling it by their own name—although their children did have some doubts about the idea.

The house was designed by William Weeks, probably the most active architect on the Central Coast during the first decade of the century. He was known particularly for designing public buildings, but his talent and versatility can also be seen in the private homes he designed. Karen calls Darling House a "Colorado Spanish" design, since Weeks and his clients the William Iliffs (cofounders of Denver University Graduate School) were all from Colorado, but Mission Revival is the true name of the popular style. The most striking features are the portico with its series of arches, the terra-cotta tile roof, and beveled, leaded-glass windows.

The imposing inn gives guests an opportunity to experience living in a period piece that is almost completely in its original state. Plumbing fixtures, for instance, date from about 1910 and still work beautifully. Tiffany lamps and Art Deco (before its time) features are just as they were designed.

Bedrooms are large, and most have ocean views. One with an especially sweeping view has a big chair and a telescope ready for serious marine watching. Antique furnishings and beautiful details of inlaid woods on pillars, beams, and floors are fascinating to examine.

The Darlings have instituted an off-season dinner bargain that is hard to resist. On weeknights, excluding holidays, for the regular room rate, you also get a complimentary dinner for two! Once in a while it is served at the inn, but usually it is at a favorite local restaurant of Karen and Darrell's—one where they often have special family celebrations.

Karen makes breakfast at the inn special. She serves it family style in the oak dining room or on the ocean-side veranda: espresso, nut breads, croissants, granola, and fresh fruits. Whatever the menu, everything you eat is fresh or made from scratch.

Two just possibly connected extras offered by the Darlings are (1) they sometimes have home-grown walnuts for sale, and (2) Darrell is a minister. So, should you decide to get married while you're at the inn, the clergy is on the premises and the rest of the guests could throw walnuts.

How to get there: From Highway 17, take Highway One north. Exit left on Bay Street, and turn right on West Cliff Drive. Inn is on the right.

J: *A stroll down West Cliff Drive will bring you to a secluded beach. This stretch of the coast is a good place for tide-pooling and for watching the dizzying magic of wintering monarch butterflies.*

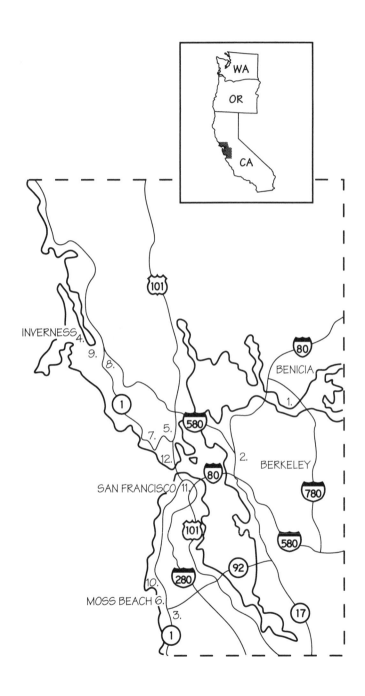

California: The San Francisco Bay Area

Numbers on map refer to towns numbered below.

olive Metcalf

The Union Hotel
Benicia, California
94510

Innkeepers: Richard Denno and Jane Wolfe
Address/Telephone: 401 First Street; (707) 746–0100
Rooms: 12; all with private bath, Jacuzzi, telephone, television, air conditioning. Wheelchair access.
Rates: $70 to $95, weekdays; $80 to $135, weekends; continental breakfast. Corporate rate.
Open: All year.
Facilities and activities: Lunch Monday through Saturday, dinner daily, brunch Sunday. Music in bar Wednesday through Sunday. Nearby: old capitol; Marine World Africa, USA; open artisans' studios in glass blowing, pottery, sculpture; antiques; marina, fishing, bird watching, picnicking.

Water, water, everywhere. Benicia is nestled on the north shore of the Carquinez Straits where the Sacramento and San Joaquin rivers flow into San Francisco Bay. When history and prosperity passed it by, this nineteenth-century town was largely forgotten. Once the capital of California, it boasts the oldest standing capitol in the state.

The stately three-story Union Hotel was restored in 1980, but even before guest rooms were ready, its authentically American food and regional dishes began attracting people to Benicia. The dining room is now presided over by Chef Lev Dagan, whose watchword is, "If it came from my kitchen and it was ever frozen, it must have been ice cream!" He varies the menu twice a day to accommodate the ever-changing availability of the best ingredients. The wine list highlights many of California's small boutique producers, and many choices are available by the glass.

The Parlour Bar is a cozy room for relaxing and has live entertainment Wednesday through Sunday. They make an especially tasty gin fizz that's a pleasant preamble to brunch or lunch.

The second and third floors have been entirely rebuilt to make the twelve bedrooms. Each is large and airy, is named for a different theme—Mrs. Miniver, Mei Ling, Summer Skies—has period furnishings, and uses large armoires for closets. The best views are from the Massachusetts Bay Room and from Louis Le Mad, where you look out at the Carquinez Straits and bridge. And the bathrooms are splendid. They're big and tiled, with some of the Jacuzzi tubs large enough for entertaining.

No, you're not roughing it at The Union Hotel. But I've always thought that was overrated, haven't you?

How to get there: From San Francisco, take Highway 80 north to Vallejo. Take Benicia turnoff; exit Second Street, turn left. Proceed to first light; turn right and go to first stoplight, which is First Street. Turn left and drive through town to the hotel on the right.

J:　*Benicia is one of the last nontouristy, semiundiscovered little towns left. I say, catch it while it's still free from the dreaded disease "Boutique-itis."*

olive Metcalf

Gramma's Rose Garden Inn
Berkeley, California
94705

Innkeeper: Barry Cleveland
Address/Telephone: 2740 Telegraph Avenue; (510) 549–2145; fax (510) 549–1085
Rooms: 40; all with private bath, color television and telephone, some with fireplace, private deck, views. Wheelchair access.
Rates: $85 to $175, double occupancy, breakfast and evening wine and cheese.
Open: All year.
Facilities and activities: Nearby: University of California, Berkeley; restaurants, shops, museums, parks.

I love Gramma's because it takes many people's preconceptions about Berkeley and knocks them for a loop. The beautiful Tudor mansion with a sweet name (and no campy implications) has an atmosphere that surprises many visitors to this city of intellect and rebellion: wholesome leaning to elegant is the feeling. It's the perfect antidote for outdated ideas of what goes on in Berkeley.

Gramma's is actually two turn-of-the-century mansions built by two brothers who were Berkeley's premier cement contractors of the era. A flower-lined walkway (some of that original cement) takes you into the check-in office in the main mansion. A sunny living room with a flower-tiled fireplace, fat chintz-covered sofas and chairs, and newspapers and magazines invites you to "sit a

120

spell." Bedrooms upstairs in the main house are the smallest and oldest, but also the best bargains. The living room adjoins a light-filled dining area, and beyond that is Gramma's back yard.

Out here is a patch of green grass, a patio with tables and chairs, and lots of flowers. At the back of the garden are two newer accommodations—Cottage House and Carriage House. I like the upstairs rooms in Carriage House. Number 8 is airy and spacious with a tile-framed fireplace, a pine armoire hiding the television, and a long desk.

Next door is the second mansion that makes up Gramma's— Fay House. You will probably go through the patio area that separates the two houses and enter a side door. But once inside, you really should walk to the front entrance to get the full effect of its magnificent staircase. Dark, flowered wallpaper, oak paneling, and touches of leaded and stained glass all make it a grand period piece. I was smitten with rooms on the third floor—not an easy haul if you're lugging much with you. But Room 8 up here is worth the trek. It is a huge room with a sitting area featuring not only love seat and chairs before the fireplace but also two 10-foot window seats.

The thing to remember about Gramma's is to make your needs known. If you prefer rooms that are newly decorated and modern, they have them. If atmosphere and period charm are what you like, you won't mind a well-aged corner or two. This is an inn where the stairs in the old houses may creak, but the fresh bouquet of lilacs seems more important.

Guests help themselves to a nourishing full breakfast buffet (would Gramma serve any other kind?) and sit at round tables for two draped to the floor. Fruits, freshly baked breads, omelets, and wonderful granola—the very thing to give you the energy to walk to the university and raise Cain all day. For dinner, some of Berkeley's best restaurants are up and down Telegraph Avenue.

How to get there: From Highway 80 (the Eastshore) through Berkeley, take the Ashby Avenue exit; turn left at Telegraph Avenue. The inn is 3 blocks on your left at number 2740.

J: *All that civility and charm . . . pretty radical stuff!*

Olive Metcalf

Old Thyme Inn
Half Moon Bay, California
94019

Innkeepers: Simon and Anne Lowings
Address/Telephone: 779 Main Street; (415) 726–1616
Rooms: 7; all with private bath, 3 with Jacuzzi and fireplace.
Rates: $65 to $210 for suite, double occupancy, breakfast and early-evening beverage. Reduced rates for weekdays and extended stays.
Open: All year.
Facilities and activities: Nearby: 1 mile to state beach; Fitzgerald Marine Reserve; whale watching, elephant seal reserve, hiking, horseback riding, fishing fleet at Princeton Harbor and pier, Main Street with shops and restaurants, Spanishtown Art Center, many annual events including October Art and Pumpkin Festival.

Medical experts would surely agree that a two-day dropout from routine can refresh spirits and do more for good marital relationships than an entire season of watching Dr. Ruth. In addition, it only gently dents a budget. All of which should have Bay Area residents, especially, zipping down to the small coastal community of Half Moon Bay. This short getaway destination is just forty-five minutes from the heart of San Francisco and a jog off the highway—an unpretentious, pleasantly unchic, and, best of all, semiundiscovered historic little town.

For lodging comfort, The Old Thyme Inn beautifully fits the bill for such a low-key holiday. The house is picturesque, dating back to

1899; it's freshly renovated, delightfully decorated, and sits right on the town's historic Main Street. You need not get in your car again until it's time to go home. (Stop by Zabella House, the oldest standing house in Half Moon Bay, and just 4 blocks away, to see still another inn beautifully restored by the Lowings.)

Actually, meeting Anne and Simon Lowings is reason enough to check into the Old Thyme. They're two of the most charming innkeepers you'll ever know. To my Anglophile ear, it helps, of course, that they speak English with a British accent—probably due to being born there. They restored this old house (and some of their stories about *that* enterprise sound like episodes from *Fawlty Towers*), Anne planted an herb garden, and Simon learned to cook. The whole family has become familiar with the joys of tide-pooling at the local Fitzgerald Marine Reserve, with the elephant seals that come ashore near here, and with walking and riding the hills and beaches all about them. You're quite likely to catch their enthusiasm for the area.

They've given a lot of care to the decorating, which has an herb theme. Each room has pretty wallpaper, comforters, English antiques, and an understated charm. The Thyme Room has a fireplace and a whirlpool tub (Simon denies it's the "Wild Thyme Room"). A Garden Suite has a whirlpool tub for two under a skylight, a four-poster bed, a fireplace, a television/VCR, and even the cachet of an English butler (Simon) who will bring breakfast in bed.

A comfortable, homey sitting area ("lounge" to us Anglophiles) has a wood-burning stove and English appointments and memorabilia. I especially liked sitting down to breakfast in the adjoining dining area under a portrait of the young Victoria. The menu would have pleased the old girl, I'm sure: fresh juice, homemade hot scones with marmalade, cold meats, and English cheeses, all topped off with a French cherry flan.

How to get there: From San Francisco, take Highway 280 south to Highway 92 and head west. At Main Street, turn left. The inn is on your left.

J: *Please understand . . . innkeepers do like to change menus. Simon tells me everyone who stays as a result of reading this guide comes "expecting those damned scones!"*

Clive Metcalf

San Benito House
Half Moon Bay, California
94019

Innkeeper: Carol Mickelsen
Address/Telephone: 356 Main Street; (415) 726–3425
Rooms: 12; 9 with private bath.
Rates: $60 to $117, double occupancy, continental breakfast. Guests receive 10 percent off in restaurant.
Open: All year.
Facilities and activities: Dinner Thursday through Sunday; Sunday brunch, reservations advised. Sun deck, sauna, croquet, complete conference and wedding facilities. Nearby: thirty minutes to San Francisco airport and Silicon Valley.

Here is a refreshing coastal wonder—an inn that takes dead aim on European-style flavor and delivers it minus the pretensions or obscene prices that often are part of the story. (Simple country charm doesn't come cheap, you know.) Carol Mickelsen is the owner and inspiration behind transforming the old Mosconi Hotel into a hostelry in the European tradition. And she offers travelers more than picturesque ambience.

Food—gloriously innovative, fresh, and colorful—is Carol's forte. She has seriously studied cooking and trained with famed French chefs Jacques Pépin and Roger Verge at Cannes. She runs the kitchen of this friendly, homey restaurant with a team of talented chefs. Carol makes all the sauces, soups, and complex parts of certain dishes; another chef does pastries, breads, and backup and a third chef works at night finishing the meals.

Diners are offered a choice of entrees that range from classic standbys done with a new twist (mesquite-grilled lamb chops with homemade peach/mint chutney served with basamatic rice pancake and sautéed greens) to dishes you may not have tasted before (homemade pumpkin ravioli with walnut sauce). Among the starters on the menu, I'm a fan of warm spinach salad with slow-roasted onions, bacon, and feta cheese. For dessert, if you can pass up a chocolate pecan pie with Chantilly cream, try a glass of Bukkuram 1986 Sicilian Moscato. Oh, so good.

Dinners are served in a dining room with brass chandeliers, blue cotton tablecloths, bright peach napkins, and a profusion of fresh bouquets. All around is an exceptional collection of original paintings by early 1900s coastal artists, particularly Galen Wolf, Greer Morton, and Joseph Cave.

French doors lead onto a large redwood deck. Here's the place to have a wedding reception on a summer day or to gather around the massive fire pit at night when the fire is lit to sip cognac and stargaze.

The stairway to the upstairs begins at an elaborate mirrored hallpiece and continues under an ornate cornice. The stained-glass partitions Carol bought are a unique touch in the bathrooms. Bedrooms on the garden side are the most elaborately decorated with antique light fixtures, brass beds, and walls painted in vivid colors, some with stenciled details. It's pleasant having coffee makings up here, and there's a small deck off the end of the hallway.

How to get there: From San Francisco, take Highway 280 south to Half Moon Bay. Turn west at Highway 92 to Main Street; turn left. Inn is on the right at the corner of Mill Street. From the south, Highway One passes through Half Moon Bay.

J: *Laudatory reviews of San Benito House have appeared in* Gourmet *and the* San Francisco Chronicle. *Now the cat's out of the bag.*

Olive Metcalf

Blackthorne Inn
Inverness, California
94937

Innkeepers: Susan Wigert and Lynn DeBarrows
Address/Telephone: 266 Vallejo Avenue (mailing address: Box 712); (415) 663–8621
Rooms: 5; 3 with private bath.
Rates: $105 to $185, double occupancy, generous breakfast buffet.
Open: All year.
Facilities and activities: Decks for sunning, hot tub. Nearby: restaurants, Point Reyes National Seashore, nature walks, wildflowers, bird watching, winter whale watching.

"This is really an adult treehouse," says Susan Wigert. This fascinating redwood, cedar, and fir structure began with a small cabin built in the 1930s. Now it rises through the treetops to four levels, joined by a 40-foot spiral staircase. Flanked with decks and balconies, approached by walkways and bridges, the building is crowned with the octagonal Eagle's Nest Room. Your first adventure after arriving will be exploring the ways around it.

The inn was designed by Bill Wigert, Susan's husband. In addition to milling some of the wood from trees on the site, Wigert made the construction quite a salvage operation. He used beams from San Francisco piers, boulders from seven counties for the walk-in fireplace, and huge doors rescued from the old San Francisco Southern Pacific building.

The main level has a large, airy living room with skylights, comfortable furniture, and a stone fireplace. The sounds of Handel (or was it Vivaldi?) came from a stereo the afternoon I arrived, cats snoozed, and the wine tray was ready. All good signs.

Adjoining the living room is a glass-enclosed solarium where a California-style continental breakfast is served: juice, fresh fruit, quiche, pastries, yogurt, and granola. This is the only meal served at the inn, but guests often walk or drive into the village to buy picnic munchies to lunch on back at the house while enjoying the decks.

Dinner choices in this coastal area used to be slim pickings, but these days in the villages there are cafes, a French restaurant, two Czechoslovakian ones, a bakery that makes a great pizza, and at Chez Madeline, a daily changing menu of fresh fish and local food prepared expertly. The innkeepers are happy to help you choose and make reservations.

Guest rooms are attractive and cozy, some with pitched ceilings and arched windows, some with small decks. A 3,500-square-foot sun deck surrounds the main level of the house—with a fireman's pole to slide down, if you're nimble. Another deck on the hillside has a complimentary hot tub. On the roof is a private sun deck for the Eagle's Nest, an octagonal, glass-enclosed tower room with wonderful views. Its private bath is across the skybridge.

This is a unique spot, for the young at heart.

How to get there: From San Francisco, take Highway 101 through Olema toward Inverness. Turn left at the Inverness Park Grocery onto Vallejo Avenue 2 miles south of Inverness. The inn is on your right.

J: *Innkeeper Susan Wigert says she has traveled in Mexico and on the East Coast but comes home to Blackthorne convinced that she lives in paradise.*

olive Metcalf

Ten Inverness Way
Inverness, California
94937

Innkeeper: Mary Davies

Address/Telephone: 10 Inverness Way (mailing address: P.O. Box 63); (415) 669–1648

Rooms: 5, including 1 suite; all with private bath. No smoking inn.

Rates: $110 to $150, double occupancy; $10 less for single; full breakfast and afternoon beverages.

Open: All year.

Facilities and activities: Books, music, fireside, gardens, hot tub. Nearby: Point Reyes National Seashore offers miles of hiking and walking trails to beaches, redwoods, picnic spots, a lighthouse. Summer swimming in Tomales Bay; winter whale watching. Explore Inverness and the other peninsula villages. Restaurants, galleries, shops.

Ten Inverness Way is the kind of rambling, comfortable house that gives bed and breakfast inns a good name. It has all the essential heart-warming ingredients: fireside and books, hot tea and music, gardens and good food. And then there are a couple of innocent extras that help explain why this inn, among a glamorous lot, is the hands-down favorite of so many inn lovers.

First, it has an intelligent, caring innkeeper who can discuss history or hiking trails, literature or good restaurants, or who knows when to simply provide the setting and leave you alone. And second, the inn has the good fortune to be situated on the

Point Reyes Peninsula, one of the most outstanding areas of sea-coast and natural wonder on the West Coast.

As in most good inns worthy of the name, the focal spot of Ten Inverness is the living room. This one looks much the same as it did seventy years ago: oriental rugs, a player piano, overflowing book-cases built into deep windows, comfortable couches, and good brass reading lamps. Sound cozy? Wait until you try one of the beds. They're not only comfortable, they're made up with crisp sheets that smell of the outdoors and pillows that prop up or punch about just right. All the beds have handmade quilts and nearby good reading lights. Any room here is a happy choice, but if you can stay for a few days, the downstairs garden room is especially comfortable. It is a suite with a love seat and chairs in a light sitting area, a small equipped kitchen, and it opens out to its own private patio garden.

For all the comforts of staying put in this snuggly inn, the area is too rich with natural wonders not to venture out, rain or shine, to experience what Point Reyes National Seashore offers. Hiking trails, beach walks, tide-pooling, or (my personal favorite) buying a bucket of oysters at Johnson's Oyster Farm and having a barbecue on the beach.

You'll want to explore the surrounding little towns, too, with unique shops, some galleries, and some fine restaurants. Mankas, a longtime favorite serving Czechoslovakian food, has changed cours-es to lighter, more eclectic fare that is wonderful.

Breakfast at an inn like this is always an opportunity to chat with interesting people—it simply seems to attract them! Mary serves warm, homemade favorites like banana-buckwheat pancakes or maybe a buttermilk spice coffee cake with her cheese-and-basil scrambled eggs, plenty of good strong coffee, fresh fruit, and good music.

How to get there: Take Highway 101 north to Sir Francis Drake Boulevard exit; follow to Olema, then jog right onto Highway One, then left about 3 miles to stop sign, then left to Inverness. Turn left at the Inverness Inn restaurant; the inn is on the right.

✳

J: *When you're in need of a comforting nest, wend your way to Ten Inverness.*

olive Metcalf

Mountain Home Inn
Mill Valley, California
94941

Innkeeper: Lynn Saggese, manager
Address/Telephone: 810 Panoramic Highway; (415) 381–9000
Rooms: 10; all with private bath and telephone, some with deck, Jacuzzi, and fireplace.
Rates: $121 to $178, double occupancy, full breakfast.
Open: All year.
Facilities and activities: Lunch, dinner, Sunday brunch; wine bar. Wheelchair access to restaurant. Nearby: Muir Woods, Mt. Tamalpais.

This inn has it all: knock-your-socks-off views of the Bay and Marin hills, fascinating architectural design, luxury rooms, a lauded restaurant, and a professional staff just dying to pamper you. Even the twisting drive up to its mountain perch is beautiful.

Longtime Marin residents remember the inn on the slope of Mt. Tamalpais through many incarnations. It was built in 1912 by a Swiss couple supposedly homesick for an Alpine view. Most recently it was a German beer-and-sandwich place serving dusty hikers. What a difference a no-expense-spared renovation makes.

A blond hardwood interior softly announces "California chic," with cathedral ceilings and pillars of redwood still covered with bark. Muted colors—beiges, apricots—are punctuated with unusual hickory furniture pieces.

Guest rooms are sleek and serene, some with a deck to enjoy

the sweeping view. Appointments include grand tubs (some with Jacuzzis), complimentary toiletries, and thick towels. During the week, inn guests have a private dining room with fireplace and outside deck. If you've stayed the night, enjoy the daily papers and a full breakfast here or in your room: hot and cold beverages and a choice of entrees, including omelets, French toast with bacon or sausage, and eggs any style with potatoes.

At the heart of the inn is the beautiful bar and intimate dining room with deck overlooking the dazzling view. Weekend guests breakfast here. The no-smoking rule in the dining rooms speaks to the serious way they regard food.

Menus reflect the availability of seasonal fresh fish and produce. The cuisine is American, but with this kitchen's own artful stamp. You will find the old reliables like rack of lamb, grilled filet with a Madeira sauce, and a smoked pork loin with orange sauce, or, on the more adventurous side, how about grilled Japanese Eggplant with a sundried tomato vinaigrette as a starter and smoked chicken fettuccine? Desserts include homemade ice cream with fresh berries, and a walnut chocolate mousse.

How to get there: From San Francisco, cross the Golden Gate Bridge, and take Mill Valley/Stinson Beach exit to Highway One junction. Turn left at light; proceed 2¹/₂ to 3 miles. Turn right onto Panoramic Highway (sign says TO MT. TAMALPAIS STATE PARK). At ⁴/₅ miles, follow middle road, staying on Panoramic, though sign still says to the park. Inn is on the right after 2 miles.

Olive Metcalf

Seal Cove Inn
Moss Beach, California
94038

Innkeepers: Karen and Rick Herbert

Address/Telephone: 221 Cypress Avenue, (415) 728–7325 (S-E-A-L); fax (415) 728–4116

Rooms: 10; all with private bath, wood-burning fireplace, private terrace or balcony, television/VCR, telephone, air conditioning. One room fully equipped for handicapped. No smoking. Children especially welcome.

Rates: $160 to $250, double occupancy, full breakfast, complimentary soft drinks, wine, evening hors d'oeuvres. $25 each additional person.

Open: All year.

Facilities and activities: Hillside garden setting, cycling (bring your own or borrow theirs), walking paths along ocean bluffs, seal watching. Excellent facilities for small conferences or family reunions up to sixteen. Nearby: sandy beach, tide pools at Fitzgerald Marine Reserve; Princeton Harbor 2 miles south offers sport fishing, whale-watching excursions, restaurants. Horseback riding, golf, Filoli tours (the "Dynasty" estate), Half Moon Bay shops and restaurants, picnic in a redwood forest.

Just a thirty-minute drive south of San Francisco is a newly built inn of such taste and comfort that it will rouse the enthusiasm of the most jaded traveler. I felt as if I were in a fine private home, much like the atmosphere in a British manor house. "Generous" is the quality that describes everything here, from the entryway and size of the rooms to the hospitality and big bouquets all around. I'll warn you ahead about these rooms—it will pain you to leave after only a one-night stay. They're that good. This is elegant comfort without gimmicks, only the finest linens and fabrics and country antiques. Our room was the Carl Larsson and featured dozens of enchanting prints on the walls by that wonderful Swedish artist. French doors lead out to your own balcony or small terrace. A bar is stocked with complimentary soft drinks and wine, a well-laid fire awaits, and a television and VCR hide in an armoire.

An electric towel warmer in our bathroom reminded me again of a British country house. Other rooms are the Ascot with a Victorian/equestrian theme and the Cypress with its king-sized "tavern" bed, private Jacuzzi, and fine views. Largest and probably most spectacular of all the rooms is the Fitzgerald. It has a canopied king bed draped in a cream and beige fabric that is repeated on the sofa in front of a fireplace, a Jacuzzi tub in the large bathroom, and views of the park and ocean.

We decided on a walk through the garden with some still-blooming wildflowers (this was November), over a path bordered by towering Cypress trees to the bluff looking down to Seal Cove. When the mists begin rolling in and the seals on the rocks below are honking, this is a moody, particularly San Francisco experience. Northern Californians will know that late fall and winter see many sunny days, whereas the fogs come during summer.

Before dinner, we feasted on hors d'oeuvres and wine in the living room with other guests. Numerous restaurants are nearby, but we chose to walk just five minutes from the inn to The Distillery, a local place on the bluffs. When you return to your room at night, the bed is turned down, and a seriously great chocolate chip cookie awaits with a note asking when and where you want to breakfast, and would you like a thermos of coffee and the paper at your door at 8 A.M.? Yes, please! We breakfasted grandly in the inn's lovely dining room and lingered talking, probably far too long.

There is a reason this inn runs so well and looks so beautiful: The Herberts are knowledgeable on-the-scene innkeepers, not mere entrepreneurs who build a stunning inn and then hire someone else to run it. Karen has been writing for fifteen years about country inns throughout Europe and California in her inn guide series. Seal Cove is the happy result of that experience.

How to get there: From San Francisco, take I–280 to Pacifica exit (Highway One). Continue south through Moss Beach to Cypress Avenue. Turn right; inn is ¼ mile on the right.

olive Metcalf

The Pelican Inn
Muir Beach, California
94965

Innkeeper: Barry Stock
Address/Telephone: Muir Beach; (415) 383–6000
Rooms: 7; all with private bath.
Rates: $130 to $150, double occupancy, full English breakfast.
Open: All year. Closed Mondays, except to inn guests.
Facilities and activities: Lunch, dinner, bar serving wine and British ales; limited wheelchair access to dining room. Nearby: Point Reyes National Seashore, beachcombing, bird watching, hiking, Muir Redwood Groves.

That fourth-generation publican who built The Pelican Inn, Charles Felix, has retired. But fear not. "Rule Britannia" still applies. Barry Stock arrived from Devon, England, to keep the British tradition of innkeeping alive and chipper.

Just twenty minutes from the Golden Gate Bridge, this replica of a sixteenth-century English country inn has white stucco and is crisscrossed with dark beams. It seems a proper spot, considering that it was here on the Marin Coast that Sir Francis Drake beached his *Pelican* (renamed the *Golden Hind*) some 400 years ago and claimed California for Queen Elizabeth I and her descendants forever.

You enter a cozy English pub with low beams, dart board, and a good stock of brews. Many of the antiques here came from an inn the Felix family previously owned in Surrey. Since his arrival, Barry has added many antiques and artifacts of his own. The four-centuries-old paneled bar is packed on weekends with San Franciscans and inn guests who enjoy traditional lunch fare like fish 'n' chips, bangers, and mash.

An adjoining dining room has a huge fireplace and sturdy, dark tables and chairs. The dinner menu appropriately offers prime rib, Yorkshire pudding, and mixed English grill among its choices. Breakfast also is served here or in your room. It is big and English: juice, eggs, bacon, bangers, tomatoes, toast, and marmalade.

The bedrooms upstairs are wonderfully English. Beds have a brocade-draped half-canopy called a "half-tester." The device was once used not for decor, but to keep small rodents who might be frolicking in the thatched roof overhead from falling on your face while you slept. Other "mod cons" (modern conveniences) are a stone with a hole hanging over each bed to ensure no rickets in case of pregnancy. Former innkeeper Felix, who claimed a trust in every known superstition, successfully kept witches and evil spirits away with buried bones under the hearth and holly over the doors. Stock continues The Pelican as a safe haven with a garlic wreath at the entrance to ward off vampires and beasties of the night.

Mr. Stock takes the profession of publican seriously and laments mere B&Bs calling themselves inns. The Pelican is in the traditional mold, where the innkeeper is a public servant and feels it his duty to see that you are lodged, fed, and looked after properly.

How to get there: From San Francisco, take Highway 101 to the Stinson Beach/Mill Valley exit. Follow Highway One to the Arco gas station; turn left and continue for 5 miles to Muir Beach.

J: *I'm a pushover for an innkeeper who calls out as you're leaving for a walk on the beach, "Better take a woolie with you, do!"*

Olive Metcalf

Point Reyes Seashore Lodge
Olema, California
94950

Innkeepers: Judi and John Burkes
Address/Telephone: 10021 Coastal Highway One (mailing address: P.O. Box 39); (415) 663–9000
Rooms: 21, including 3 suites; all with private bath, direct-dial telephone; most have fireplace, whirlpool tub; suites have wet bar, refrigerator, bedroom loft. One room with facilities for the handicapped.
Rates: $85 to $175, double occupancy, with deluxe continental breakfast. $15 each additional person. Ask about midweek and off-season rates.
Open: All year.
Facilities and activities: Lodge specializes in small conferences and intimate weddings. Game room with antique billiard table; small library; wines, champagnes, and snack baskets available. Nearby: Point Reyes National Seashore facilities, hiking trails, beach, horse and bike rentals, San Geronimo Golf Course. Explore local shops, restaurants in nearby fishing villages.

Let's say you're eager to explore the endlessly fascinating Point Reyes Peninsula. You're up for a hike to Chimney Rock and a walk on the beach. You're ready for some serious tide-pooling, a bit of bird watching, and a bike ride. You're even hoping to experience a misty rain, a fog rolling in, or gale-force winds—all frequent elements in a Point Reyes stay. But when you've had enough nature for the day, you may want to indulge yourself in comfort with more than a touch of luxury. This lodge is a choice that will please.

Attractive as the wooden structure is on the outside, the two-story wings extending from either side of the lobby entrance with cars parked in front appears, initially, to be an upscale country motel. I didn't have a hint of the elegance inside.

The lobby area sets the tone immediately with its soaring open beams, mellow wood, fresh flowers, and local art. A few steps above, the library is an open, light-filled common area for guests to enjoy. We sat at a long reading table with a glass of wine and looked at pictures and books of the area's history.

Down a level is another sitting area and a game room with a stone fireplace, antique billiard table, games, and puzzles. One exit to the surprising back-lawn area is also here. The rolling green lawn is dappled with old shade trees and dotted with Adirondack-style chairs. This peaceful green expanse is the view from every room.

Ours was one of the rooms with both a fireplace and a whirlpool tub. All the tubs have a screen that can open to the living room. And before you think, "so what?," let me tell you that sitting in a tub with bubbles up to your nose while gazing at a crackling fire in the living room and out to the tranquil back lawn gives the word *sybaritic* full meaning.

Should your stay at the lodge be a special occasion, you might like either the Rancho Garcias or the Sir Francis Drake suites. These accommodations are stunningly decorated and have sitting areas, wet bar, refrigerator, and an upstairs sleeping loft with feather beds. This is all in addition to the whirlpool and fireplace. These rooms sleep four people.

Our breakfast was a generous continental buffet. In a breakfast room down a few steps from the lobby, we helped ourselves to juices, fruit, wonderful granola, pastries, and muffins.

For other meals, it's fun to explore the nearby villages. You will find charming local cafes and bistros serving specialties from fresh mussels and oysters to excellent pizzas. For dinner, a longtime favorite is Mankas restaurant in Inverness.

How to get there: From San Francisco, take Highway 101 north to the San Anselmo turnoff; continue on Sir Francis Drake Boulevard to Olema.

J: *Bring your bicycles or your horse to Point Reyes. The lodge will arrange storage and stabling for either.*

Olive Metcalf

Roundstone Farm
Olema, California
94950

Innkeeper: Inger Fisher
Address/Telephone: 9940 Sir Francis Drake Boulevard (mailing address: P.O. Box 217); (415) 663–1020
Rooms: 5; all with private bath and fireplace. Smoking on the deck.
Rates: $115, double occupancy, full breakfast. Two-night minimum on weekends.
Open: All year.
Facilities and activities: Point Reyes National Seashore. Nearby: Earthquake Trail, lighthouse, Chimney Rock; picnics, bicycles, horses available; bird watching; whale watches January through April; Inverness with small shops, unique crafts; excellent restaurants.

Just an hour's drive north of San Francisco is Point Reyes National Seashore, an ink blot–shaped peninsula of dramatic impact. This stunning convergence of land and sea, of hammering surfs and treacherous riptides, of windswept beaches and steep cliffs is a thrilling place for nature lovers. You don't go in the water here; you watch it respectfully. There are carpets of California poppies in the spring, tide pools of sea life, tule elk, sea lions, migratory birds, seals, and, in winter, whales migrating to Baja. The weather varies from hour to hour: warm and sunny to sudden chilling fogs.

Fresh from exploring this wild seashore, how lovely to return to the tranquil comforts of a country inn, beautifully designed and tastefully decorated. Roundstone Farm is a contemporary inn in the area with just those qualities. Its understated, fresh look is a complement to the Point Reyes terrain. Inger Fisher is both the designer and owner of Roundstone. She has owned the land a long time, but she waited and planned until she could build just the inn she wanted. "I've accomplished my dream—so far," she says.

The farmhouse of cedar batten and board has a long living room with a 16-foot ceiling and skylights. Books, a stereo, and comfortable upholstered furniture are inviting. One long side opens to a broad deck overlooking a pond and meadow where deer and horses graze. Mrs. Fisher also raises horses on the ten-acre ranch. Her Connemaras and Arabians are beautiful sights, too. What a fresh-air spot to read in and gaze at the rolling hills with Tomales Bay beyond.

Each of the guest rooms is a quiet retreat. Ours had sea-spray soft colors, a handsome pine armoire, and fireplace with tiled hearth. With a cozy down comforter, excellent bed, and good reading lights, what more could you want? Breakfast, that's what.

Inger serves in a raised dining room that looks over the living room and out to the new patio garden and beyond to the meadow and hills. Some of us had taken an early-morning walk along the earthquake trail of the San Andreas Fault, and her hearty breakfast was thoroughly enjoyed: fresh juices, egg and sausage torte, homemade chunky applesauce, hot homemade bread, jams, and coffee that kept coming while we sat around the table and talked.

How to get there: Ten miles north of the Golden Gate Bridge on Highway 101, take the San Anselmo/Richmond Bridge exit. Proceed west on Sir Francis Drake Boulevard approximately 20 miles. Roundstone Farm is 300 yards before (east) the intersection with Highway One.

ે

J: The legacy of good innkeeping has traveled a reverse direction in this instance: from son to mother. Jackie and Ron Fisher, Inger's son and his wife, became innkeepers first at the beautiful Mangels House in Aptos.

cli ve Metcalf

Holly Tree Inn
Point Reyes Station, California
94956

Innkeepers: Tom and Diane Balogh
Address/Telephone: 3 Silverhills Road (mailing address: Box 642); (415)
663-1554
Rooms: 4, all with private bath; 2 cottages with private bath, hot tub, and
fireplace.
Rates: $100 to $175, double occupancy, full breakfast. Some rooms suitable
for families with young children.
Open: All year.
Facilities and activities: Nearby: 1 mile to Point Reyes National Seashore; area
offers horseback riding, hiking, fishing, boating, bird watching, mush-
rooming, nature walks; unique shops, fine restaurants.

There is something especially pleasing about fine houses built
before World War II: They're modern enough for comfort, yet old
enough to have a spacious elegance few of us enjoy at home. Holly
Tree Inn has those qualities, and sits on nineteen lush acres of
lawns and gardens. It was built in 1939 by a Swede with a British
wife, who probably accounts for the arbor of holly trees, the English
laurels, lilacs, privet, and the herb garden.

The house is decorated in understated British taste that suits it
perfectly: English and continental prints, plump upholstered chairs
and sofas, antiques, fresh flowers, and whimsy. A row of tiny
wooden buildings ranges across both fireplace mantels in the dining

and living rooms. A guest sipping a sherry in the big sofa might look at it for some time before realizing it is Point Reyes in miniature—made by innkeeper Tom Balogh.

Bedrooms are each different and delightfully English. The smallest, Mary's Garden Room, is done in a green-and-blue sprigged print, has a fireplace and love seat, and opens onto a patio and perennial flower garden. The larger rooms are equally tasteful and have beautiful views.

For a special occasion, something very intimate and cozy, you will love Sea Star Cottage, a small rustic house built on pilings above the tidal waters of Tomales Bay. A 75-foot dock leads to the front door, opening to a living room with wood-burning fireplace, a four-poster queen-sized bed, blue-and-white tiled bathroom, fully equipped kitchen, and solarium with hot tub. Breakfast is prepared for you in advance, ready for you to warm up and serve in the sunny breakfast room or out on the deck.

Christmas at Holly Tree Inn is special. Polished wood gleams in the glow of both blazing fireplaces, and there are decorations galore. Santa made an unexpected appearance once by way of a working electric dumbwaiter beside the fireplace, usually used for bringing up logs.

Mid-January is whale-watch time on cool, misty Point Reyes Peninsula. If you've always intended to read up on this phenomenon, nestled by the large brick fireplace in the living room is the place to choose; then take a short drive out to the coast to watch the migration.

A fine breakfast is served in the dining room—juice, fresh fruit, bran muffins or croissants, homemade poppy-seed bread, several cheeses, and then something special, like individual asparagus soufflés. For other meals, there is a wide choice of good restaurants in the area.

How to get there: From San Francisco, exit Highway 101 north at Sir Francis Drake Boulevard. Stay on Drake forty-five minutes to Olema and turn right onto Highway One. Drive 1 block north, then turn left onto Bear Valley Road. At Holly Tree Inn sign, turn left onto Silverhills Road. Turn left at second driveway. Look for Holly Tree Inn sign.

Olive Metcalf

Pillar Point Inn
Princeton-by-the-Sea, California
94018

Innkeeper: Dick Anderton
Address/Telephone: 380 Capistrano Road (mailing address: P.O. Box 388, El
   Granada); (415) 728–7377
Rooms: 11, including 1 room equipped for handicapped; all with private
   bath, fireplace, media center, refrigerator, telephone. No smoking inn.
Rates: $125, single, to $140, double occupancy, Sunday through Thursday;
   $145 to $160 weekends; full breakfast. $20 additional person.
Open: All year.
Facilities and activities: Facilities for weddings, business meetings; conference
   room. Nearby: active harbor and marina; gray whale migration
   December through March; Año Nuevo Reserve 35 miles south; con-
   ducted nature tours at Fitzgerald Marine Reserve; walking tour of Half
   Moon Bay; fine coastal restaurants.

Just 25 miles south of San Francisco on Highway One, the new
construction is taking on a New England look. In the Princeton-by-
the-Sea/El Granada area they're even calling themselves Cape Cod
on the California coast. The Pillar Point Inn is one of the newer additions to the scene, a handsome Cape Cod–style building that opened
in 1985.

There's a clean, windswept look to the frame structure with a
white picket fence and flowers running along its length. A recep-
tion/parlor area looks smart with floral print sofas arranged before a
fireplace decorated with blue-and-white tiles. Beverages are set out

here and may be taken to the second-floor harbor-view deck. Touches of wood and brass against soft blue-gray colors and fresh flowers tell you at once that this is an impeccably maintained inn. All but one of its eleven luxurious rooms overlook the colorful Pillar Point Harbor. The fussiest traveler should be happy with the soft, easy-to-take colors, cuddly European-style feather beds, and beautifully tiled fireplace and hearth. Hidden behind cupboard doors is an entire media center: television, video player, and radio. Topping off this full slate of appointments is a minirefrigerator, telephone, and first-rate bathroom. Some rooms have a private steam bath. One room has wheelchair access and a bathroom specially fitted for a handicapped guest.

A cheery breakfast room with pine-top tables and cottage curtains is another pleasant spot. Innkeeper Dick Anderton serves a full breakfast here including fresh fruits, juices, and a variety of homemade hot dishes.

This is a great stretch of the coast to explore: a busy fishing fleet and wharf, a variety of vessels, both commercial and pleasure craft, and an active boat-building industry, where you can watch even wooden boats in various stages of completion. Just 4 miles south, the old town of Half Moon Bay is wonderful to walk with its distinctive shops and an art center called Spanish Town. The town is the scene every fall of an enormously popular pumpkin festival, but most of the time you'll find far fewer people around here than in other coastal communities. Best of all is the nature and marine life to observe here, from the great elephant seal herds to the California gray whales' migration.

How to get there: From San Francisco, drive south 25 miles on Highway One to Princeton-by-the-Sea. Turn into the harbor on Capistrano at the traffic light.

Olive Metcalf

Alamo Square Inn
San Francisco, California
94117

Innkeepers: Wayne Corn and Klaus May

Address/Telephone: 719 Scott Street; (415) 922–2055 or (800) 345–9888; fax
 (415) 931–1304

Rooms: 13, including 4 suites; all with private bath, telephone. Television
 available.

Rates: $85 double bed, double occupancy, to $225 for 2-bedroom suite,
 including full breakfast, afternoon tea, wine.

Open: All year.

Facilities and activities: Facilities and catering for weddings, small private parties, and seminars. Nearby: restaurants; historic Alamo Square District
 for walking, viewing Victorian architecture; 10 blocks west of San
 Francisco Civic Center; close to Golden Gate Park.

These two San Francisco mansions on Alamo Square, lovingly
restored and now maintained as an elegant inn, are just another
grace note added to this historic district. The area escaped the great
fire of 1906 and still has hundreds of picturesque houses that have
survived since it was a popular suburb in the 1880s and 1890s.
Some of the city's most beautiful examples of Victorian architecture
face Alamo Square, a small park on a sloping hillside.

Innkeepers Corn and May have constructed a solarium and
conservatory filled with flowering plants and greenery that joins an
1895 Queen Anne mansion to an 1896 English Tudor. Just looking

at this verdant space makes you think of the possibilities, like hosting an elegant little party.

You see why prospective brides frequently choose the inn as the scene of both their wedding ceremony and reception; it's a romantic house. There are two parlors furnished in a blend of Victorian and oriental styles, a grand staircase for a smashing entrance, and a large formal dining room.

The innkeepers have been restoring the two mansions for over ten years, but Corn says it is still an inn in transition. Guest rooms are comfortably decorated with antique touches. Some have gas fireplaces, and one unit overlooking the rose garden has a full kitchen. Some rooms overlook the park, others have garden views, and one of the suites has a balcony with a panoramic view of the city. This suite in Art Deco style also has a sunken Jacuzzi.

Klaus, a native of the Rhineland-Pfalz area of Germany, is a professional chef and takes pride in his breakfast productions. It's a hearty, sit-down meal in the dining room, but it can also be delivered to your room or served in the garden. Gorgeous fresh raspberries were the stars of the fruit selection when I visited. Then there was juice, cheese omelets, and the chef's specialty, homemade Danish and other breakfast pastries. (He makes special hors d'oeuvres too.)

Both Wayne and Klaus know San Francisco well. They're ready to help guests with information about what's happening in town, the best play, or the newest restaurant.

How to get there: From Highway 80 going north to the Golden Gate Bridge, take Fell Street west about 7 blocks. Turn right at Scott Street to number 719, on the left.

J: This is just the kind of neighborhood to walk when you want to get a feel for San Francisco: a park and greenery, picturesque houses, hills, and views.

Olive Metcalf

The Archbishops Mansion
San Francisco, California
94117

Innkeepers: Kathleen Austin; proprietors, Jonathan Shannon and Jeffrey Ross

Address/Telephone: 1000 Fulton Street; (415) 563–7872 or (800) 543–5820

Rooms: 15; all with private bath, cable television, and telephone, 13 with fireplace.

Rates: $125 to $325, double occupancy, continental breakfast, afternoon refreshments. Two-night minimum on weekends.

Open: All year.

Facilities and activities: Dinners, business meetings, private parties, weddings catered by arrangement. Nearby: San Francisco Opera House, Davies Symphony Hall, Galleria Design Center, Moscone Convention Center.

Let us not pussyfoot about the kind of establishment this is: *opulent, romantic, dramatic,* and *grand* will do for starters. Messrs. Shannon and Ross call themselves innkeepers, but the lodgings and service they offer give the term a new dimension.

This impressive mansion in the Alamo Square District was built in 1904 as the private residence of the archbishop of San Francisco and his entourage. It survived the 1906 earthquake and became headquarters for a citywide effort to rebuild San Francisco. Pope Pius XII stayed here in the mid-1930s while he was still a cardinal. High standards of taste, talent, and lots of money have brought the mansion back to architectural prominence, but the tender loving care lavished on guests is what ultimately makes it an exceptional inn.

You enter a great hall with an elegant parlor on one side and ahead a magnificent three-story open staircase covered by a 16-foot stained-glass dome. The architecture is French Empire. The intricate ceiling details, splendid rugs, antiques, and lush draperies could convince you that it was a European palace. But there are unexpected treasures, too, like Noel Coward's 1904 Bechstein grand piano in the reception hall and a large Victorian pier mirror from Abraham Lincoln's Springfield home.

Each of the luxurious bedrooms is designed to reflect the atmosphere of a particular opera. The most opulent is the Gypsy Baron Suite with its large sitting area before a baronial fireplace and a stunning four-poster canopied king-sized bed. The Rosenkavalier Suite has gracefully curved construction, even in the thresholds and bookcases.

Cosi fan Tutte, La Tosca, and Madama Butterfly all have exceptional antiques and exquisitely embroidered linens. Don Giovanni has an intricately carved bed that is just one of the prizes in a house full of treasures. Some of the bathrooms are like good-sized rooms (Carmen's has a fireplace) with oriental rugs, chandeliers, and tall stands for keeping the champagne cold while you soak in a hot tub. Surely, *you* don't tub without champagne at the ready?

Guests gather for complimentary refreshments in the afternoon in a downstairs parlor. Breakfast is served in the enormous dining room or delivered to your room in a French picnic basket. Several salons are available for small conferences or where the hosts cater dinners or cocktail parties by prior arrangement. The surroundings are palatial but warm, with all the personal attention you could desire.

How to get there: From Van Ness, take Fulton Street west to Alamo Square. Inn is on the right, number 1000.

❖

J: *Jonathan Shannon says: "Innkeeping is a theatrical event; it's nice to provide guests with an environment they don't have at home."*

Olive Metcalf

The Bed and Breakfast Inn
San Francisco, California
94123

Innkeepers: Marily and Robert Kavanaugh
Address/Telephone: 4 Charlton Court; (415) 921–9784
Rooms: 10, including penthouse; 6 with private bath, some with telephone
and television.
Rates: $70 to $140, double occupancy; $215, penthouse; light breakfast.
Open: All year.
Facilities and activities: Located on one of the most fashionable shopping
streets in San Francisco. Nearby: restaurants, shops, Victorian architec-
ture, bus line to downtown.

You say you want intimate ambience . . . Cotswolds-cozy
atmosphere . . . in San Francisco? It awaits you, with elegance,
down a narrow cul-de-sac off Union Street.

Occasional guests have been heard to utter the word *alley*—
probably some down-to-earth Midwestern types—but the preferred
location description here is "mews," or possibly "courtyard." Whatever you call it, it *is* adorable. Red geraniums in window boxes
stand out against the green and white exterior of the inn, which is
really three restored Victorian houses. You'll be greeted like an old
friend. Sit down on the white wicker settee and have a glass of
sherry.

The breakfast room just off the entrance can entertain a china lover for hours. Much of Marily's collection of Spode, Copeland, and Wedgwood, among others, is displayed along with a vast number of teapots. Even better, it's all used on pretty linen settings for morning and afternoon tea. You can breakfast on a different china setting every day in a garden patio, or be served in your room. You'll get the *San Francisco Chronicle* and freshly ground coffee or English teas, fruit, and hot "good things" like croissants or scones.

Rooms are decorated with extraordinary flair using family heirlooms from England. They all have the bright, fresh look of just having been redone. Dainty Laura Ashley print is in a delicate room called Celebration; grass cloth and rattan furniture in Mandalay. Other rooms are Covent Garden, Green Park, and Kensington Garden, which opens to a flower-filled deck behind the inn. The Mayfair is a private flat with living room, kitchen, latticed balcony, and spiral staircase to the bedroom loft.

A small library room downstairs is a cozy retreat with a television, games, and books. You're invited to brew yourself a cup of tea, if you like. Very personal service is the pride of everyone around here.

Within a 2-block circle around the inn are dozens of interesting restaurants. Perry's is one that's always fun—one of San Francisco's most famous bars, specializing in interpersonal relations and great hamburgers.

How to get there: From Van Ness Street, take Union Street west. Between Laguna and Buchanan streets, turn left into Charlton Court.

J: *As a dyed-in-the-wool "Masterpiece Theatre" buff, I love the English ambience here, not to mention the "upstairs" treatment they give you.*

olive Metcalf

The Mansions Hotel
San Francisco, California
94115

Innkeeper: Robert Pritikin
Address/Telephone: 2220 Sacramento Street; (415) 929–9444
Rooms: 25, including some suites; all with private bath and telephone, some
  with fireplace and television.
Rates: $89 to $325, double occupancy; $74 to $300, single; full breakfast.
Open: All year.
Facilities and activities: Restaurant serves dinner weekends and most
  weeknights; concerts, billiards, Bufano Sculpture gardens; weddings,
  parties, and conferences catered. Nearby: a neighborhood of splendid
  San Francisco homes; cable car 4 blocks away; tennis courts.

In the words of Monty Python, "and now for something completely different": two grand mansions interconnected; nightly magical séances; real British masters like Turner and Reynolds on the
walls; pigs, rendered in all media, throughout the mansions; rooms
of fine antiques, sculpture, funky junk, and cages of macaws; a
neighborhood polling place whose costumed staff offers voters beverages and venison pâtés from silver platters . . . it's all The Mansions!

Ad man Robert Pritikin has been called eccentric and whimsical, but he also may be the most original innkeeper in the city. His
inn is a little quirky, but it's lavishly decorated and great fun. One
of the mansions is a twin-turreted Queen Anne Victorian, the other

a 1903 Greek Revival house. Together they are a spectacular and very "San Francisco" sight. The atmosphere inside can only be called elegant, with billiard room, handsomely furnished parlors, crystal chandelier, and, most especially, the magnificent collection of marble and bronze Bufano sculptures. Pritikin's is the definitive display of this artist's works.

It's the pigs, in porcelain, painting, and sculpture, that tell you a sense of humor is loose here. The perfectly reasonable explanation for the swine element in the midst of Victoriana is that they're to pacify Claudia, the Mansions ghost. She kept pigs in the Queen Anne house, where she lived and died, and according to demonologists her "extremely heavy" (but not negative) presence is still in the mansion.

Claudia often appears in the music room in her empty Victorian wheelchair and invisibly plays selections requested by the guests. Sometimes the concert closes with ragtime or a Sousa march, assisted by the audience members, who have been supplied with cowbells, maracas, and tambourines. Weekend concerts feature innkeeper Pritikin on the Concert Saw and other class acts.

Up the grand staircase are guest rooms in turn-of-the-century-style decor with modern plumbing, telephones, and other contemporary comforts. Some have balconies and marble fireplaces; each has a private speaker that plays classical music when you wish. Bedrooms in the west wing have a more contemporary, light-filled feeling. On the third floor, The Green Gables and The Petite Suite are charmers.

Dinner is served in a lovely stained glass–appointed dining room opening onto a garden. David Pore is the chef, winning raves from critics and guests. The weekday a la carte and weekend prix fixe four-course dinners are a bargain in this city. He also does a splendid full breakfast, from fresh-squeezed orange juice and crumpets to eggs and sausage and au gratin potatoes.

How to get there: Entering the city from the east or south, follow signs to the Golden Gate Bridge until you come to the Van Ness exit. If you are entering over the Golden Gate Bridge, follow signs to downtown and Lombard Street. Go east on Lombard to Van Ness and turn right. From Van Ness Avenue, turn west on Sacramento to the inn on your right.

Olive Metcalf

Petite Auberge
San Francisco, California
94108

Innkeeper: Rich Revaz
Address/Telephone: 863 Bush Street; (415) 928–6000
Rooms: 26, including 1 suite; all with private bath, 18 with fireplace.
Rates: $105 to $215, double occupancy, full breakfast served buffet style and afternoon tea. Parking $15 per day.
Open: All year.
Facilities and activities: Nearby: walk to San Francisco's theater district, shopping, Nob Hill, Union Square, fine restaurants, cable-car connections.

Hard to believe, but in the very heart of downtown San Francisco is an inn with all the ambience of a French country inn. Not rustic-country, mind you, but classy-country. Step into the green canopied entrance from busy Bush Street and you enter a warmly inviting lobby of large, brick-colored tiles that look old (but probably aren't), oriental rugs, fresh flowers, and a carousel horse that for some reason looks French.

But everything looks French with bright Pierre Deux fabric designs on lampshades, picture mats, and French Provincial furniture. (At the desk I was told that the Pierre Deux company, by the way, was begun by two men both named Pierre; thus the "deux.") White porcelain ducks sporting ribbons around the neck, and grapevine wreaths entwined with ribbons give the impression of perennial springtime, French style.

Upstairs, even the smallest rooms are impeccably decorated with every possible convenience. Handsome armoires hide televisions. Good reading lights are on either side of the beds, which have beautiful linens, fluffy quilts, and extra pillows. A hand-addressed welcome letter for the expected guests awaits on the bed.

One of the medium-sized rooms has space for a creamy tiled fireplace, rose love seat, blue wingback chair, and a window seat. Bathroom fixtures have elegant porcelain handles, and special toiletries and thick towels await.

What makes this an inn instead of an elegant small hotel? Hands-on taking care of you, that's what. Do you want to arrange transportation from the airport, have your car parked, or have your shoes shined? Do you need someone to handle those tiresome details of dinner reservations and theater tickets? Would you like to lay on a smart dinner party but abhor the crassness of a public restaurant?

Relax, mon ami. All can be arranged. Downstairs from the lobby is a comfortable lounge, dining room, and courtyard garden. The attractive dining room is painted with a scene from an outdoor French cafe. (There is no smoking in the dining room.) Breakfast is served here mornings; tea, wine, and nibbles in the afternoons. The inn offers an attractively presented and satisfying breakfast, with fresh fruit, juices, cereals, homemade breads and pastries, and an ever-changing main dish.

How to get there: From Union Square, go left (west) on Sutter Street to Taylor; turn right, go to Bush; turn right. Inn is on the right at number 863.

J: *I've always loved the pastoral life. It's good to see it thriving here on Bush Street.*

olive Metcalf

Victorian Inn on the Park
San Francisco, California
94117

Innkeepers: Lisa and William Benau, Paul and Shirley Weber
Address/Telephone: 301 Lyon Street; (415) 931–1830 or (800) 435–1967; fax
(415) 931–1830
Rooms: 12, including 1 suite; all with private bath and telephone, some with
fireplace, television on request.
Rates: $88, double occupancy, to $250 for suite for 4, generous continental
breakfast. Two-night minimum on weekends.
Open: All year.
Facilities and activities: Accommodates small meetings. Nearby: restaurants,
the Panhandle and Golden Gate Park for walking and bicycling; De
Young Museum, California Academy of Sciences, Japanese Tea Garden.

When Queen Victoria celebrated her Diamond Jubilee in 1897,
the Victorian Inn on the Park was built by a local lumberman for
his son Thomas Clunie. The Clunie House reflected the family business with its intricately paneled entry and parquet floors lavishly
inlaid with oak, mahogany, and redwood. The history of the ornate
house progresses from first owner, Clunie, who became a state sen-
ator and United States congressman, to a cult group who held
rebirthing rites in a hot tub in the basement!

Since the Benaus and Lisa's parents, the Webers, rescued it,
they have restored and decorated the house as an inn with faithful
attention to turn-of-the-century details. Lisa and her mother chose

the antique pieces. There are fascinating old photographs on the walls and a red velvet upholstered Queen Anne sofa and chair in the parlor. They've found, or had designed, some of the most flamboyant fringed lampshades I've ever seen . . . and they look wonderful in rooms this size.

Six guest rooms are upstairs, another four in what was once the ballroom on the top floor, and two more bedrooms in the basement. The largest room has a fireplace and a good view of the Panhandle, but one of the loveliest is the Iris Suite, with whimsical iris wallpaper from the Bruce Bradbury collection, a multitude of pillows, and a sitting area tucked under a dormer window. All the rooms have pretty comforters and down pillows.

My favorite room is the library downstairs. It's rather dark, with lots of wood and books, and very cozy. The Benaus will pour the sherry.

Breakfast, served in your room or in the dining room (be sure to look at the ceiling mural here), consists of fresh fruit, juice, croissants, homemade breads, and cheese. The morning *Chronicle, New York Times,* and *Wall Street Journal* are on hand. The innkeepers will give you good ideas for dinner choices nearby, or they'll arrange small catered dinners at the inn.

How to get there: From Highway 101 north, take Fell Street toward Golden Gate Park. Inn is on the right at Lyon Street.

J: *One of the world's zaniest races, the annual San Francisco Bay to Breakers, goes right by the inn's front door. Each May for seventy-five years, world-class runners have raced from San Francisco Bay, up the murderous Hayes Street hill, and out Fell to Ocean Beach. The event has grown to be the city's best party, with 100,000 runners, many in outrageous costumes. You could have a front-row seat here to see all the sights—and they're astounding.*

olive Metcalf

The Washington Square Inn
San Francisco, California
94133

Innkeepers: Nan and Norman Rosenblatt
Address/Telephone: 1660 Stockton Street; (415) 981–4220 or (800) 388–0220
Rooms: 15; 10 with private bath. Telephones; television available on request at no charge. No smoking inn.
Rates: $85 to $170, double occupancy, continental breakfast.
Open: All year.
Facilities and activities: Nearby: great walking area of San Francisco, restaurants, shops, markets, cable car line; 1 block from Telegraph Hill; easy walk to Ghirardelli Square, the Cannery, financial district.

The inn faces Washington Square, in the heart of North Beach, to my eye the most colorful neighborhood in the city. Saints Peter and Paul Church dominates one side of the square; on the other sides are wonderful restaurants (the Washington Square Bar and Grill is the mecca for politicians and literary types), shops, and markets displaying fresh pasta, salamis, and produce. In the park a covey of shining black bangs clutching brown bags (a Chinese kindergarten class) settles down on the grass for a picnic lunch. Several old men practice *tai chi* exercises, oblivious to the bustle on all sides. Over all is the aroma of freshly ground coffee.

You can see much of this scene from the comfort of the inn's lobby/sitting room. There is a handsomely carved fireplace, comfortable provincial furniture on a blue rug, magazines, and books. A big basket of fresh fruit looks as if you're actually supposed to take a piece. Continental breakfast with freshly squeezed juice is served here or in your room. Since this is North Beach, with some of the best restaurants and bakeries anywhere, the croissants and pastries will be the best. Afternoon tea is served here, too, with tiny sandwiches and shortbread.

The inn is as convenient for business travelers who want a personal atmosphere as it is for families who want bedroom-sitting room combinations with sofa beds. From hiring you a stenographer, to packing a picnic lunch, to arranging baby-sitting or tours, the staff is ready to help. High-anxiety types may find that the most considerate personal service is an innkeeper who will find at 10:00 P.M. that aspirin or Alka Seltzer you forgot to pack.

The rooms are pure pleasure. Nan Rosenblatt is a San Francisco designer and has decorated them with English and French antiques and a good eye for comfort. She has chosen bright French floral fabrics for quilted comforters and matching canopies. Some rooms look out on a small courtyard, and those in front overlook the square and a bit of city skyline.

The colors, aromas, and sights of North Beach are the very essence of San Francisco. And you can walk to most of the city's attractions from this location.

How to get there: From Van Ness, take Union Street east; turn left on Stockton. The inn is on your right.

J: *This sophisticated urban inn is actually delighted to have children!*

olive Metcalf

Casa Madrona Hotel
Sausalito, California
94965

Innkeeper: John Mays
Address/Telephone: 801 Bridgeway; (415) 332–0502 or (800) 288–0502
Rooms: 34; all with private bath, some with fireplace, private deck, water view.
Rates: $95 to $200, double occupancy; cottages, $140 to $160; 3-room suite, $325; continental breakfast and wine and cheese social hour.
Open: All year.
Facilities and activities: Dinner, wine and beer bar nightly; lunch Monday through Friday; Sunday brunch. Outdoor Jacuzzi. Nearby: Sausalito's shops and galleries, ferryboat rides across the bay, fine dining, hiking, bicycling.

John Mays knows how to create an atmosphere. He's turned this luxurious old mansion perched on a hill above Sausalito into one of the most romantic inns you'll find. Of course, he has a lot going for him with a town almost too winning for words and spectacular views of the yacht harbor.

Casa Madrona is more than one hundred years old. Time had taken its toll on the former residence, hotel, bordello, and boardinghouse when John Mays rescued it in 1978. It nearly slid off the hill during the rains of '82, but renovations already begun saved it from gliding away.

Since then Mays has added an elegant tumble of cottages that cascade down the hill to Sausalito's main street. Each one is different, with dormers, gables, peaked roofs, and hidden decks. Amazingly, the whole gray-blue jumble lives perfectly with the old mansion.

You've seen "individually decorated" rooms before, but these beat all. Mays gave each one of his new hillside cottages over to a different Bay Area decorator. The range of their individual styles resulted in rooms with themes from nautical to equestrian (The Ascot Suite), to a Parisian Artist's Loft. Most have private decks and superb views. And since it *is* fabled, sybaritic Marin, there are luxurious tubs for two (sometimes elevated and open to the room), refrigerators stocked with fruit juice and mineral water, and fresh flowers. (But no peacock feathers.)

If you're indifferent to unique rooms surrounded by lush gardens, exotic bougainvillea and trumpet vine spilling over decks and walkways, perhaps elegant food will ring your bell. A beautiful wine bar and uncluttered dining room in the old house on top of the hill are lighted and decorated to enchant. Only white linen on round tables and fresh flowers compete with the view from the deck of the bay and Sausalito Yacht Harbor . . . that is, until the food is served.

We began with what I thought was a California cuisine standard but that has become a part of American cuisine: radicchio and Belgian endive salad with baked chèvre (goat cheese). Perfection. Our waiter was agreeable when I ordered another first course (angel hair pasta with roasted peppers and mussels) instead of an entree. (I love places that encourage you to order by *your* appetite instead of *their* rules.) Others at our table raved about linguine with Parma prosciutto, roasted shallots, baby turnips, and balsamic vinegar cream, and rack of lamb with minted gremolata and roasted garlic glaze. The meal could not have been lovelier.

How to get there: Cross the Golden Gate Bridge; take Alexander Street exit to center of town. San Francisco Airport pickup available. Ferry service from San Francisco.

J: *If this inn can't rekindle a dying ember, no place can.*

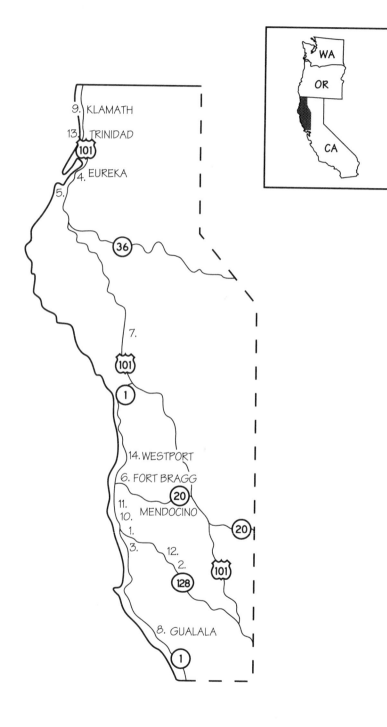

9. KLAMATH

13. TRINIDAD

101

4. EUREKA

5.

36

7.

101

1

14. WESTPORT

6. FORT BRAGG

20

11.

10.   MENDOCINO

1.

3.

12.

2.

128

101

20

8. GUALALA

1

WA

OR

CA

California: The North Coast

Numbers on map refer to towns numbered below.

olive Metcalf

Fensalden
Albion, California
95410

Innkeepers: Frances and Scott Brazil
Address/Telephone: Highway One (mailing address: Box 99); (707) 937–4042
Rooms: 7, plus water-tower suite and bungalow with kitchen; all with private bath. No smoking inn.
Rates: $80 to $135 for suite, double occupancy; bungalow, $115; breakfast.
Open: All year.
Facilities and activities: Nearby: 7 miles to Mendocino for fine restaurants, shopping, art center, galleries, theater; 1¹/₂ miles to Albion and Navarro rivers for more restaurants and swimming, fishing, canoeing; hiking, biking terrain.

I first discovered this inn as I was humming down California Highway One, roof back, sea breezes blowing, and tape deck playing full blast. I nearly ignored a small sign reading FENSALDEN but fortunately I followed the narrow road a quarter of a mile back into the hills and found this stunning inn. You will have to be more alert, since Cal Trans has insisted the sign be removed, but Fensalden is worth looking for.

It belongs to Frances and Scott Brazil, who fell in love with the place when they were guests, bought it, and moved north from Los Altos to make it their "early retirement" home. No wonder! The twenty acres of rolling, wooded land overlooks the spectacular Mendocino Coast, and the two ramshackle buildings that were once

162

an 1860s stagecoach stop and tavern were transformed by the former owners into a handsome country inn.

The two-storied, cedar-shingled structure with dormers and balconies looking out to the ocean seems to blend naturally into the land. Every step of renovation and decorating has been done with reverence for this beautiful site. It was named Fensalden (accent the middle syllable), which in Norwegian means "home of the mist and the sea."

The interior walls are the original rough-hewn redwood with each window and door framed in oiled redwood trim. A hall leads to a large common room with an ocean view through rows of cypress trees lining the headlands meadow. A grand piano (Frances plays) dominates the room that also holds comfortable sofas and chairs, a wood-burning stove, and a couple of Charles Russell prints.

At the east end of the room, windows look out at the flower garden entrance. Here is the large oak claw-footed table where Frances serves a full breakfast. Her apple puff pancake is a favorite, but she has a variety of egg dishes, hot muffins, and plenty of fresh juice and coffee. For other meals, there are excellent restaurants within a short drive.

The seven bedrooms are beautifully simple. Down comforters are inside colorful cotton covers—such a fresh, clean idea, I wonder why more innkeepers don't use them, instead of quilts that can't be laundered after each guest. The baths are particularly attractive. Ceramic tile showers and sinks made by local potters are works of art.

Separate from the main house are two unique accommodations. The two-story water-tower suite has a fireplace, sitting area, kitchen, exposed beams, and a beautiful view from its deck. The rustic bungalow, which sleeps four, is a particularly quiet, private retreat.

How to get there: Driving north on Highway One, the inn is 1¹/₂ miles past the intersection of highways 128 and One. Driving south on Highway One, the inn is 1¹/₂ miles past Albion and 7 miles south of Mendocino.

Olive Metcalf

The Boonville Hotel
Boonville, California
95415

Innkeepers: John Schmitt and Jeanne Eliades
Address/Telephone: Highway 128 and Lambert Lane (mailing address: P.O. Box 326); (707) 895–2210
Rooms: 8, including 2 suites with sitting room and private balcony; all with private bath. No smoking inn.
Rates: $70 to $145, double occupancy, continental breakfast.
Open: All year except January.
Facilities and activities: Restaurant serves dinner Wednesday through Sunday, Sunday brunch; wheelchair access to restaurant. Nearby: local pub; hiking, fishing, biking area; wine tasting.

Restaurant groupies will remember The Boonville Hotel from the mid-'80s, when it had a short-lived moment of fame as *the* country place for avant-garde food. Dining there was so highly touted, the three-hour drive from the Bay Area became an obligatory pilgrimage for serious foodies. You wouldn't dare contemplate a drink before dinner (interferes with the taste buds, you know), and customers sat in an uncomfortable hush, whispering and waiting respectfully as the courses slowly appeared and were almost reluctantly surrendered.

Erase all that nonsense from your memory and prepare to fall in love with my idea of what a California country inn should be—fresh, innovative, and fun. The Boonville Hotel has been rescued, restored, redecorated, and joyously brought back to life by its young owners. The old building, painted a sparkling white, sits directly on the road through the town, a small herb and flower garden on one side, a deck and more gardens on the other. Inside, clean white walls and pale oak floors are the background for a few brilliantly colored rugs, abstract paintings, and outrageously beautiful fresh flower arrangements. An attractive bar and a small sitting room are on the first floor in addition to the restaurant.

Upstairs, eight understated bedrooms, some with vaulted ceilings, some with decks and views out to the surrounding hills, are crisply fresh with a slightly Southwestern feeling. I liked the copper sinks and especially the fresh duvet covers on beds of natural-finish hardwood. Both suites have a sitting area and refrigerator. Jeanne has gradually added more furnishings to the bedrooms and the sitting room downstairs with the same good taste shown in her other choices. But I found something very attractive about the clean, minimal look the inn has at this writing.

The food that owner/chef John Schmitt is doing here is reason enough to drive to Boonville. John comes to the restaurant business with impressive credentials. He not only studied in France, but to many Californians, it says a lot to hear that his parents own The French Laundry Restaurant in the Napa Valley and that John has worked under his mother Sally's tutelage. We enjoyed a casual lunch outdoors on the deck. (Sadly, the owners have since made the decision to serve only dinners and Sunday brunch.) Even though we were in the heart of wine country, we had to try the local brew from the Anderson Valley Pub and Brewing Co. across the road.

A few words more must be said about the stunning flowers throughout the inn. Karen Bates arranges them, using flowers from the organic farm gardens in nearby Philo, the source, also, of many of the restaurant's ingredients. They're not elaborate arrangements, but rather such simple, artful combinations that each one is a painting—a bouquet of lilac and red poppies in a blue pottery pitcher; a tall jar with a wavy bunch of cosmos; a pitcher on the bathroom sink of fat, pale pink roses. Very special.

How to get there: From San Francisco on Highway 101, go north to Cloverdale, then follow Highway 128 west through the beautiful Anderson Valley to Boonville.

Olive Metcalf

The Toll House
Boonville, California
95415

Innkeeper: Betty Ingram and Barbara McGuinness

Address/Telephone; 15301 Highway 253 (mailing address: P.O. Box 268); (707) 895-3630

Rooms: 4; including 1 suite; all with private bath and telephone, suite with fireplace, Jacuzzi tub, private deck. No smoking inside.

Rates: $115 to $190, double occupancy, generous breakfast and afternoon refreshment.

Open: All year.

Facilities and activities: Restaurant and bar serving lunch, dinner, Sunday brunch. Deck and gardens for country weddings, receptions; catering on- and off-site, facilities for small conferences; outdoor hot tub, massage therapy available. Nearby: hiking, picnicking, fishing and swimming in Navarro River; local pub, shops; wine tasting at many outstanding wineries.

The Toll House looks the picture of simple, apple-pie, rural America nestled in the beautiful, secluded Bell Valley in the heart of Mendocino County. Actually, it is a sophisticated country inn with handsomely furnished guest rooms and common areas, beautifully landscaped grounds, and cutting-edge fine food. Things have changed at The Toll House, but you who have known its special charms and the glorious land surrounding it can put your minds at ease. The present owners have such a love affair going with this house and the area, they've purchased even more land, and the result is that 350 acres now encircle the inn.

The 1912 house, remodeled and expanded by Ingram and McGuinness, is 6 miles up the road from Boonville and was once the headquarters for the vast sheep-grazing Miller Ranch. It became known as The Toll House because the family, who maintained the road, charged loggers to haul their redwood over it to the inland mills. This valley is the home of "Boontling," a peculiar, contrived jargon spoken here and even taught in the schools between 1880 and 1920. A sprinkling of it survives today. A cup of coffee at a Boonville cafe is a *horn of Zeese*. The *Buckey Walter* is a pay telephone.

This is a house that draws you into its homey atmosphere— huge old shade trees, lovely gardens of flowers and herbs, and a wide veranda wrapping the front and sides of the house where there are chairs and a cushioned porch swing. I like the inviting living room and the small bar adjoining it.

Betty Ingram came to innkeeping from the airline and travel industries, and her partner, Barbara McGuinness, was a software developer. They are both concerned with the ecology of Mendocino County. Their concerns extend to the foods served in the attractive Toll House Restaurant. Organically grown fruits and vegetables from the Toll House gardens are supplemented with the finest locally grown meats, poultry, and dairy products. Chef Michael Wiggins creates some elegant meals with these superior ingredients.

Even if you never leave the inn while you're at The Toll House, it will be a wonderful experience in refined country living. But there is so much to do in this area. You ought to try Betty's very special private swimming hole, or a tour of Nessgram Farms organic gardens, or a picnic in the redwoods or along the coast, or wine tasting at the increasingly renowned local wineries.

How to get there: Traveling north from San Francisco, take Highway 101 to Cloverdale. Turn west on Highway 128 for 27 miles to Boonville, then east on Highway 253 to the inn about 6 miles up the road. This is a winding but scenic route. Or take Highway 101 to Ukiah and then Highway 253 (Boonville Road) west for 11 miles as it twists over the mountains to Boonville. Airport pickup available at either Ukiah or Boonville airports by advance request.

Elk Cove Inn
Elk, California
95432

Innkeeper: Hildrun-Uta Triebess
Address/Telephone: 6300 South Highway One (mailing address: Box 367);
   (707) 877–3321
Rooms: 8; all with private bath, some with fireplace, most with ocean view.
   No smoking inn.
Rates: $108 to $128 Monday through Thursday, $118 to $138 Friday
   through Sunday, double occupancy, full breakfast.
Open: All year.
Facilities and activities: Easy beach access, beach walks, secret caves, seals,
   exotic birds. Nearby: white-water tours, restaurants, wineries; 15 miles
   to Mendocino galleries, shops, theater; six state parks.

   Elk is a small village on a bluff overlooking the ocean, as fresh
as the winds that blow over it. There are a few surviving Victorian
houses, including this 1883 inn, but it is ocean lovers who come to
Elk. From the bluffs behind the inn there is a spectacular ever-
changing view of the Pacific. A short staircase leads down the bluff
to an expansive, driftwood-strewn beach with a fresh-flowing creek
that meets the ocean.
   The main house where breakfast is served has four individual
units, recently remodeled, adjacent to it. Two of these have free-
standing fireplaces, high beamed ceilings, and skylights. All of them
have bay windows looking out to the ocean view.

Hildrun-Uta is the energetic owner/innkeeper, continually working on ways to improve her inn. Her decor is nicely done, with appealing individual touches in each cottage. One has handmade doors more than a hundred years old; another has bits of stained glass worked into the framework; still another has a sunken bedroom from which the bay window looks to the ocean. Given the dramatic beauty of this stretch of coastline, I applaud her determination not to squander any opportunity for viewing it. There is a window seat in one cottage that is seemingly on the very edge of the bluff, and even a shower (with a mural of hand-painted tiles) has an ocean view. Decanters of sherry or wine and fresh flowers welcome you.

Hildrun-Uta's latest improvement offers the best accommodations of all: three newly done rooms on the second floor of the main house, all with huge dormer windows opening out to a spectacular ocean view. A delightful common room up here has a library and French doors leading to an ocean-view deck.

Breakfast is an important part of the experience. Hildrun cooks everything herself. With the help of two daughters, she serves on fresh linens and pretty china in her newly remodeled dining room that runs across the ocean side of the inn. Her German background is reflected in the French and German specialties she prepares. The breakfast star is *Eierkuchen,* an impressive German eggcake served with fresh berries, applesauce, or raspberry sauce.

How to get there: From San Francisco, take Highway 101 to Cloverdale, then Route 128 to the coast. Turn left on Highway One; go 5 miles to Elk. The inn is on the ocean side of the highway south of Elk.

J: *Take your sneakers and a sweater for brooding (and usually blustery) beach walks.*

Olive Metcalf

Harbor House
Elk, California
95432

Innkeepers: Helen and Dean Turner
Address/Telephone: 5600 South Highway One (mailing address: Box 369); (707) 877–3203
Rooms: 10, including 4 cottages; all with private bath, 5 with private deck, 9 with fireplace.
Rates: $155 to $230, double occupancy, breakfast and dinner. Each additional person $45. Ask about midweek winter rates. No credit cards.
Open: All year.
Facilities and activities: Dinner by reservation. Private beach, fishing, ocean kayaking with guide. Nearby: Mendocino shops, galleries, restaurants, forest walks, local wineries; golf, tennis, horseback riding.

The windswept solitude of this stretch of Northern California's shore is one of nature's tens. And for an inn on the bluffs above the rocky coast, Harbor House has it all: a dramatic location, unique architecture, fresh decor, and fine food.

The house was built in 1916 entirely of virgin redwood by the Goodyear Redwood Lumber Company as a place to lodge and entertain their executives and guests. In the 1930s it was converted to an inn and has variously faded and flourished over the years. The inn's newest owners are warm hosts who understand exactly what a spell this inn casts.

The large living room, completely paneled in redwood with a

high-beamed open ceiling, sets the tone: quiet and unpretentious. Comfortable sofas and a piano are grouped on a rich Persian rug before a huge fireplace, with books and a stereo nearby. (Christmas here sounds wonderful—the redwood room glowing in firelight, a giant tree, roasting chestnuts, festive dinners, and music from local musicians.) Bedrooms and cottages are freshly decorated, many with pastel watercolor prints by a local artist of flowers and birds indigenous to the area.

Ocean views from the dining room are breathtaking. On blustery North Coast days, some guests choose to spend the day in this redwood-paneled room watching the churning surf. It's comforting to know you don't have to leave this warm atmosphere to find a restaurant. Wonderful food is in store for you here.

The Turners subscribe to that old verity of California cooking: Use only the freshest, best ingredients possible, and keep it simple. Many ingredients are plucked right from the inn's own garden. What they don't grow, they purchase from the finest local sources, like baby potatoes and the locally raised lamb. Fresh fish is often featured, prepared with Harbor House nuances. All the breads and breakfast pastries are homemade. Desserts also tend to reflect whatever is fresh. Typical are poached pears with raspberry sauce, or a sweet flaky pastry stuffed with apricots and cream. A fine California wine list and a good selection of beers are available. Dinner is a fixed menu, changing every night, but with advance notice, they'll try to accommodate any special dietary needs.

Mendocino's attractions are only twenty minutes farther north, but I'm all for staying right here. Walking the beach, discovering the secluded patios and paths—one leads to a waterfall and grotto—these are the quiet seductions of the inn. If you're in during the day, a bottle of local wine and a cheese platter from the kitchen are available to hold body and soul together until dinner.

How to get there: From the Bay area, take Highway 101 to Cloverdale, then Highway 128 west to Highway One. The inn is 6 miles south on the ocean side of Highway One.

J: *Plan on long romantic dinners.*

Olive Metcalf

Carter House
Eureka, California
95501

Innkeepers: Mark and Christi Carter
Address/Telephone: 1033 Third Street; (707) 445–1390
Rooms: 7, including 1 suite; 5 with private bath.
Rates: $95 to $185, double occupancy, full breakfast and evening beverage.
Open: All year.
Facilities and activities: Dinners and special events catered at the house; dinners Thursday through Sunday at Hotel Carter across the street. Nearby: renovated Old Town waterfront, shops, restaurants, Victorian architecture tours, salmon fishing, Fort Humbolt; drive south to Avenue of the Giants, north to Redwood National Park.

Sitting in the splendid parlor of Carter House sipping wine, a guest from Ohio declared that he had "built a good many houses in my time" and this house couldn't possibly be new. "No one *does* work like this anymore."

But you do if you're Mark Carter and grew up in Eureka near the famous Carson Mansion, probably the single finest example of Victorian architecture in the country. Carter renovated other houses by the same architects, and, with an old book of their designs, he decided to construct one from scratch.

With a crew of three, Carter built the four-story redwood mansion, handcrafting the intricate wood moldings and detailings. Instead of heavy Victorian decor, Mark and Christi kept the walls white (allowing the beautiful wood to stand out even more), put down white marble in the hallway, and decorated with a few outstanding antiques and oriental rugs on polished oak floors. A changing gallery of paintings and ceramics by local artists, plants, and fresh flowers complete the remarkable, *new* Victorian.

One of the seven guest rooms is a suite, complete with sitting room, fireplace, private bath, and Jacuzzi. Three rooms with high-vaulted ceilings, designer linens, and antiques are on the top floor; three more rooms and a sitting room with a television are below the parlor.

Mornings begin with a newspaper at your door, then a lavish breakfast served in the dining room. On my visit, we started with fresh raspberries and juice, proceeded to hot breads and eggs Benedict, and finished with Christi's wonderful apple tart.

Be sure to walk across the street and check out another lodging Mark has built—the Hotel Carter. Guests at this elegant small hotel enjoy room appointments like Jacuzzi tubs, televisions, and telephones and have a generous continental breakfast included in their rate. Some of the finest food on the north coast is being served in the intimate dining room with stunning works of local artists on the wall.

The Carter lodgings are hospitable places to get acquainted with Eureka—and you should. Mark smiles at people who think that because the town is remote, it must be a cultural wasteland. The truth is, it's a stimulating community of writers, artists, and craftspeople, with five theater companies and higher theater attendance per capita than in San Francisco!

How to get there: Highway 101 into Eureka becomes Broadway. At L Street, turn left. Inn is on the corner.

✳

J: *A friend of Mark tells that some years ago he'd often lock up the restaurant he managed and see Mark drive by—at 2:00 A.M. He wondered what his married friend was doing out at that hour and learned later that new father Mark, rather than have his guests disturbed, lulled his crying son back to sleep out driving. Is that an innkeeper?*

olive Metcalf

Hotel Carter
Eureka, California
95501

Innkeepers: Mark and Christi Carter
Address/Telephone: 301 L Street; (707) 444–8062
Rooms: 20, including 2 suites; all with private bath, television, telephone, 8
with whirlpool baths, suites with fireplace. Smoking in lobby only.
Rates: $95 to $250, including full breakfast, evening wine and hors d'oeu-
vres.
Open: All year.
Facilities and activities: Restaurant serving elegant cuisine Thursday through
Sunday. Lobby and dining-room showcase of contemporary art. Near-
by: walk along brick pathway bordering marina, through restored Old
Town with specialty shops, restaurants; hundreds of restored Victorian
homes, many art galleries in town.

Ever since first hearing Rodgers and Hart's "There's a Small
Hotel," I've thought the song—and small hotels—were the
quintessence of sophisticated romance. In Eureka's charmingly
restored Old Town district, the Hotel Carter brings the essence of
that lovely song to mind. It is a perfect rendezvous—intimate, glamorous, and serving some of the most elegant food and wines available north of San Francisco.

Most first-time visitors assume that Mark Carter restored the
yellow Victorian-style building, but it is newly constructed, modeled after a nineteenth-century Eureka hotel. It blends the exterior
look and ambience of the past era with today's luxurious conve-

niences, all done with Carter's impeccable taste in detailings and furnishings. (He also built from scratch the magnificent Victorian-style B&B across the street.)

You may very well fall in love with the hotel the minute you step into the lobby. The old-world elegance of 14-foot-high ceilings here and in the adjoining dining room looks both chic and inviting with plump sofas and chairs, and the work of local Humbolt County potters and painters is showcased brilliantly against the salmon-colored walls. The Carters set out fine regional wines and hors d'oeuvres before a marble fireplace here each evening.

But your outstanding taste treats will come at breakfast and dinner in the intimate dining room. Since the days when Christi Carter, while managing two babies, cooked at their B&B what came to be known as the famous Carter Breakfast, she has always taken the lead in searching for the best chefs, the finest ingredients, and true cutting-edge cuisine. The Hotel Carter has become the right place to see that concern for truly excellent cooking come to fruition.

Our dinner one night began with baby greens dressed with a strawberry vinaigrette, fresh, grilled swordfish with lemon butter, three perfect vegetables grown in the Carters' garden, a new small grain (something akin to couscous), and crusty baguettes. A local chardonnay and a pinot noir *had* to be sampled. A scrumptious apple-walnut tart served with homemade ice cream and coffee saw us off to our room impressed with the quiet service and fine food.

The twenty guest rooms are decorated in pale earth colors, with peach and white linen, and are furnished with handsome antique pine furniture combined with appointments we appreciate—telephones, remote-controlled televisions hiding in wardrobes, and whirlpool tubs. Our suite on the second floor with a fireplace, window seat, and view of Humbolt Bay was a spot we would love to return to often.

How to get there: From Highway 101 in downtown Eureka, proceed west on L Street through Old Town to the hotel.

J: *You may think of Eureka as logger/fisherman country, a perception that makes this elegant hideaway all the more surprising. If it weren't that the Carters are such nice people, I'd say, "keep it a secret."*

Olive Metcalf

Old Town Bed & Breakfast
Eureka, California
95501

Innkeepers: Leigh and Diane Benson
Address/Telephone: 1521 Third Street; (707) 445-3951
Rooms: 6; 4 with private bath. No smoking inn.
Rates: $75 to $185, double occupancy; singles deduct $10; full breakfast and
afternoon refreshments.
Open: All year.
Facilities and activities: Hot tub. Nearby: waterfront, Old Town, Victorian
architecture, Carson Mansion, shops, restaurants, theaters, museums;
fishing.

I can almost feel sorry for the thousands of visitors to California every year who think everything worth seeeing is contained
between Los Angeles and San Francisco. Tell them about the Redwood Empire that stretches more than 400 miles from San Francisco into Oregon and their eyes glaze. But that's okay with the rest of
us. That reluctance to go beyond the well-traveled areas of the state
is what keeps vast regions of California still an unspoiled scenic
wonder.

After living in many countries and states, Leigh and Diane
Benson decided to put down roots in the heart of the redwood
country. Their decision brought them to Eureka, the commercial
center of Northern California, and to this 1871 Victorian. The house
is the one-time residence of William Carson, a local lumber baron.

Its location at the entrance to Old Town is ideal for walking that ambitious waterfront revival of Eureka's Victorian past.

The Bensons have obviously found a new life they love. Their inn is neat as a pin, with fresh flowers in every room from their almost year-round gardens. Much of the artwork in the house was done by Leigh's daughter (I have a copy of one of her charming line drawings of the inn) or by his mother. Diane likes touches of whimsy, such as teddy bears on all the beds and rubber ducks by the claw-footed tubs. There are also two cats in residence.

Bedrooms are spacious, airy, and attractively decorated. The largest room is Carlotta's, with a king-sized bed, private bath with old-fashioned bathtub and shower, and a wood-burning stove. But it's hard to resist one called Sarah's Rose Parfait, with a raspberry carpet, lace curtains, and pretty floral wallpaper. The Maxfield Parrish Room features his artwork, oak antiques, and a shared bath with tub. This is the room for watching sunsets. Sumner's Room, the smallest, has a double bed and a private bath with shower.

This is one of the few inns that give a break to the solo traveler. A deduction of $10 from the rate schedule offers an attractive package to a single traveler or $20 off to a single business traveler who wants an inn atmosphere rather than a hotel.

A full breakfast is served in the country kitchen near (though not cooked on) an old wood-burning stove. A typical Diane menu might be baked apples, Cast Iron Breakfast Pie, yogurt dill biscuits with homemade jam, or decadent French toast with fancy syrup, fruits with crème fraiche, and sausage links.

How to get there: Going north on Highway 101, proceed through Eureka and turn left on I Street. Go 2 blocks to 3rd Street and turn right. At the fork at 3rd and Myrtle take the turn to the left. The inn is on the left a block and a half down. Southbound on 101, turn right on P Street. Go 1 block to 3rd Street and turn right and park. Inn is on the left.

J: *Diane has had so many requests from guests for her breakfast recipes that she's put together her own cookbook, which is now in its sixth edition.*

Olive Metcalf

The Gingerbread Mansion
Ferndale, California
95536

Innkeeper: Ken Torbert

Address/Telephone: 400 Berding Street (mailing address: P.O. Box 40); (707) 786–4000

Rooms: 9; all with private bath, 2 with claw-footed tubs, 3 with fireplace. No smoking inn.

Rates: $85 to $175, double occupancy; singles deduct $15; generous continental breakfast and afternoon tea.

Open: All year.

Facilities and activities: Bicycles loaned, formal English garden. Nearby: Victorian Ferndale, theater, art galleries, shops, restaurants; June Scandinavian Festival, August Ferndale Fair, May three-day World Champion Kinetic Sculpture Race (in which "cheating is not a right—it's a privilege"); bird-watching reserve at Russ Park; walking tours of Pacific Lumber Co.; Humbolt Redwoods State Park.

The Victorian village of Ferndale is far enough off Highway 101 to have remained a secret for a long time. Now, the entire town is a State Historic Landmark, and increasing numbers of travelers are discovering it and experiencing that special pleasure of finding a still-little-known treasure.

Except that every owner of a Victorian has obviously hired a color consultant and a painstaking crew with brushes to decorate his or her fairy-tale house, the town has virtually not changed since the 1800s. There are no traffic lights, no parking meters, no mail

178

delivery (citizens pick up at the post office). A village blacksmith is more than local color for the tourists; he uses his hammer and anvil to fabricate practical tools and decorative items. And one of the few remaining Carnegie-endowed public libraries is still in business, circulating books.

Visitors can sample this slice of old-time Americana from a spectacular turreted, gabled, and elaborately trimmed Queen Anne inn. The Gingerbread Mansion is renowned for being one of the most photographed Victorians in northern California, but fame hasn't turned its head. Ken runs a first-class inn, paying attention to little things that you'll remember: robes and luggage racks, a turned-down bed at night, reading lights on both sides of the bed, extra pillows, a hand-dipped chocolate at bedside, and an early morning tray of coffee in your room. He'll provide boots and umbrellas if you forget yours and lend you a bicycle, too, from the yellow-and-orange fleet painted to match the inn.

All the bedrooms have been decorated elegantly, romantically, and amusingly. I never miss a chance to tour around the mansion for a view of any rooms that aren't occupied. The Gingerbread Suite has a prim and proper sitting area *and* twin claw-footed bathtubs sitting toe to toe on a raised platform surrounded by a Victorian railing. The Fountain Suite bath has twin tubs side by side facing a mirrored wall reflecting the flames in a Franklin stove and a full view of the room. What a marvelous place for a leisurely, meaningful conversation.

When breakfast is served, you'll have homemade muffins and cakes along with fresh juice and fruits, locally made cheeses, cold cereals, and hard-boiled eggs. In the afternoon, tea and cake is spread in one of the downstairs parlors.

How to get there: Exit Highway 101 just north of Fortuna. Cross over Eel River Bridge, and proceed west 5 miles to Ferndale's Main Street. At the blue Bank of America, turn left. Go 1 block to inn on corner.

Olive Metcalf

The Grey Whale Inn
Fort Bragg, California
95437

Innkeepers: John and Colette Bailey
Address/Telephone: 615 North Main Street; (707) 964–0640; or (800) 382–7244
Rooms: 14; all with private bath and telephone, some with deck, fireplace, or ocean view. Wheelchair access, handicapped-adapted room. No smoking inn.
Rates: $80 to $160, double occupancy; single $20 less; full buffet breakfast. $25 additional person.
Open: All year.
Facilities and activities: Ground-floor lounge with television, fireplace, VCR, pool table; conference room for small meetings. Nearby: restaurants; shops, walk to depot for Skunk Train; drive to redwood forests, hiking trails, state parks, beaches, Noyo Harbor fishing, tennis, golf; local March Whale Festival; July Salmon Barbecue; September Paul Bunyan Days.

The Grey Whale was the first bed and breakfast in Fort Bragg, and every time I visit it is better than ever. The weathered redwood building has the spare, straight lines of New England and looks suitably sea-bleached and salty. The perception is enhanced by the hand-carved whale on the front lawn, done by Byrd Baker, an artist and a leader in the "Save the Whales" movement.

The inn was originally built as the Redwood Coast Hospital in 1915, but that history fades more with every year of John and

Colette Bailey's ownership. They converted the building to an inn in 1976, adding their own warm, colorful touches.

Wide, carpeted hallways and larger-than-usual rooms afford unusual privacy and quiet. Both the prices and the variety of facilities make this one of those (all too rare) inns where you can safely take a husband and not hear a complaint. Small wonder. He'll see a comfortable, uncluttered room where he can relax and not knock over some doodad. He'll hear the nostalgic whistle of a steam engine as the Skunk Train leaves the depot. When he picks up a morning newspaper in the hallway and strolls on to survey the breakfast buffet feast, he will probably decide coming to The Grey Whale was his idea all along.

Some rooms sleep up to four and have kitchenettes, some have a fireplace, and others have ocean views. The Sunrise room with its whirlpool tub for two, private sun deck, and king-sized bed is a good choice for the seriously romantic.

On the ground floor, the fireplace lounge is stocked with magazines and games, and has a television and a pool table. A service area on the second floor has an ice machine and refrigerator guests can use. In the morning a beautiful buffet is spread here of juices and fruits, breads and muffins, and something hot, sometimes a baked omelet or homemade waffles, or Impossible Pie with spinach.

One reason things work so well around here is that the owners still live on the premises and are the real live innkeepers, not just the name on the brochure. They also are blessed with a staff that is loyal. It all adds up to being warmly welcomed and in good hands.

Straight directions don't begin to tell the story of driving to the North Coast. For about a three-and-a-half hour drive from San Francisco, take Highway 128 west out of Cloverdale over to the coast. You'll maneuver steep climbs and tight curves before dropping down into beautiful Anderson Valley with many wineries to explore. Once through the redwood groves along the Navarro River, you'll meet Highway One and climb to the headlands looking out at the Pacific. Don't take your eyes off the road until you pull over, but the views are breathtaking. The point is . . . *great scenery takes time.* If you drive Highway One all the way from San Francisco, allow about six hours to Fort Bragg.

How to get there: In Fort Bragg, Highway One becomes Main Street. Driving north, the inn is on your left.

Pudding Creek Inn
Fort Bragg, California
95437

Innkeepers: Garry and Carole Anloff
Address/Telephone: 700 North Main Street; (707) 964–9529 or (800) 227–9529
Rooms: 10; all with private bath. Smoking in Garden Court or outside only.
Rates: $65 to $115, double occupancy, full breakfast.
Open: All year except January.
Facilities and activities: Hot tub room; TV room. Nearby: western depot for Skunk Train; walk to Glass Beach, shops, restaurants; party boats at Noyo Harbor; July Salmon Barbecue; Mendocino Coast Botanical Garden 3 miles south; Pudding Creek State Beach open for picnicking, swimming, fishing.

What's an inn without a story? Pudding Creek's tale is that a Russian count with a mysterious past came to the area in the mid-1800s, bringing money that everybody assumed to be ill-gotten. He started a bottling plant, prospered, and built four houses in Fort Bragg, including this one. He changed his name to Mr. Brown, and he took a bride who wore the first wedding dress advertised in the Montgomery Ward catalog. Pictures of the couple, and the wedding dress, are displayed in the parlor.

If this adds an information overload to your historical trivia quotient, simply enjoy the cheerful, easy atmosphere you'll find here. The inn is really two houses connected by an enclosed garden courtyard. Even on the blustery day I visited, it was pleasant in the protected garden with fuchsias, begonias, and ferns thriving. This is a choice spot, weather permitting, to have afternoon tea and relax. And if you need serious relaxing, the hot tub room at one end of the garden will be an attraction.

Guests can also gather in the main parlor or in a television/recreation room, transformed from an unused kitchen in one of the houses.

A buffet breakfast can be taken in either of two dining rooms, and it is done with style—lace tablecloths, pretty dishes, and linen napkins. Carole serves her own homemade coffee cakes or breads, a hot egg dish or casserole, and juice and fresh fruit along with coffee and teas. Guests with more moderate breakfast appetites will appreciate also seeing dry cereals and low-fat milk. When you're ready for dinner, the Anloffs have plenty of suggestions close by that will suit your taste.

The bedrooms are decorated in a combination of early American and Victorian furniture, colorful quilts, and pretty flowered wallpaper. A room named for the count is, naturally, a touch more royal, with cranberry velvet accents, redwood paneling, a king-sized brass bed, and stone fireplace. If you should be traveling with a third person, the Pot Pourri room is a pretty choice. In addition to having a queen-sized bed, the room, decorated in a blue floral print and wicker furniture, has a built-in captain's bed. The private bath and shower are directly across the hall.

How to get there: Highway One becomes Fort Bragg's Main Street. Traveling north, the inn is on the right just past the heart of town, corner of Main and Bush streets.

ॐ

J: *If you don't know about the Skunk Train—it is a 40-mile trip on a standard-gauge passenger and cargo railroad through redwoods and mountainous terrain between Fort Bragg and Willits. A big tourist attraction.*

clive Metcalf

Benbow Inn
Garberville, California
95440

Innkeepers: Patsy and Chuck Watts
Address/Telephone: 445 Lake Benbow Drive; (707) 923–2124
Rooms: 55, including terrace- and garden-level rooms with television and VCR; all with private bath.
Rates: $88 to $250, double occupancy, breakfast extra. Off-season rates: April 1 through June 15; October and November.
Open: April 1 to December 1; December 18 through January 2.
Facilities and activities: Bar, dining room open to public for breakfast, lunch, dinner, Sunday brunch. Hiking, swimming, picnics at Benbow Lake; bicycles, boat rentals, tennis, horseback riding; 9-hole golf course; Shakespeare-on-the-Lake, mid-August; Halloween Ball, November wine tasting, Christmas and New Year's Eve celebrations. Nearby: scenic drives through redwoods.

Californians call this territory the Redwood Empire, and the Benbow Inn is surely one of its castles. Driving north on Highway 101, you see it rising four stories high in Tudor elegance, situated among tall trees and formal gardens on the shores of Benbow Lake and the Eel River. It was designed in 1926 as an inn and enjoyed some grand years. In 1978, the Wattses rescued it from fading elegance and have been steadily restoring and improving it.

For all the fresh refurbishing and additions, Patsy and Chuck have managed to keep a kind of old Hollywood baronial feeling in the main lobby that's fun: a large stone fireplace, oriental rugs, antiques, and grand-scale furniture. Tea and scones in the after-noon and an Afghan hound that lounges about looking elegant add to the Hollywood atmosphere. Looking at an old guest register, I saw that fifty years ago Mr. and Mrs. Basil Rathbone checked in—with valet/chauffeur. Charles Laughton stayed here, too, memoriz-ing his lines for *Mutiny on the Bounty* and reading in the evenings to the Benbow family and staff.

Nostalgia stops when it comes to accommodations. New bath-rooms, thick towels, great beds, and attractive decor are the rule in the main building. A nice touch in every room is a basket stocked with paperback mysteries. Garden- and terrace-level rooms are even more deluxe, all with decks overlooking the garden and river.

Dinner in the handsome dining room is a dressy to casual (in California, that means shoes), candlelit affair. If you're a guest at the inn, you'll be greeted by name at the door. The menu is not trendy, but includes a variety of fresh fish, good beef, and veal, and pasta in particular. Several low-fat entrees are offered with calorie count listed for guests who notice those things. For those who don't, there's a gorgeous white chocolate mousse with fresh berries.

How to get there: Two hundred miles north of San Francisco, 2 miles south of Garberville, on Highway 101.

J: *The Benbow is not inexpensive, but it's not for snobs either. When I visited, it had a full house of mostly affluent-looking middle-aged couples and honeymooners. But when a party of latter-day hippies arrived for dinner, infant in arms, they were greeted as warmly as any other guests.*

The Old Milano Hotel
Gualala, California
95445

Innkeeper: Leslie Linscheid
Address/Telephone: 38300 Highway One; (707) 884–3256
Rooms: 9, including 2 cottages; 3 rooms with private bath. Smoking outside
only. Wheelchair access to 1 suite.
Rates: $75 to $160, double occupancy, full breakfast. Two-night minimum
Saturday.
Open: All year.
Facilities and activities: Dinner served Wednesday through Sunday, $19;
wheelchair access to dining room. Hot tub, massage therapy available,
wedding facilities. Nearby: beach walks, fishing; explore coastal towns.

The Old Milano Hotel has the right patina of age to look
engagingly romantic. At the same time, it's a pleasure to stay where
all appointments are fresh and clean and where everything *works.*
This well-maintained country inn has a special setting—three
sprawling acres on the Mendocino Coast. You can stroll through the
English gardens or relax on the broad lawn and watch the churning
surf.

Two indoor sitting rooms have plants, fresh flowers, and cozy
chintz-covered sofas to snuggle in by the huge stone fireplace.
Afternoon wine tastings here give you a chance to sample some of
Mendocino's vintages.

Guest rooms upstairs blend antiques, armoires, floral wallpapers, and handmade quilts. Five of them have ocean views, and one overlooks the garden. The rooms are refined, but not exclusively feminine. Men will enjoy the spacious master suite, which has a private bath and a separate sitting room with a superb view of the ocean and "Castle Rock." The inn's facilities are not well suited to children under age sixteen.

Two cottages on the grounds give you the ultimate in privacy. The Passion Vine Cottage has a sitting area and Franklin stove. The Caboose, which really is an old caboose, is tucked among the cedars.

Breakfast is served in your room, outside on the patio, or in the dining room. Along with the standard fare of homemade breads, fresh fruits, and yogurt are the Old Milano's private blend coffee and unique teas.

Dinner, even though it is open to the public, has an intimate atmosphere. At least six entrees are offered each night, usually three meat and three fish. The inn's chef makes up a different menu every day, so that the freshest foods can be used. The inn is known for things like fresh mussels and miniature thick-crusted pizzas made with goat cheese and tarragon. Their desserts are worth the calories, maybe an apple custard cake or a deep-dish fruit pie. Many brides who choose The Old Milano for their reception ask this kitchen also to provide the cake.

Don't miss trying the terrific outdoor hot tub on a point over-looking the surf. Guests reserve it to assure privacy. Nearby are several skilled massage therapists the innkeeper will schedule for you also.

Does this sound like a place to drop in for a few days and recharge your batteries? You're right.

How to get there: On the ocean side of Highway One, 1 mile north of Gualala; 100 miles north of San Francisco.

St. Orres
Gualala, California
95445

Innkeepers: Rosemary Campiformio, Ted Black, Eric Black; reservations, Jan Harris

Address/Telephone: 36601 Highway One (mailing address: Box 523); (707) 884–3303 or 884–3335

Rooms: 8 in the inn share 3 baths; 11 cottages, all with private bath.

Rates: $50 to $65, double occupancy, in the inn; $75 to $180 in the cottages; full breakfast.

Open: All year.

Facilities and activities: Dinner; beer and wine bar; wheelchair access to upper dining room. Hot tub, sauna; beach access, picnics. Nearby: Fort Ross.

Non-Californians see the spectacular Russian architecture of St. Orres tucked away above Highway One and tend to think it is another example of the native penchant for theater. Actually, a historical basis for the style is found only a few miles south at the trading fort the Russians built in the nineteenth century when they traded in furs and employed the Aleut Indians to hunt the sea otter.

Fort Ross is restored to look as it did while the Russians were in residence, but St. Orres stands as an architectural fantasy of the heritage. It's an intimate hideaway built of hundred-year-old timbers and hand-carved redwood, with stained-glass windows and onion-top turrets capped by copper octagonal roofs.

You enter through a trellis-covered patio to a cedar lobby, an attractive bar, and plant-filled solarium. The dining room is in one of the stunning domed towers that rise more than 38 feet, with row after row of windows and stained glass.

Each bedroom in the inn is a cozy redwood snuggery with a built-in double bed covered with a unique handmade quilt. The baths are "his," "hers," and "ours," the third one being a large, tiled tub with dual shower heads. Two front rooms have French doors that open onto ocean-front balconies.

The more spacious accommodations are the eleven cottages surrounding the inn. The most rustic is The Wildflower cabin, one of the original buildings on the property. It has a double bed on a sleeping loft, with a skylight above. There's a kitchen, bath, wood-burning stove, and an outdoor hot-water shower.

For more luxury, try The Tree House, with architectural details similar to those of the inn. It has a carpeted living room with wood-burning stove and French doors opening onto a sun deck with an ocean view. Pine Haven is the newest cabin. All the cottages have breakfast delivered to their doors in a basket.

You should not be surprised that the food is as outstanding as the architecture. Begin with goat cheese in a flaky crust or with a smoky-flavored black bean soup and close with Chocolate Decadence; in between, the menu is sometimes continental, always uninhibited. It changes according to what is fresh and available. One specialty is rack of lamb with a Dijon mustard crust. Another is quail marinated in tequila and garlic, served with yam and green onion pancakes.

How to get there: On Highway One, between Gualala and Anchor Bay, the inn is on the inland side.

J: *Gualala, by the way, is pronounced "Wallala." It's not Spanish, but rather a Spanish version of the Pomo Indian word meaning "where the waters meet."*

Whale Watch Inn
Gualala, California
95445

Innkeepers: Jim and Kazuka Popplewell, owners
Address/Telephone: 35100 Highway One; (707) 884–3667
Rooms: 18, including 4 suites, in 5 buildings; all with private bath, some
with fireplace. Smoking on decks only.
Rates: $160 to $250, double occupancy, full breakfast. Two-night minimum
may apply on some weekends.
Open: All year.
Facilities and activities: Selected wines and champagnes available, whirlpool
baths; private stairway offers beach access. Nearby: restaurants, hiking,
golf, tennis.

If the quaint appeal of the North Coast's old accommodations
escapes you, Whale Watch may be just the contemporary luxury
answer to your desires. On two cliff-side acres, it consists of five
architecturally striking buildings with spectacular ocean views. It is
the ultimate adult getaway designed for privacy, personal service,
and with incomparable scenic beauty.

Every bedroom is stunningly decorated with elegant furniture,
some custom-designed Queen Anne, some hand-carved pieces, a
fine Bombay chest here, a yew-wood library table and chest there.
Amenities? Merely fine linens and down comforters, ice makers,
skylights, fireplaces in most rooms, and your private deck looking
out at the rugged surf.

190

If sybaritic bathrooms are your thing, these take you to the outer limits of the bathing experience. In the Silver Mist, a spiral stairway flows from the bedroom up to the second level capped by a skylight roof to a two-person whirlpool, separate shower, and lounging area with a fabulous view of the Pacific below.

Some rooms are on two levels, and all of them are large. Four suites in the Sea Bounty, designed for longer stays, are self contained, and include fully equipped kitchens.

The original Whale Watch building has a large, hexagonal common area with a circular fireplace and a sweeping Pacific view. The area is used as a gathering place for inn guests and has comfortable sofas and chairs, game tables, taped music, books, and wonderful spots to enjoy the view. The two modestly sized bedrooms in this building open off this impressive room.

In keeping with the atmosphere of quiet privacy (no television, no telephones), a full breakfast is served to guests in their rooms. A short drive up or down the coast brings you to some excellent restaurants—St. Orres, for one; The Old Milano, for another.

How to get there: Take Highway 101 to Petaluma and proceed west to Highway One. Or, take Highway 101 to 4 miles north of Santa Rosa and proceed west on River Road to Highway One. Follow Highway One north to Whale Watch at Anchor Bay, 5 miles north of Gualala on the ocean side. Fly-in: Ocean Ridge Airport.

Olive Metcalf

The Requa Inn
Klamath, California
95548

Innkeepers: Paul and Donna Hamby
Address/Telephone: 451 Requa Road; (707) 482–8205
Rooms: 11; all with private bath. No smoking inn.
Rates: $50 to $75, double occupancy, full breakfast and afternoon tea.
Open: All year except January and February.
Facilities and activities: Dinner. Walk to riverside, sandy beaches; watch abundant marine life, birds. Nearby: fishing, canoeing, hiking trails, Redwood National Park.

The town of Requa is fairly remote territory of Northern California—almost on the Oregon border. If a historic inn up here, nestled in the redwoods on the lower Klamath River, doesn't pique your interest, pass on. But—you'll be missing a taste of one of California's unique areas, and not so incidentally, some of the best fishing in the state.

The thing I like about The Requa Inn is that you don't have to fish to be drawn to this old white inn in the woods. The place has staying power, that's for sure. The present building has been here since 1914, but the original inn was built across the street in the 1880s; it moved to its present site in 1885, burned, and was rebuilt in 1914. The inn was first called The Pioneer, then the Klamath Inn.

Bedrooms are simply furnished, uncluttered, and immaculate.

The parlor, or common room, is a pleasingly unplanned mixture of chairs, sofas, tables, and lamps grouped near a big brick fireplace that almost always has a fire burning. What will captivate you is a nonstop view of the Klamath from a window running the length of the room. It could be raining nonstop and the fish all gone on holiday, but you would still enjoy relaxing with a book in this cozy room. Especially since there is food nearby.

Meals are as unpretentious as are the accommodations, but just right. Paul says his philosophy about the food they serve is "you should recognize everything on the plate with no questions about what it is when it's set before you. Fresh ingredients, simply cooked is our style." Fresh local fish, of course, halibut and salmon, char-broiled steaks, and chicken are regular items on the menu. For dessert, you're likely to find something homey like fresh blackberry cobbler. At breakfast, guests have a choice of a full breakfast from the menu or a continental breakfast. All meals are served in a pleasant dining room with lace curtains at the windows and a view of the river.

It's taking in the nature surrounding you that is the lure of The Requa Inn. Walking among the redwoods, fishing, boating, and swimming are all available. Bird watching is wonderful here, and nature photographers will delight in the possibility of catching shots of sea lions, pelicans, or even the occasional whale that comes up the river.

How to get there: On Highway 101, about 62 miles north of Eureka, you will see a well-marked sign for Requa Road and a left turn lane. Follow Requa 1¹/₁₀ miles to the inn.

J: *I am personally acquainted with people who fish who seem to feel it's part of the nature of a fishing trip to be uncomfortable and stay in disgracefully shabby lodgings. If you know people like that, you might advise them (tactfully, of course) to wise up.*

olive Metcalf

Glendeven
Little River, California
95456

Innkeepers: Jan and Janet deVries
Address/Telephone: 8221 North Highway One; (707) 937–0083
Rooms: 12, including 2-bedroom Barn Suite; 10 with private bath. No smoking inside.
Rates: $90 to $195, double occupancy, weekends, holidays, and August; continental breakfast. Off-season rates Monday through Thursday. $20 less for single occupancy; two-night minimum on weekends.
Open: All year.
Facilities and activities: Art and craft gallery, small meeting area, well-tended gardens. Nearby: beach walks, picnics on headlands, close to Mendocino galleries, restaurants, and shops; July Mendocino Music Festival, September Winesong.

The delights of California's North Coast have little to do with sunshine and blue skies. It's the bluffs, the rugged coastline, and the misty cool climate that seduce those of us who love it. But unpredictable weather makes the comfort of your lodging all the more important. Glendeven is an inn that pleases, rain or shine.

It is an 1867 farmhouse of Maine-style architecture, set back on a headland meadow from the Mendocino Coast, surrounded by fields and trees. The atmosphere in the pleasant sitting room pulls you in to nestle before the fire and enjoy the view through a wall of windows to a brick patio and the meadow beyond. A piano for impromptu musical urges, a good stereo for those of us less

194

inclined, books, a tray of sherry, and a quiet country setting—this is the stuff of a country inn.

The deVrieses, both with a design background, have an eye for contemporary art and craft. To display their collection, and the handcrafted chair line of owner Jan deVries, they have a new addition, The Gallery at Glendeven. Art is also integrated throughout the inn, combined with fine antiques, country wallpapers, and lace curtains.

The guest rooms are beautifully done. Every one is a pleasure with fireplaces, commanding views—some with French doors leading to private balconies—and attention to detail. In the farmhouse, one of my favorites is The Garret, a large attic room with dormer windows and splendid vistas. Stevenscroft, a separate building in back, has four elegant rooms with fireplaces and tiled baths. The Barnhouse Suite, an 1800s hay barn, is now a spacious two-bedroom suite that works out well for two couples traveling together or for a family. Like the others, it exudes the Glendeven style: warm, comfortable, subtle elegance.

Breakfast included excellent coffee (ready for the early risers), a fresh fruit bowl, boiled eggs, and just-baked raisin-bran muffins. It seems to be a good time to hear the latest reports on local restaurants. There are some outstanding choices in the vicinity that the innkeepers are prepared to tell you about.

Two acres of grounds and gardens invite you to stay right where you are, even though Mendocino is just up the highway. A path to the beach or to State park headlands is an easy walk and are wonderful places to spend the day. With notice, the innkeepers will prepare a tidbit basket for you to take along.

How to get there: On California Highway One traveling north, just past Van Damme State Park, the inn is on your right.

J: *If you don't enjoy Glendeven, you're just not inn material.*

Olive Metcalf

Heritage House
Little River, California
95456

Innkeeper: Gay Dennen Jones
Address/Telephone: 5200 Highway One; (707) 937–5885
Rooms: 75; all with private bath. Wheelchair access.
Rates: $105, single, to $335 for 2-person suite, full breakfast and dinner.
    Each additional person $65.
Open: All year except December and January.
Facilities and activities: Full bar, restaurant. Walking paths through woods,
    along beaches. Limousine service available for anything from wine
    tasting to sightseeing tours. Nearby: Mendocino for art galleries, shops,
    restaurants, theater.

Above the dramatic Mendocino Coast in 1949, the late
innkeepers L. D. and Hazel Dennen set about restoring an 1877
farmhouse of Mr. Dennen's grandfather. Since then, Heritage
House has become a classic. Defying time and fashion, it goes on
pleasing and setting a high standard for a country inn. It is now run
by their daughter, Gay.

The site is magnificent: Forests of eucalyptus and redwood
meet green pasturelands and then stretch to a rocky, churning sea-
coast. The present sedate atmosphere belies a fairly wild past. In the
early 1930s, Baby Face Nelson used the cove below the house for
his bootleg operations, concluding one of his last deals in the house.
As late as the 1940s, Chinese immigrants were smuggled into the

country here. Today it is one of the more formal inns along the coast, with gentlemen "encouraged" to wear jackets and ties at dinner.

A few guest rooms are in the main building, but most are in cottages tucked into the landscape. As the rooms were built and remodeled through the years, the spirit of 1877 has been kept with furnishings and names inspired by early-day buildings of the area, like Scott's Opera House and Schoolhouse. A two-story unit, The Watertower, has a circular stairway leading from a living room to a bedroom. Most rooms have fireplaces or Franklin stoves; some have Jacuzzi tubs and wet bars.

A domed dining room (entirely nonsmoking) has superb ocean views and a fresh, airy feeling that make it as inviting at breakfast as it is for candlelit dinners. Breakfasts are hearty: a cereal, fruit, and juice buffet, followed by eggs Benedict, a choice of breakfast meats, and dollar-sized pancakes. By the time you return to your room, the sharp staff has made the bed and refreshed your bathroom. Dinner menus change nightly. Perhaps a creamy potato soup, greens mixed with pine nuts and Smithfield ham, rare beef tenderloin or Pacific snapper with sauce mousseline, fresh vegetables, and fettuccine, ending with an almond cream cake. The wine list is extensive.

The comfortable lounge has an enormous fireplace and sweeping views of the rocky coastline. Don't expect television or video games; you come here to read, look, and relax. And the walks are major pleasures.

How to get there: On Highway One, the ocean side, between Albion to the South and Little River to the North.

J: *Anyone who gets bored on the Mendocino Coast should apply for a new soul.*

olive Metcalf

Little River Inn
Little River, California
95456

Innkeepers: Charles D. Hervilla and Susan Kimberly
Address/Telephone: Highway One; (707) 937–5942 reservations; 937–5051 restaurant
Rooms: 54, including inn rooms, cottages, motel-type units; all with private bath, some with fireplace.
Rates: $72 to $100, ocean-view rooms without fireplace; $110 to $235, with fireplace; breakfast extra. $10 per extra adult; no charge for children under 12. No credit cards.
Open: All year.
Facilities and activities: Breakfast, dinner daily; bar. Lighted tennis courts; golf course (nine holes), pro shop, putting greens. Nearby: hiking, bicycling Van Damme State Park, beachcombing, good tide-pool exploring; minutes from Mendocino art galleries, antiques shops, restaurants.

Anyone who has driven north on Highway One along the dramatic Mendocino coastline has seen this rambling white inn off on the right. It looks "New England" because it was built in 1853 by a pioneer from Maine, Silas Coombs.

Three generations later, the parlors are lobbies and dining rooms, and the conservatory is the bar. The long front porch used to be the place to watch for arriving schooners. Now it's where you follow the movements of the salmon fleet and, during the winter months, a favorite place for watching the migration of gray whales.

The range of accommodations here means you can have exactly what tickles your fancy. Rooms in the inn are decorated in early California style with antiques. If you prefer more modern appointments, try the motel wing. The pleasant, single-story rooms have big decks looking out at the ocean. They are quiet spots to read, interrupted occasionally by deer wandering in the meadow below.

The cottages are especially cozy when you want to snuggle in for a few days. They have one or two bedrooms, some with sitting areas and fireplaces. One of my favorites for many years and through several refurbishings is the Van Damme Property. It sits across the road from the inn with three other units directly above the rugged coastline.

A continuous refurbishing of the inn goes on, and the rooms are all quite comfortable, if not particularly stylish. I do miss, however, a coffeepot in the room (since breakfast is not part of your rate), and perhaps a radio, too, would be pleasant to have.

Little River's dining room is known up and down the coast for fine cooking. Whatever is freshest from the sea will be on the menu, along with good steaks and other choices. Salmon, abalone, snapper, and ling cod are specialties, and they are prepared with the delicate touch fresh fish deserves. (It ought to be a crime for kitchens to *claim* that they specialize in seafood when their only technique is to beat, batter, and deep fry!)

There's a down-to-earth quality about food here that you get only when things are homemade. This kitchen makes soups from scratch and its own breads. For dessert, try a fresh berry cobbler with tender crust and softly whipped cream.

How to get there: Three hours north of San Francisco on Coast Highway One. The inn is on the right just south of Mendocino. Fly-in: Mendocino County Airport, 2 miles from the inn.

Olive Metcalf

Rachel's Inn
Little River, California
95460

Innkeeper: Rachel Binah
Address/Telephone: 8200 North Highway One; (707) 937–0088
Rooms: 8, including 2 suites; all with private bath, 5 with fireplace.
  Wheelchair access.
Rates: $96 to $125, main house; $125 to $165, "The Barn"; double occu-
  pancy, full breakfast. $18 for third person. Two-night minimum on
  weekends; three nights on holiday weekends.
Open: All year.
Facilities and activities: Dinners by special arrangement. Weddings and small
  receptions catered; walk fields, headlands, and beach; whale watching.
  Nearby: skin diving cove; Van Damme State Park; Fern Canyon; Men-
  docino restaurants, galleries, shops, theater.

If you like the wild, natural Mendocino atmosphere but still
want comfort, even elegance, in light-filled space, try Rachel's Inn.
What a pleasure to see someone with Rachel Binah's talent and
flair go into the inn business. She had been catering for ten years
when she found a dishearteningly ramshackle 1870s house on the
Mendocino Coast and decided to make it an inn. It took the confidence of a riverboat gambler to believe that an inn was hiding in
that ruin, but Rachel has accomplished an impressive renaissance of
the house.

The site is very special—ocean views, tall trees, and windswept meadows. And adjoining her property are eighty-two acres of state-owned land that runs right down to cliffs overlooking the ocean and that will remain in the natural state it is in now.

The interior of the inn is as fresh and airy as the outdoor Mendocino breeze. Each room's construction and decor reflect a feeling for the coast setting and make the most of the superb ocean views. High, vaulted ceilings, white walls, and redwood trim detailings are in the large living/dining room. A crackling fire felt good, even on an August morning.

The bedrooms have the same uncluttered good looks as the rest of the house. Linens on the queen-sized beds are in soft muted colors—mauves, grays, and florals. The Blue Room has a private balcony, and the Garden Room has a fireplace and an outside entrance, convenient for a wheelchair. Several rooms have an extra single bed. There are three comfortable sitting rooms for guests to use. In the parlor downstairs off the dining room, a piano and an ocean view are added attractions.

As I write, Rachel is putting final touches on her four quite special accommodations in a new building on the property. Unless inspiration dictates another name, she's calling it "The Barn," since it's designed in the traditional style of a California barn and blends with the 1870s main house. Inside, luxury and contemporary flair set the style. All four units have fireplaces; two are suites with sitting room, balcony, wet bar, refrigerator, and extra beds. One room is totally handicapped accessible—ramp to the main house and special shower.

For someone with Rachel's catering experience, breakfast is a piece of cake. She offers juices, fresh fruits, homemade sausage or bacon, muffins, and an egg dish. But give her an event and she'll really start cooking—buffet receptions, weddings, or a seven-course dinner, like the one she was preparing the day I visited. She has a wine cellar at the inn.

How to get there: On Highway One immediately north of Van Damme State Park and 2 miles south of Mendocino, the inn is on the ocean side.

J: *Your first sight of this inn, painted a daring soft mauve, will tell you that there's a stylish innkeeper at work.*

Olive Metcalf

The Victorian Farmhouse
Little River, California
95456

Innkeepers: Carole and George Molnar
Address/Telephone: Highway One (mailing address: Box 357); (707)
    937–0697
Rooms: 10; all with private bath, 6 with fireplace.
Rates: $80 to $115, double occupancy, full breakfast and evening sherry.
Open: All year.
Facilities and activities: Conference room. Nearby: walk to ocean; whale
    watching; picnics; 2 miles to Mendocino restaurants, galleries, shops,
    theater.

When the Molnars were looking for an inn to buy, Carole
favored gold rush country, but George had his heart set on the
Northern Coast of California all along. When he talks about "the
historic North Coast," you hear real feeling for the beauty and history of this rugged area. The Molnars had long collected antiques,
so when they found this picture-perfect Victorian farmhouse near
Mendocino, it was kismet.

The house was built in 1877 by John Dennen as a home for
him and his wife, Emma. The Molnars' pride in it is apparent, and
they've lavished their time and attention on making it a completely
captivating inn. With just four guest rooms in the farmhouse, it has
as intimate and cozy an atmosphere as you'll find. Each room is a
picture of Victorian charm with period antiques, white eyelet dust

ruffles, quilts on the beds, and wicker furniture. One room has an appealing cushioned window seat and a small sitting room that opens onto a deck. The Garden Room looks onto an old-fashioned flower garden that is lighted at night. The views from upstairs are of apple orchards and ocean.

In the apple orchard behind the farmhouse, the Molnars have added six rooms, all with private baths and fireplaces. They're decorated with antiques and dainty flower prints on the walls. Pretty views from here are of redwood and fir trees and the creeks around the farmhouse.

Each room has a small, round table set with crochet lace over a soft-color cloth and pretty china where you'll be served breakfast. The tray brought to your room will have whatever beverage you want—tea, coffee, hot chocolate—juice, fresh fruits, perhaps baked apples, yogurt, and homemade muffins and breads. Carole never wants guests to have the same breakfast twice during a visit, and when people settle in for a week or more, she laughs that she has to get creative.

In the small downstairs parlor, sherry is offered in the evening, and you'll see some of the clocks George has restored. Carole and George will show you menus of nearby restaurants, and there are some fine ones on this part of the coast. When I was there, an antique desk in the room held wine, stuffed animals, and family photographs—all recent gifts from guests who left feeling they had found a home away from home with the Molnars.

How to get there: Driving north on Highway One, the inn is on your right between Heritage House and Little River.

J: *The Molnars say you should see it in the spring when the daffodils flower and the orchard is in bloom.*

Olive Metcalf

Agate Cove Inn
Mendocino, California
95460

Innkeepers: Sallie McConnell and Jake Zahavi
Address/Telephone: 11201 North Lansing Street (mailing address: P.O. Box 1150); (707) 937–0551; in Northern California, (800) 527–3111
Rooms: 10; all with private bath, ocean view, and cable television, 9 with fireplace. No smoking in rooms.
Rates: $75 to $175, double occupancy, full country breakfast. Ask about cash discount rates, midweek rates.
Open: All year.
Facilities and activities: Accommodations for weddings and special occasion parties. Nearby: short walk to Mendocino Village galleries, Art Center, restaurants, specialty shops; hiking, canoeing, horseback riding, tennis, golf accessible.

Our friend knew I looked at a lot of inns, but she still insisted that she had discovered a jewel in Mendocino that I had missed. "Fabulous views," she raved. "Best breakfast I ever had at an inn," she went on. Naturally, I had to check it out immediately—besides, traveling the Northern California coast is hardly a tough assignment. As it was an election year, I was ready to forgive a little exaggeration from a friend, but I was also prepared to be underwhelmed. Score one for my friend.

Agate Cove Inn is indeed a jewel. Sitting above and behind Mendocino Village on a bluff above the ocean, it appears to be an old farmhouse. That is just what the main house is, built in the

1860s by Mathias Brinzing, who established the first Mendocino brewery. Some of the original candlestick fence still runs through the beautiful old-fashioned garden.

Scattered through the grounds are the cozy cottages, each (except for one room where you have to make do with only a lovely garden view) with views of the ocean, a fireplace, a decanter of sherry, and a private deck for watching the sea.

The rooms have king- and queen-sized four-poster or canopied beds, handmade quilts, and country decor that goes for comfort rather than excessive cuteness. The luxury cottages have large double showers or oversize tubs, and considering California's water problems, it would be a crime to use one of them alone.

The main house has a spacious living room for guests to enjoy. A red-brick fireplace, colorful wingback chairs, love seats, quilts, antiques, and books all bring a country warmth. The room opens onto the breakfast room, with stunning ocean vistas. For some of us, breakfast really begins with the morning San Francisco newspaper on the doorstep—and that's the way they do it at Agate Cove, too—then a short walk through the garden to the main house. Select your juice and fresh fruit and choose a table, already set with fresh, home-baked bread and jams. You must divide your view between your entree being cooked on an antique wood stove nearby and the drama out the window of crashing waves on the rocks.

Mendocino is an enchanting seaside village, but it is not undiscovered. Agate Cove puts you close to all the village attractions but just enough removed to feel you're in a very special, romantic hideaway. For quiet, uncrowded—some say the most beautiful times—come during the winter season.

How to get there: About a three-hour drive from San Francisco via Highway 101 and 128. When your each Mendocino, take Lansing Street exit after the traffic light. The inn is ¹/₂ mile north of the village.

clive Metcalf

The Headlands Inn
Mendocino, California
95460

Innkeepers: Pat and Rod Stofle
Address/Telephone: Corner of Howard and Albion streets (mailing address: Box 132); (707) 937–4431
Rooms: 5; all with private bath, king or queen bed, and wood-burning fireplace; 1 with parlor stove. No smoking inn.
Rates: $98 to $150, double occupancy, full breakfast and afternoon tea. Two-night minimum on weekends; three or four nights on holiday weekends. No credit cards.
Open: All year.
Facilities and activities: Hiking the Mendocino Headlands or beaches. Nearby: walk to galleries, shops, restaurants, Art Center, theater; Mendocino Botanical Gardens; 4 state parks; redwoods; wineries.

The lumber industry flourished along this coast a century ago, leaving this all-wooden New England–style town as a legacy. Among the remaining buildings is The Headlands Inn, named for the spectacular bluffs above the rocky shore. The shingled, rather stern exterior belies an exceedingly warm and well-furnished interior.

The building began in 1868 as a small barbershop on Main Street. It also had a history as a "high class" restaurant, The Oyster and Coffee Saloon. In 1893, the house was moved to its present location on the corner of Howard and Albion streets by horses pulling it over logs used as rollers. From here, it has white-water ocean views looking over the inn's English-style garden, toward the tree-covered mountains beyond.

I could happily move into any one of these guest rooms. The decor is restful with impeccable housekeeping. Fresh flowers, apples, candy, extra bed pillows, and current magazines are some of the thoughtful appointments. Everything from bed coverings to upholstery looks fresh and inviting. Most of the rooms have wonderful views, and each has a fireplace or country stove. Much of the furniture is antique, and other pieces, like several of the beds, are handsome products of contemporary craftsmen.

A parlor on the first floor, with a fireplace and common bathroom, and another sitting room on the second floor, with games, books, and good reading lights, are two additional rooms where guests can relax. A full tea service, including mineral waters, cookies, and mixed nuts, is provided every afternoon in the sitting room.

Breakfasts are served on trays directly to each room. In comfortable surroundings like these it's an indulgence that pleases. The W. J. Wilson Room has a private balcony for breakfasting outside, but most chilly Mendocino mornings you'll prefer inside, perhaps in the Bessie Strauss Room with a view from its bay window of the English garden and the ocean.

Full breakfasts include a hot entree that changes daily, always something original and beautifully presented. It might be Pat's curried breast of chicken and ham crepes with pecan garnish, or individual apple, onion, and sausage pies with puff-pastry crust. And all are garnished with edible flowers from the garden. There also are home-baked muffins, the freshest fruits available, an assortment of teas, and specially blended coffee.

Beyond breakfast, the area offers some outstanding dining opportunities. You can walk to the renowned Cafe Beaujolais and the popular 955 Ukiah Street, or just a few minutes' drive takes you to the intimate Little River Restaurant.

How to get there: Entering Mendocino from the south on Highway One, proceed 2 blocks on Lansing Street to Howard Street. Turn right, go 1 block to inn on the left.

J: *The flower gardens here, like so many others in Mendocino, are English style and quite special. They appear to be completely natural, as if the flowers had popped up spontaneously.*

Olive Metcalf

Joshua Grindle Inn
Mendocino, California
95460

Innkeepers: Jim and Arlene Moorehead
Address/Telephone: 44800 Little Lake (mailing address: Box 647); (707)
937–4143
Rooms: 10; all with private bath; some with fireplace or Franklin stove. No
smoking inn.
Rates: $90 to $135, single or double occupancy, full breakfast.
Open: All year.
Facilities and activities: Nearby: walk to coast headlands or beach; all Mendo-
cino activities, shops, restaurants, Art Center, galleries, theater.

The beautiful Joshua Grindle Inn looks every bit as New England as it sounds. It is named for the man who built it in 1879, situated on two acres several streets above the bustle of Main Street,
Mendocino. The white house is a picturesque sight itself, but from
the slight hill it sits on, the views of ocean and rocky coast are glorious.

New England flavor at its best is throughout the house—comfortable, tasteful, and immaculate. Antiques that decorate each
room are early American rather than Victorian. Fine woods and
some pieces Arelene has refinished herself lend a classic, unfussy
feeling to the decor.

Guests are invited to use the light, airy living room with a fireplace. You should note especially a beautiful antique pump organ

restored by Arlene. At the sideboard, guests may help themselves to fruit, cream sherry, or local mineral water.

The Mooreheads serve a full breakfast at an antique 12-foot-long pine refectory table. A fine old hutch and a grandmother's clock make exactly the kind of cheerful, cozy ambience that draws people to country inns. Conversation hums over fresh fruit, frittata or quiche, and homemade coffee cakes and breads.

It is a short walk to explore the town's galleries and excellent restaurants, but you might choose this inn merely to experience the misty air of Mendocino in a comfortable, country atmosphere. All the guest rooms are appealing. The Library is a warm room with a four-poster queen-sized bed and a fireplace trimmed with tiles depicting Aesop's *Fables*. The Grindle, with a view of town and ocean, has a queen-sized bed and, for a third person, a twin bed. In the grounds behind the main house are two additional buildings with accommodations: two rooms in the cottage, and three in the newest addition, The Watertower. The decor is early American with pine antiques and wood-stove fireplaces.

The things that captivate me most about the Joshua Grindle are the fresh, clean smells in the guest rooms, the books and comfortable chairs, the breezy vista toward Mendocino and the ocean, and the wonderful gardens. They're a joy to see growing, seemingly so wild and casual (I *know* that's not the case), on this beautiful site.

How to get there: Going north on Highway One, turn off to Mendocino at Little Lake Road (the exit past the main road into town). Inn is on your right in the first block.

※

J: *Even with the crowds that flock to Mendocino during summer tourist time, the atmosphere here is tranquil and rural.*

olive Metcalf

MacCallum House
Mendocino, California
95460

Innkeeper: Melanie Reding
Address/Telephone: 45020 Albion Street (mailing address: Box 206); (707)
937–0289
Rooms: 21; 6 in the main house with shared bath, sinks in rooms; other
accommodations around the garden, 7 with private bath.
Rates: $65 to $160, continental breakfast. Special family and midweek rates.
Open: All year.
Facilities and activities: Restaurant serves dinner; full bar. Nearby: walk to
everything in Mendocino: beach, restaurants, shops, galleries, theater;
whale watching; fishing; hikes.

Daisy MacCallum was the lucky bride who in 1882 moved into
this beguiling New England–style Victorian house, a gift from her
father. Gingerbread trim, gables, and a white picket fence decorate
the yellow house that sits on three acres.

This is an inn for lovers of flowers and flounces, quilts and old
trunks. In the old house, the rooms have been cheerfully preserved,
many still containing the original furnishings, Tiffany lamps, and
Persian rugs. Facilities are down the hall, but most rooms have a
sink. The third floor is a cozy haven, with walls papered with
rotogravures of the period, and has a small parlor with splendid
views of the town.

Other accommodations are in cottages around the garden.
Among these, The Watertower and The Green House have private

baths and wood-burning stoves. The Carriage House is convenient for families or two couples, with two separate units, each with a Franklin fireplace and privacy. The most luxurious rooms are those in The Barn. The upstairs unit has a private deck with sweeping views and a sitting room with a massive stone fireplace.

The Gray Whale Bar and sun porch are additions so skillfully done you would think they were part of Daisy's house. Remember, a bar means music and laughter (naturally), so if you plan to rise early for bird watching, you might want one of the garden or barn suites, a little more removed from the action.

Dinners are served in the book-lined dining room at tables set with fresh flowers and oil lamps, before a huge cobblestone fireplace. The chef is Alan Kantor, a graduate of the prestigious Culinary Institute of America. Like all good chefs, he uses the freshest and best-quality ingredients, and with them he has created an adventurous California menu. Some of his specialties are grilled Italian eggplant with wild mushrooms, herbs, tomato, and fontina; braised Sonoma rabbit with grilled polenta; Canadian salmon grilled with orange-lime salsa; and tenderloin steak with a balsamic vinegar demiglace and caramelized onions. Kantor also prepares the bistro menu served in the Gray Whale Bar or outside on the porch. That's where I had tasty homemade linguine with red peppers and snow peas. A continental breakfast is served strictly for house guests.

How to get there: From Highway One, enter Mendocino on Main Street. On Lansing, turn right and go 1 block to Albion; then turn left. The inn is on the right in the center of the village.

olive Metcalf

Philo Pottery Inn
Philo, California
95466

Innkeepers: Sue and Barry Chiverton
Address/Telephone: 8550 Route 128 (mailing address: Box 166); (707) 895–3069
Rooms: 5, including 1 cottage; 3 with private bath. No smoking inside.
Rates: $80 to $95, double occupancy, full breakfast, evening wine, tea and cookies.
Open: All year.
Facilities and activities: Available for small group retreats or business conferences. Nearby: many Anderson Valley wineries, restaurants in Boonville and Navarro, ocean thirty-minutes' drive, bicycling. Hendy Woods State Park with walking trails through the redwoods.

If you like an atmosphere more laid back than elegant, favor conversation and good music rather than fine antiques and solitary splendor, you'll find a haven at the Philo Pottery Inn. And as for the innkeepers, the Chivertons, it seems to me, have exactly the right attitude. Sue says they try to see that their guests enjoy the Anderson Valley by making suggestions for activities and any reservations required. But ". . . if they don't want to do anything except relax, we leave them alone!"

The 1888 redwood house was once a stagecoach stop. The setting is still rural, with tall trees and an English flower garden. The main house is redwood inside and out, an intimate lodging with high-ceilinged common rooms, antique furnishings, and an extensive library that guests can use. The name of the inn, by the way, comes from former owners who had a pottery studio in the back yard.

Behind the inn, a garden cottage is a quiet, cozy accommodation with its own wood stove and porch. The bathroom is detached from the cottage, but only a few steps away. In the main house, two bedrooms upstairs share a bath, making a convenient family suite.

Each of the two downstairs rooms has a private bath, one with an old claw-foot tub (bubble bath provided) and brass shower. These are cozy rooms appointed with patchwork quilts, down comforters, and lots of pillows.

The living room has everything you could require for relaxing with a glass of sherry or a cup of tea and a homemade sweet—loads of books and current magazines, a stereo and classical cassettes, and Barry's collection of jigsaw puzzles.

If you're just getting acquainted with this area, get Sue and Barry's suggestions for all there is to see and do. A few minutes away in Boonville, a popular pub called the Buckhorn serves the owner's homemade brew, and the Boonville Hotel has reopened, serving dinner and Sunday brunch.

Whatever else you do, be sure to visit some of the Anderson Valley wineries. Navarro Vineyards, Husch, Handley Cellars, Obester, Kendall-Jackson, and Scharffenberger Cellars are names that may not be familiar to you, but their wines are among California's finest. Those mentioned all have tasting rooms open to the public.

Sue serves a big breakfast as guests drift in—fresh fruits, homemade granola, and juices are the starters, followd by home-baked breads and muffins and an ever-expanding repertoire of hot entrees such as spinach cheese strata or pecan-stuffed French toast. The coffee is locally roasted, and, being English, Barry promises a really great pot of tea.

How to get there: From San Francisco, take Highway 101 north to Cloverdale; follow Highway 128 west through the Anderson Valley to Boonville, then Philo. Driving south on Highway 101, exit at Highway 253, and drive through the Bell Valley to Boonville and Philo. Both are beautiful drives.

J: *This is a beautiful area for mountain bicycling. Sue says some of her more adventurous guests do a loop out to the coast and back.*

olive Metcalf

The Lost Whale
Trinidad, California
95570

Innkeepers: Susanne Lakin and Lee Miller

Address/Telephone: 3452 Patrick's Point Drive; (707) 677–3425

Rooms: 6, including 4 suites; all with private bath and ocean view, 2 with step-out balcony, some with sleeping loft. No smoking inn.

Rates: $85 to $120, double occupancy, full breakfast and afternoon tea. $15 additional adult; children 2–16 $10.

Open: All year.

Facilities and activities: Jacuzzi, play area, farm animals, bicycles, wooded path to private beach. Nearby: restaurants, scenic wooded trails, secluded coves, Patrick's Point State Park, redwood forests, Fern Canyon, fishing village of Trinidad, deep-sea or surf fishing, golf, surfing.

How's this for a courageous concept: Build a handsome new inn on a spectacular piece of property; cater particularly to families; and set your prices at rates that make it hard to beat.

Susanne Lakin, a graphic artist, and her musician husband, Lee Miller, built this slate blue and gray Cape Cod–style inn on the ocean at Trinidad (about 50 miles below the Oregon border) with just those intentions. With two young children of their own, they know that people sometimes do want to travel with their family, and they designed the inn to fill that need. The decor is practically childproof: sleek bare wood plank floors, bleached pine furnishings, cozy homespun fabrics, easily cleaned surfaces, and no knickknacks. This may be a first, as far as I know, but maybe they'll start a trend.

What I particularly like is how pretty and fresh it all looks. Too often, when an innkeeper says children are welcome, it's because the place is already so well worn the kiddies couldn't possibly harm it. The Lost Whale, on the contrary, is stylish and sparkling. The main-floor Great Room is delightfully bright and cheerful, with white walls and pine trim, blue overstuffed sofas and big chairs, an iron stove, floor-to-ceiling bookcases, and games and puzzles. A wall of windows looks out to a deck where I saw tricycles and toys, and a Jacuzzi, but most impressive of all, the inn's gorgeous ocean view.

Guest rooms upstairs are not large, but each has its distinctive appeal. There are peaked ceilings; some have sleeping lofts and futons, cozy sitting alcoves, or balconies. Here too the decor is simple but tasteful, with Laura Ashley comforters on queen beds and the fresh colors of Williamsburg blue and rose carried through. The walls, by the way, are soundproofed.

The inn sits on such a spectacular site you'll want to be outdoors most of the time. Children have the run of the enclosed grounds with a playhouse and some small farm animals for entertainment. But it's the winding staircase that takes you down to the private, unspoiled Agate Beach that will have you wondering how you might possibly make a living in Trinidad. Tide pools, driftwood, and interesting rocks will keep even the littlest ones enchanted for hours.

If barking sea lions don't wake you first, the aromas from the kitchen will. Lee and Susanne serve a full breakfast at two pine tables in The Great Room, brightened with fresh flowers and colorful place mats. The menus vary, but you will see home-baked bread and muffins, perhaps bagels and the locally smoked salmon, and quiches made from the inn's own eggs and vegetables. For other meals, you'll find a range of options nearby, from pizza and Chinese take-out to the popular Larrupin Cafe just down the road.

How to get there: From Highway 101 about 22 miles north of Eureka, exit on Patrick's Point Drive and continue south 1 mile to the inn. Fly in: Arcata-Eureka airport, 15 minutes from the inn.

olive Metcalf

DeHaven Valley Farm
Westport, California
95488

Innkeepers: Jim and Kathy Tobin; chef, Ben Kemp
Address/Telephone: 39247 North Highway One; (707) 961–1660
Rooms: 8, including 2 cottages and 1 suite with sitting room; 6 with private bath, some with fireplace and individual thermostat. No smoking inn.
Rates: $85 to $125, double occupancy, full breakfast. $20 each additional person; children under 5 free. Two-night minimum weekends, except by wait list.
Open: All year except January.
Facilities and activities: Dinner by reservation, wine and beer service. VCR, telephones, computer, modem, fax available; hot tub, farm animals, hiking, picnicking. Wedding facilities. Nearby: walk to ocean, tide-pooling, abalone fishing; drive the Avenue of the Giants; thirty-five minutes to Mendocino.

Three and a half hours north of San Francisco, an 1870s farmhouse of immense appeal sits above the Mendocino Coast, its twenty acres of rolling hills, woods, meadows, and a stream sloping down to the ocean. You can walk the beach and explore life in a tide pool, or tramp the hills and chase butterflies, or sit on the roof deck and brood as the ocean mist rolls in. And all the while, your creature comforts are being attended to by thoughtful innkeepers and a first-rate chef.

Talk about getting away from it all for a few days! If you're a city person, you may not know that places like this exist, but this inn cozily fills that occasional need for a little isolation.

I was first drawn to the spot many years ago and felt sad to see the inn fall on hard times. But the Tobins have brought the old house back to life, even introducing touches of luxury while still keeping the warm, comfortable feeling so right for this peaceful countryside. Most of the rooms have access to a second-floor deck that overlooks the hills and rocky coast—just about the most perfect reading, gazing-out-to-sea, or star-watching spot you can imagine.

If the day is raw, you'll be comfortable in the pleasant living room by the fireplace. This is my idea of a reading room, but there is also a telescope at the window, a piano, games, and a VCR. A help-yourself policy extends to cold drinks or the nearby decanter of sherry to ward off major chills.

In addition to a hearty breakfast, the Tobins are among those few West Coast innkeepers who also offer other meals. Using the abundance of fresh locally grown produce, cheese, lamb, chickens, and fish, Ben Kemp oversees four-course dinners. He grows many of the ingredients himself. Breakfast and dinner are served in an intimate, eight-table dining room.

Outside, ever more ambitious herb and flower gardens flourish. The hillsides were blooming with wildflowers and California poppies the day I visited. It's an easy walk to the beach, where the tide-pooling is wonderful.

How to get there: From San Francisco, take Highway 101 to Cloverdale, then west on Highway 128 through the Anderson Valley and Navarro Redwoods to the Mendocino Coast. Turn north on Highway One past Fort Bragg to 1⁷/₁₀ miles north of Westport; inn is on the right.

J: *A midwinter afternoon, rain and wind pelting the windows, tempting aromas wafting in from the kitchen . . . This is the kind of snug inn tales are told about.*

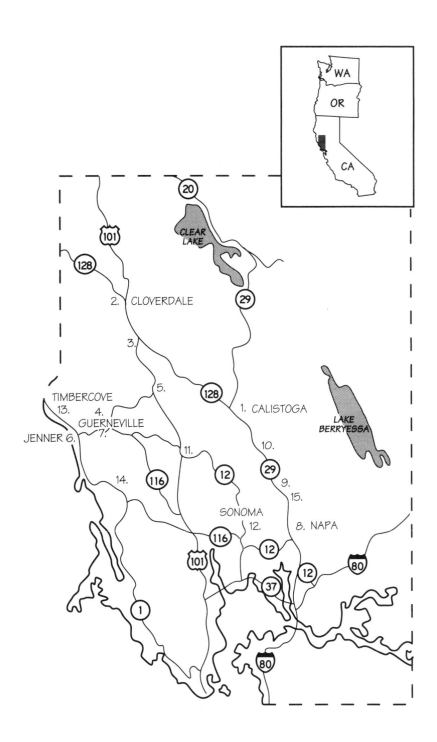

California: The Wine Country

Numbers on map refer to towns numbered below.

olive Metcalf

Calistoga Country Lodge
Calistoga, California
94515

Innkeeper: Rae Ellen
Address/Telephone: 2883 Foothill Boulevard; (707) 942–5555
Rooms: 6; 4 with private bath. Smoking restricted to patios.
Rates: $85 to $115, double occupancy, continental breakfast.
Open: All year.
Facilities and activities: Swimming pool, hike, bicycle, picnic, small group
    events welcome. Nearby: restaurants, wineries.

The silhouette of a weary Indian warrior on his tired horse is
the sign at the lodge's entrance. It is Frazier's "End of the Trail," a
fitting theme for an inn situated at the north end of the trail
through the heart of Napa Valley wine country. The beautiful
wooded property promises a peaceful retreat at trail's end.

When you open the door to the rambling, white 1930s stucco
house nestling in trees, you enter a thoroughly *uncommon* common
room. Tom Scheibal, the inn's first owner and a furniture designer,
removed all distractions to create one long open-beamed space, as
clean and bleached as a desert scene. The floors are wide planks of
whitewashed pine with textured rugs scattered about. At one end is
an old stone fireplace with a caribou head over it surveying the
room.

The rustic pine furniture arranged in several groupings down
the room was designed and built by Scheibal. Chairs and settees are

softened with pads and pillows covered in natural canvas. On some he has splashed the fabric with ragged black splotches to resemble cowhide. The only color in the room comes from vivid Indian rugs on the walls and leafy green potted trees. Some aptly chosen black-and-white photos are a wonderful touch: Gary Cooper in a cowboy hat; Georgia O'Keeffe and Alfred Stieglitz.

A marble-topped table is used for a continental breakfast buffet served on bright pottery. Very pleasant to help yourself and mosey out to the swimming pool terrace. (The pool is heated mid-April through mid-October.) A gazebo in the garden beyond the pool has facilities for microphone/music, so desirable for a wine-country wedding. Another pleasant sitting area is the upstairs roof deck with wicker seating.

Bedrooms down the hall keep the Southwest feeling with Indian artifacts and rugs and four-poster pine beds. The Mt. Helena room has a fireplace with deer antlers, Indian baskets, and a beige-and-caramel-spotted calfskin rug. The common bathroom in the hall will make you smile. This "Bovine Bathroom" looks as if it is lined with cowhide. Every surface, walls and porcelain alike, is spotted with black and outlined with rope. In chic decorator circles, this is known as the "bovine motif." Downstairs, a low-ceilinged room with a stone fireplace is quiet and cozy, but you do have to go upstairs for the bath. The upstairs Lookout Room is appealing with its western-pine bathroom with a dormer window and access to a roof deck.

A basket of local restaurant menus is in the common room. The valley has such an embarrassment of famous places that you may arrive with several names you want to try. Tre Vigne is the trendy one of the moment, and you'll also hear good reports about the Green Valley Cafe and Terra for Italian-style food. Rae Ellen is happy to make any reservations you want.

How to get there: Follow Highway 29 through the Napa Valley to Calistoga; at the intersection of Highway 128, continue straight ahead a mile. The inn is on the left side of Highway 128.

olive Metcalf

Culver's, A Country Inn
Calistoga, California
94515

Innkeepers: Meg and Tony Wheatley
Address/Telephone: 1805 Foothill Boulevard; (707) 942–4535
Rooms: 6 share 3¹/₂ baths; all with air conditioning. No smoking inn.
Rates: $85 to $115, double occupancy, full breakfast and complimentary
sherry.
Open: All year except December 23 through 26.
Facilities and activities: Swimming pool, Jacuzzi, sauna. Nearby: tour wineries; mineral waters and mud baths; biking; hot-air ballooning; Calistoga restaurants, shops.

Calistoga has been famous since the nineteenth century as a health-spa town with mineral waters and mud baths. One of the mansions built in the resort community then was that of editor and publisher John Oscar Culver. His large, three-level Victorian is now an immaculate, well-decorated inn.

The inn sits on a hillside with a view of the Napa Valley and Mount St. Helena from the big covered front porch. The grounds are dotted with old shade trees, and a path leads around to a swimming pool (it's not heated, but you won't miss that during a Calistoga summer), sun deck, and Jacuzzi elegantly nestled into the back hillside.

Inside, there is a comfortable, colorful sitting room with mellow pine floors, vivid oriental rugs, a red-velvet sofa, antiques, and a fireplace. The Wheatleys' British background is evident in curios and family photos, the china and silver collections, and the Delft displayed in the dining area.

At breakfast, guests gather at round tables in a light-splashed room adjoining the spiffy kitchen that recklessly sports an oriental rug. French doors open onto a patio for summer breakfasts. It is a fresh, appealing atmosphere with a dividend to the arrangement: While you sip juice, you can savor the aroma of homemade goodies baking and get suggestions about restaurants and local attractions. Scones or home-baked breads or muffins are usually on the menu along with an egg entree. Fresh fruit, coffee, and a variety of teas are accompaniments.

Bedrooms are as light and airy as is the main floor. The upstairs four are furnished in Victorian and early-twentieth-century style. Rooms on the lower floor range in decor from Edwardian to Art Nouveau. They are uncluttered and simply done, each benefiting from a few carefully selected furniture pieces and accessories.

At the end of the hall on the lower level is a first-class sauna with a shower beside it. Guests who are really into body shock can hop from one to the other. For really major body rejuvenation, the innkeepers will arrange for massage or mud baths—"the works"—at a nearby spa.

How to get there: Follow Highway 29 through the Napa Valley to Calistoga and intersection of Highway 128. The inn is ¾ mile north of Calistoga on the west side of Highway 128.

❀

J: *Meg hopes you'll notice her antique hutch in the breakfast area. It is dated 1875, the same year that the inn was built.*

olive Metcalf

Larkmead Country Inn
Calistoga, California
94515

Innkeepers: Gene and Joan Garbarino
Address/Telephone: 1103 Larkmead Lane; (707) 942–5360
Rooms: 4; all with private bath and air conditioning.
Rates: $110 to $125, double occupancy, continental breakfast and early-evening refreshment.
Open: All year.
Facilities and activities: View vineyards from porch. Nearby: wineries, Calistoga restaurants, shops, mineral waters, mud-bath spas.

Between the Silverado Trail and the Sonoma Mountains runs the fertile Napa Valley. Acres of vineyards are crisscrossed with lanes. On one of them is a splendid white clapboard house with broad porches. You will not find a fluttering flag or a cute sign announcing the inn, merely a burnished brass plate with LARKMEAD on it. Drive through the old fieldstone gates and around the house to a wisteria-covered loggia.

The main-floor living room and bedrooms are really on the second floor. Early in the century, the house was purposely built high by the Swiss owner, says Joan Garbarino, in order to catch the evening breezes and look out over his vineyards.

Guests are encouraged to enjoy the ambience of the sprawling house and grounds. The large living room is beautifully furnished with the Garbarinos' collection of antiques, handsome upholstered furniture, books, and paintings. Their Persian rugs are brilliant contrasts to dark wood floors. A crackling fire and a decanter of sherry invite arriving guests to a private, tasteful world.

The house is large, but Joan offers only four bedrooms. It is a matter of high standards ("I'm death on cleanliness!") and wanting to give personal attention to every guest. Bedrooms, named for Napa Valley wines, all overlook the vineyards and hills beyond. Beaujolais uses the open porch over the loggia. Chenin Blanc has a fresh green-and-white floral print on the walls, draperies, and a chaise. Chardonnay is decorated in Art Deco, and Chablis has an enclosed sun porch.

You breakfast in the formal dining room on Imari china with Grand Baroque sterling. Joan serves a beautiful arrangement of fresh fruit followed by individual baskets of hot breakfast breads with freshly ground coffee.

This is the only meal served, but the recent appearance of some exceptional restaurants in the valley attracts many people. The Calistoga Inn is a great favorite, with fresh menu changes daily and an adjoining pub.

How to get there: From San Francisco, take Highway 101; or from the East Bay, take Highway 80 to Highway 37. At Highway 29 continue north, and turn right on Larkmead Lane between St. Helena and Calistoga. For a more picturesque route, take any cross-valley road from Highway 29 to the Silverado Trail; follow north, turn left on Larkmead Lane.

J: *You can step right next door to the Hans Kornell Winery and see the process of making bottle-fermented champagnes.*

olive Metcalf

Vintage Towers
Cloverdale, California
95425

Innkeeper: Garrett Hall
Address/Telephone: 302 North Main Street; (707) 894–4535
Rooms: 7, including 2 suites; 5 with private bath, all with air conditioning.
Smoking on verandas and gazebo only.
Rates: $70 to $110, double occupancy, full breakfast.
Open: All year except January.
Facilities and activities: Dinner by special arrangement. Bicycles; television,
VCR in parlor; will cater small conferences, weddings under seventy-
five. Nearby: wine tasting tours; Russian River 6 blocks away for
canoeing, swimming, tubing; Lake Sonoma boating, fishing, skiing;
equestrian trails, hiking.

Vintage Towers is another of those grand Victorians built by a
lumber baron for himself. Simon Pinschower built this Queen Anne
in 1901, and it's had loving care through the years, most recently
with innkeeper Garrett Hall and his partner Jim Mees.

Every one of the antique-appointed rooms is freshly decorated
and pleasant, but the suites are especially choice. The Vintage
Tower is furnished with some fine Eastlake-style furniture. A settee
and chair upholstered in royal blue sit in the bay window formed
by the tower, bedroom furniture that has remained in Cloverdale
families for more than one hundred years.

One owner of the house had a penchant for adding huge floor-
to-ceiling, many-drawered cabinets to the bedrooms. An overnight

guest is hardly going to use them, but I enjoyed just thinking about how I could fill them if they were in my house.

Pinschower did not scrimp on space. At the top of the stairs, what could have been an ordinary landing is, instead, an entire sitting room furnished with a wood-burning stove, a pair of English chairs, and a barber's chair. As you explore the house, you will see even more fascinating furniture and objects—a collection of old posters, an extensive display of old pottery, and a wonderful antique radio collection.

The library is fascinating. More than 1,000 volumes are in the house, including handsome old sets of Dickens and Carlyle. Across the hall is the Music Room with a piano and a collection of offbeat instruments and more antique radios. The most unusual is a piano player—no, that is *not* a player piano. The old Chase-and-Baker oddity is fitted up with a roll of music, say a Scott Joplin rag, rolled up next to the piano, and its wooden fingers dash over the keyboard banging out the tune.

Garrett's backgound includes some pretty upscale cooking (he was pastry chef at the trendy Los Angeles restaurant Citrus), so it is no surprise his breakfast production is substantial. Homemade *everything*, of course, from muffins and jams to unique entrees. Just two of his original recipes are a raspberry/blackberry biscuit pudding served with a fruit plate, and the individual fruit cheesecakes he does for dessert. For dinner, he will suggest several restaurants in town, or you might want to drive to Healdsburg for a big splash at Madrona Manor.

How to get there: From San Francisco, follow Highway 101 to center of Cloverdale. At first stoplight in town, turn right on First Street. Go 1 block to North Main; turn left. Inn is 3 blocks on the right.

Olive Metcalf

Campbell Ranch Inn
Geyserville, California
95441

Innkeepers: Mary Jane and Jerry Campbell

Address/Telephone: 1475 Canyon Road; (707) 857–3476

Rooms: 5; all with private bath, king-sized bed, and air conditioning, 1 with fireplace, most with balcony; 1 cottage. No smoking inn.

Rates: $100 to $145, double occupancy, full breakfast. $25 for additional person. Two-night minimum weekends, three on holidays.

Open: All year.

Facilities and activities: Swimming pool, hot tub, professional tennis court, horseshoes, Ping-Pong, bicycles available; facilities for small business seminars; hiking. Nearby: Russian River 3 miles, Lake Sonoma 4 miles for water recreation and fishing, many wineries, restaurants.

Bring your camera to this 35-acre hilltop ranch. The spectacular view over rolling Sonoma vineyards and a profusion of flowers and plantings will have you snapping memories of your stay. It's a quintessential Northern California scene, with the fresh air and vast open skies thrown in with the room rate.

Suppose you want to stay a few days in the wine country, but you don't want to spend all your time touring and sipping. This is just the kind of inn you'll want: a modern ranch house with comfortable, impeccably maintained surroundings, an atmosphere of utter relaxation, and plenty to keep you entertained.

The Campbells are transplanted Pennsylvanians who raised a

family in this home and haven't lost their knack for making it a place to have fun. There's an elegant terrace and swimming pool and a professional tennis court. They even keep an unlimited supply of lemonade and iced tea available. A big family room has a television, Ping-Pong, games, and a collection of model trains that will amuse a lot of people. There's an attractive living room with a large fireplace, where you can relax or read.

The bedrooms are spacious, most with a deck overlooking the pool and the hills and vineyards beyond. Every room had a fresh bouquet from the garden. The cottage, which is separate from the house, has been redecorated as a more casual accommodation than those in the house, but its flexible sleeping options work well for a family. Jerry Campbell's model-train room is between the cottage and the coops needed for his other hobby, raising pigeons.

Save Room for Dessert is the name of Mary Jane Campbell's cookbook and a kind of second name for her. Those are usually her words as guests leave for dinner. When they return, she's ready with a warm fresh-fruit pie and coffee every evening. Jerry says it's one of the most sociable times at the inn, sitting around the kitchen table or on the terrace under the stars. These are the special moments that get people hooked on country inns.

When you check in at the ranch you'll get a menu with a bounteous choice of fruits, breads, and breakfast entrees. All you do is make your selections and say what time you'll want it. Could you get used to this life?

How to get there: From Highway 101 at Geyserville, take the Canyon Road exit and follow west 1³/₅ miles to the inn.

J: *Nearly sixty wineries are scattered through the Russian River area, many with famous names like Korbel and Simi. Different from Napa Valley wineries, most here are small, family operated, with tasting rooms less crowded and time to visit, sometimes with the winemaker.*

olive Metcalf

Hope-Merrill House
and Hope-Bosworth House
Geyserville, California
95441

Innkeepers: Bob and Rosalie Hope
Address/Telephone: 21238 Geyserville Avenue (mailing address: Box 42);
(707) 857-3356
Rooms: 5 in Hope-Bosworth; 2 with private bath, 1 with half-bath. 7 in
Hope-Merrill; all with private bath. No smoking inn.
Rates: $65 to $90 at Bosworth House; $95 to $125 at Merrill House, double
occupancy, full breakfast.
Open: All year.
Facilities and activities: Picnics, vineyard tours arranged. Nearby: restaurants,
explore backroads, many small wineries, Russian River, redwoods,
Lake Sonoma, Warm Springs Dam.

Geyserville is a small town in the Alexander Valley, one of the
most beautiful—and least traveled—areas of California wine country. On the first day of September, the vines were hanging heavy
with ripe grapes, and the aroma of the crush just begun pervaded
the valley.

This pair of houses, facing each other across Geyserville's main
street, was restored as inns by the Hopes in 1980. The Hope-Merrill
is the more splendid of the two, a redwood Victorian of the Eastlake
Stick style popular in the 1880s. It was once an early stage stop. It

has exceptionally beautiful dining and living rooms, with handsome silk-screened wallpapers, antique furniture, and a collection of Victorian curiosities. The seven bedrooms are strikingly decorated. Ceiling fans are a modern touch that *look* old but do a good job of cooling on hot days.

Both houses retain an atmosphere of the time they were built—old-fashioned yards, grape arbors, and, at Hope-Merrill, a white gazebo. The gazebo sits in an enchanting Victorian garden that, even if you're ho-hum about gardens, will have you taking pictures with abandon.

Many old houses are on the list of National Register of Historic Places, but Hope-Merrill has won first-place honors for its owners as the outstanding bed and breakfast inn in the Great American Home competition of the National Trust for Historic Preservation. High praise went to the Hopes for the excellence of the job they have done. Much of the exterior work and almost the entire interior restoration was done by the Hopes over four years.

The Hopes have devised a treat they call "Pac A Picnic." It's a gourmet (and I use the word literally) picnic lunch featuring almost exclusively Sonoma County foods—local cheeses and smoked meats, seasonal fresh fruits and vegetables locally grown, and Rosalie's own prizewinning breads. Appetizer, main course, salad, dessert, fruit, and a bottle of Bob's estate bottled wine are packed in a beautiful wicker basket that you keep. Lunch for two is $30.

How to get there: From Highway 101, take Geyserville exit to 128; follow it into town past the Bank of America. Check in at Hope-Merrill on the left.

J: *Get a map and drive or bike as many of these back roads as you can. They're special.*

Olive Metcalf

Applewood, An Estate Inn
Guerneville, California
95446

Innkeepers: Darryl Notter and Jim Caron
Address/Telephone: 13555 Highway 116; (707) 869–9093
Rooms: 10; all with private bath, television, telephone. No smoking inn.
Rates: $115 to $185, single or double occupancy, full breakfast. Two-night
minimum on weekends.
Open: All year.
Facilities and activities: Fixed-price dinner available some evenings. Swimming pool, spa; facilities for private parties, small business seminars. Nearby: restaurants, golf, tennis, horseback riding; canoeing and other river activities; Guerneville shops; many local wineries; Sonoma Coast beaches. Armstrong Redwood State Reserve.

Applewood, formerly called The Estate, is an unexpected taste of glamour in the forested hills hugging the Russian River. As it twists through the Guerneville area, the river's beautiful natural setting has long been a popular choice for "resorts," cabins, cottages, and campgrounds. But . . . this is something quite different.

It's not always easy to relax in handsome surroundings, but that's not the case in this Mission Revival–style house. It was built as a private residence in 1922 by a financier, Ralph Belden, and you know what grandiose ideas the wealthy in those days had when it came to building even their vacation homes. This one is imposing, but it remains an inviting country home. On the main floor, a large rock fireplace divides the living room from a many-windowed solarium. On the lower level, bedrooms open to still another comfortable sitting room.

The decor is *Architectural Digest*—with warmth. Darryl studied design in San Francisco, and the house shows it. There's no one "look," but rather an individual, personal style. He's designed stylish slipcovers for some of the chairs and smart duvet covers for the beds. There are fine antiques among some just comfortable furniture. Both he and Jim are always looking for interesting pieces, but they admit that as much as they've bought, it seems to disappear in the large house.

Bedrooms are wonderfully romantic, and there's not a Laura Ashley in the lot. Billowing cotton draperies at an expansive bow of casement windows graced Number 4, my room. ("Cute" room names are out, says Darryl.) A sitting area had two cushy lounge chairs, a settee, and a fresh bouquet of roses. The room had everything for comfort: television and telephone, down pillows and comforters, even the rarest of all inn appointments—good reading lights. When I returned from dinner, the drapes were drawn, bed turned down, and my robe laid out. (Next time I'll pack a prettier robe.)

Breakfast was prepared and served as elegantly as everything is done around here. On a terrace by the pool a table set with heavy silverware, linen napkin, silver coffeepot, and newspaper at hand was the right place to be on the sunny morning of my visit. The beautiful fresh fruit, hot muffins, and a bacon-avocado-tomato-sour-cream omelet were perfection.

This is a terrific place to entertain—one other person or a party. If you have four or more, the innkeepers will sometimes cater special lunches or dinners. They're working hard to make this classic house a class-act inn by applying a simple philosophy: only the best of everything.

How to get there: From 101 north, take River Road/Guerneville exit just past Santa Rosa; go west 14 miles to Guerneville. At the stop sign at Highway 116 and River Road, turn left, cross the bridge over River Road. The inn is ½ mile beyond the bridge on the left. Local airport pickup.

olive Metcalf

Ridenhour Ranch House Inn
Guerneville, California
95446

Innkeepers: Diane and Fritz Rechberger
Address/Telephone: 12850 River Road; (707) 887–1033
Rooms: 8; 5 with private bath. Wheelchair access. No smoking inn.
Rates: $65 to $115, double occupancy, full breakfast. Two-night minimum
   on weekends.
Open: All year.
Facilities and activities: Dinners served Saturday night to house guests, by
   request. Private parties, meetings, and weddings catered when entire
   inn is booked. Hot tub. Nearby: hiking, bicycling, winery visits, Russian
   River beaches, good restaurants.

The Russian River winds over two hundred miles of northern
Sonoma County. Near Guerneville (pronounced Gurn-ville, please),
it flows west through wooded mountains, redwood forests, and
vineyards to the Pacific. In this beautiful countryside, Louis Riden-
hour built a ranch house in 1906 on part of the 940-acre spread
that his family had on both sides of the river.

Diane and Fritz have owned the house since 1989 and a restaurant in Southern California prior to that. They have achieved an inn
that blends a laid-back atmosphere with all the comforts of a private
country home. There is a large country kitchen with a professional-
sized stove, freezer, and cooking equipment, a dining area, and a
redwood-paneled living room. This is the kind of space that invites

you to relax by the fireplace with lots of comfortable furniture, attractive rugs, greenery, and big-window views of the forested area along the river.

A smaller sun parlor–type room they call a "guest kitchen" is off the living room. It's a convenient place for guests to keep wine cold that they might have bought on a tour, or even to make themselves a sandwich.

Each bedroom has individual touches that please, fresh flowers, and tranquil views of the wooded setting. Some rooms have an early American look with brass beds and quilts; others have English antiques. The inn's facilities are not well suited to children under ten years.

You can enjoy breakfast in the big kitchen or out on the patio: freshly ground coffee, fresh juices and fruits, strudels, crepes, or eggs Florentine.

Food is the aspect of innkeeping that particularly interests Fritz. (I haven't met an innkeeper yet who claims making beds is the best part.) At this writing, besides the big breakfasts, he is doing elegant Saturday night dinners for house guests. The menus, which change seasonally, are quite elaborate—among the five entree choices might be rack of lamb, duck breast a l'orange, salmon Wellington, or an eggplant dish for vegetarians, and desserts like profiteroles.

Paths meander around the inn's informally landscaped grounds, under oak and redwood trees, and past a hot tub. One can walk to the neighboring Korbel Winery and visit their champagne cellars, or to secluded river beaches nearby.

How to get there: From Highway 101 north of Santa Rosa, take River Road exit. Drive west 12¹/₂ miles to entrance to the inn on the right, just 500 yards east of Korbel Winery.

✳

J: Your fresh breakfast fruit is often from the inn's own orchards: figs, pears, plums, apples, and, oh joy . . . fresh raspberries!

Olive Metcalf

Camellia Inn
Healdsburg, California
95448

Innkeepers: Ray and Del Lewand
Address/Telephone: 211 North Street; (707) 433–8182
Rooms: 9; all with private bath, 4 with gas fireplace, 3 with Jacuzzi for two. No smoking inn.
Rates: $70 to $125, double occupancy, full breakfast buffet and afternoon wine.
Open: All year.
Facilities and activities: Beautiful gardens, swimming pool. Nearby: 2 blocks from town plaza's shops, restaurants; Russian River wineries; canoeing, fishing, swimming on the river.

This graceful Italianate Victorian is a wonderful setting for indulging fantasies of the leisurely "good old days," with you starring as master or mistress of the mansion.

Because you're decently rich, you have not one but *two* connecting parlors with twin marble fireplaces. The rooms have long elegant windows, 12-foot ceilings featuring medallions, and other architectural details. Oriental rugs and inviting sofas and antiques fill the rooms, which are decorated in warm salmon tones. Crystal decanters and fresh flowers are appointments you insist upon.

As the proper owner of one of the finest houses in town, you must perambulate the grounds to see that the roses and camellias are thriving and to pause by the tiled fish pond to count the stock.

After a vigorous property inspection, you rest by the villa-styled heated swimming pool—just the shady spot for a sip of something bracing.

If your fancy today is a winery tour or dinner at a restaurant, your household staff is knowledgeable about both. For dinner, a suggestion might be that you leave the carriage at home and stroll to Jacob Horner on the town plaza, or Tre Scalini, just a few steps from the plaza. Most agreeable.

Later that night you step from an upholstered footstool to your four-poster, canopied, queen-sized bed and slip between crisp sheets. You prop yourself up on fluffy pillows and survey your big bedroom with lace at the windows and antiques. Soothing music lulls you to a well-deserved sleep. In the morning, confident that someone *else* is grinding Viennese coffee and squeezing fresh juice, you linger in your private bath with its marble shower, antique sink, and thick towels.

What a pleasure to enter a dining room that looks the way God meant it to look—spacious and substantial, with a massive hand-carved mahogany mantel surrounding a tiled fireplace. Help yourself from the buffet offering fresh fruit, just-baked breads, a hearty main dish, and homemade jams. Have another cup of coffee and, if you *must* spoil the dream, face the morning newspaper.

How to get there: Driving north on Highway 101, take the second Healdsburg exit. Follow Healdsburg Avenue to North Street, and turn right. Inn is on the left.

J: *I can't see why some people are always complaining about life's hardships. The world seems altogether orderly and pleasant to me at Camellia Inn.*

Olive Metcalf

Grape Leaf Inn
Healdsburg, California
95448

Innkeeper: Karen Sweet
Address/Telephone: 539 Johnson Street; (707) 433–8140
Rooms: 7; all with private bath and air conditioning. No smoking inn.
Rates: $85 to $130, double occupancy, full breakfast and afternoon premium local wines and cheeses.
Open: All year.
Facilities and activities: Nearby: Healdsburg Square, restaurants, shops; wine touring; bicycling; Russian River boating, rafting, fishing; Lake Sonoma water sports; Fish Hatchery.

This sedate lavender Queen Anne with the grape-color trim is a gingerbread deceiver. Who would think that behind its Victorian facade are seventeen skylight roof windows, air-conditioned bedrooms, and seven private bathrooms, four with a two-person whirlpool tub/shower?

The 1900-vintage home has undergone major renovations, including the addition of an entire second floor under the existing roofline. The four bedrooms and baths up here have an abundance of appeal, due in large part to all the natural light from the roof windows. They can be opened for fresh air, but even when closed, you have magnificent views of the trees, mountains, and blue sky of Sonoma.

Each of the upstairs guest rooms has a sloping roof, and you know how cozy that is. They are named and decorated after the varietal grapes grown in the surrounding countryside: Chardonnay, Cabernet Sauvignon, Merlot, Zinfandel, Pinot Noir, and Gamay Rosé. Colorful linens and puffy comforters decorate the iron and brass beds, all king- or queen-sized. The Chardonnay has a separate sitting area with a daybed covered in white eyelet and two stained-glass windows in shades of blue and purple.

Downstairs, guests can enjoy a colorful parlor with a gray-floral-patterned sofa before the fireplace, as well as a living room, dining room, and kitchen. They are fresh, pleasant rooms to relax in, read, or sip a glass of wine. Outdoors under the trees, the umbrella tables are inviting, too.

A full breakfast is served in the dining room at a lace-covered table with fresh flowers. Fresh juice and fruit, home-baked breads and muffins, and an entree, such as a frittata, are typical.

For dinner, stroll to the square and try Tre Scalini, a wonderful Northern Italian restaurant just off the plaza. Also on the square is the Salame Tree Deli. It's a good supply station for picnickers. Choose from an assortment of cold cuts, cheeses, and wines; then head for the back roads—on bikes if you've brought them. And who would go to Sonoma without a bicycle!

How to get there: Driving north on Highway 101, take the Central Healdsburg exit and follow into town. At Grant Street, turn right 2 blocks. The inn is on the right at the corner of Johnson Street.

J: *Can anyone doubt that we Westerners are ready for hardship and sacrifice when necessary? The popular duo-bathing phenomenon proves we'd do anything to conserve water!*

olive Metcalf

Healdsburg Inn on the Plaza
Healdsburg, California
95448

Innkeeper: Genny Jenkins
Address/Telephone: 116 Matheson Street (mailing address: Box 1196); (707)
   433–6991
Rooms: 9; all with private bath and air conditioning. Smoking only on roof
   garden.
Rates: $75 to $150, double occupancy, full breakfast and afternoon refreshments, evening sweets. Substantial discounts midweek and off-season.
Open: All year.
Facilities and activities: Television lounge. Nearby: Healdsburg restaurants,
   shops; wine tours; Russian River for canoeing, fishing; picnics; bicycling; Lake Sonoma.

Genny Jenkins looks around the small Victorian hotel she has
restored, shakes her head, and grins. "I didn't *need* this!" She
already owns The Cinnamon Bear, a small B&B in St. Helena, but
given her enormous energy, the beautiful old Krause building on
the Plaza had too much potential to pass by.

Healdsburg is a heart-tugger of a town, built around a Spanish-
style plaza with quaint storefronts and historic houses on its back
streets. Genny has decoratively painted and trimmed her building
with bright colors, divided the lower floor into attractive shops, and
created a comfortable inn upstairs. The street-level entry and lobby
are part of a gift shop and gallery showing original local art. Daugh-

ter Dyanne runs this operation. A paneled stairway leads up to a wide, tall-ceilinged hallway with ornamental architectural details, period lighting fixtures, and a lounge where guests can enjoy a collection of classic novels or watch television or video.

Rooms facing the plaza have graceful bay windows that make delightful sitting areas, and some have fireplaces. Genny is constantly decorating with an eye for turn-of-the-century furniture and whimsy. Several bathrooms have new spectacular skylights over big, claw-footed tubs. "We really go in for an abundance of plush towels, bubbles, and rubber ducks," she says.

The room that captivated me is in back. Long ago, it was a photography studio. An entire wall—and these are 12-foot ceilings—is a slanted skylight. Besides the large bath and queen-sized bed, at no extra cost, you get a ceiling of clouds and sky. Imagine it for full moons!

A large flower-filled roof garden is one of Genny's best innovations. Breakfast is usually served out here at fancy white iron tables and chairs: fresh fruit and juice, homemade goodies, and an entree of cheese, eggs, or meat combination. Sunday morning breakfast expands into a champagne brunch served until noon that is open to the public as well as house guests.

Many guests walk around the corner to Tre Scalini for Northern Italian food for dinner. It is not just trendy—it's fine cooking.

How to get there: Driving north on Highway 101, take second Healdsburg exit; turn right on Matheson Street to town plaza. Inn faces the plaza. Coming from the north, take Mill Street exit to the plaza.

J: *In 1901, the local paper said that this building was "a substantial ornament to the town." Healdsburg is lucky that the description holds true once again.*

Madrona Manor
Healdsburg, California
95448

Innkeepers: John and Carol Muir
Address/Telephone: 1001 Westside Road (mailing address: Box 818); (707) 433–4231, or fax (707) 433–0703
Rooms: 18 and 2 suites; all with private bath, telephone, and air conditioning, 18 with fireplace. Wheelchair access.
Rates: $110 to $200, double occupancy, full breakfast, Sunday through Thursday. $190 to $280, double occupancy, Friday, Saturday, and holidays, Modified American Plan (breakfast and dinner included).
Open: All year.
Facilities and activities: Dinner nightly, Sunday brunch. Swimming pool. Nearby: golf, tennis, hiking, canoeing, fishing, winery tours, picnics, bicycling.

Country inns continue to spring up in northern California faster than yuppies are going out of style, but Madrona Manor stands alone. First, it is a truly dramatic Victorian mansion sitting in the midst of landscaped grounds and eight wooded acres. But even more notable is its outstanding California restaurant, the only one in Sonoma County rated three stars by *Chronicle* food critic Patricia Unterman.

Approaching the Italianate mansion up the long driveway brings feelings of pleasant anticipation. Elegant accommodations await inside: antique furnishings, period wallpapers and rugs, and rooms with original plumbing and lighting fixtures. The third floor has renovated rooms with fireplaces, queen-sized beds, and antique reproduction furniture from Portugal. Less opulent but more modern rooms are in two other outbuildings and the Carriage House, where a fireplace has been added to the lounge.

The fine cooking is served in two high-ceilinged, attractive dining rooms. Former Chez Panisse cook Todd Muir runs the kitchen. He and his staff work in a modern kitchen (contrasting with the rest of the 1881 setting) complete with a mesquite grill and a smokehouse in back that produces smoked trout, chickens, and meats. The gardens produce all the flowers for the dining room and guest rooms as well as herbs and specialty produce for the kitchen.

An à la carte menu of salads, pastas, and grilled main courses, or an elegant prix-fixe dinner ($40 at this writing for weekend guests on the Modified American Plan) are available seven nights a week. My first course of individual goat-cheese soufflé was perfectly crusty on top with a softly oozing middle. Every element of the meal, down to dessert of amaretto-soaked cake with chocolate-ricotta filling, was meticulously prepared.

The wine list is both extensive and reasonably priced, which, even though this is the heart of the wine country, is not always true up here. Some selections from small local wineries are at near-retail prices.

Breakfast for guests is as carefully done as dinner. It includes their wonderful house bread, toasted; a perfectly timed soft-boiled egg; loads of seasonal fruit; oatmeal and granola; ripe, room-temperature cheeses; and house-smoked meats. When the weather allows, take this meal outside on the palm terrace.

How to get there: From San Francisco, drive north on Highway 101, 12 miles north of Santa Rosa; take the Central Healdsburg exit; follow Healdsburg Avenue north to Mill Street, turn left, and it becomes Westside Road. Inn is ³/₄ mile on the right. From the north, take Westside Road exit from Highway 101; turn right. Inn is ¹/₂ mile on the right.

১ৢ

J: *What a beautiful place for a special celebration.*

Olive Metcalf

Murphy's Jenner Inn
Jenner, California
95450

Innkeepers: Jenny Carroll; owners, Richard and Sheldon Murphy

Address: 10400 Coast Highway One (mailing address: P.O. Box 69); (707) 865–2377

Rooms: 11 rooms, suites, and cabins; all with private bath, suites with living room, kitchen, wood stove, deck.

Rates: $65 to $150, double occupancy, including continental breakfast, tea and aperitifs in the salon. $10 each additional person.

Open: All year.

Facilities and activities: Restaurant and wine bar; hot tub. Weddings, receptions, group retreats, conferences can be accommodated. Nearby: canoeing on Russian River, miles of sandy beaches, hiking trails through redwoods, wine tasting along Russian River Wine Road, historic Fort Ross, Terra Nova Institute Conference & Retreat Center.

Where the Russian River meets the blue Pacific is where I'll meet you, baby . . . blues. Sounds like a song somebody should have written, doesn't it? Actually, the tranquil spot fitting this description is so peaceful, someone did exactly the right thing back in 1907 when they established Murphy's Jenner Inn. The calming spirit of water and sand and this welcoming inn have continued over the years to work their magic on wayfarers along Highway One.

The main lodge building where you check in faces the Russian River and consists of a parlor, a fine restaurant, a deli/gift shop, and a gas station. The cozy parlor (they call it a salon) is a warm gathering place on foggy coastal mornings or chilly nights. Burgundy sofas flank a wood stove standing in the center of the room. Port and sherry standing by are also helpful in chasing away a chill. Old photographs on the walls and fringed lampshades are an old-fashioned flavor, and the flowers are exuberantly plastic. A simple continental breakfast is served here in the morning—fresh fruit, various muffins, and store-bought pastries.

Guest accommodations are in a variety of buildings surrounding the main lodge. Some are up the hill on the back of the property, and some are across the road and built directly over the water. All have private entrances and private baths, but if you want a hot tub, balcony, or kitchen, that's available too. The Captain's Cabin, situated behind the lodge, has a wonderful view, a loft, wood-burning stove, deck, and full kitchen. It sleeps eight.

The Crew's Quarters is the smallest unit of all, but if you intend to be out most of the time, it is the bargain room. The two-story River House on the banks of the Russian River is one of the best. The Heron Room in blue and white and wicker has a pretty sitting room and a great view. We liked watching the birds from our deck on the second floor of River House.

Dinner will be the evening event at this quiet inn, and Chef Ron Klaus will not disappoint. The room itself is warmly attractive—white linen, blue napkins, dark woods, and large windows. Klaus began his career in Zurich but seems to know exactly what to do with California ingredients. We had a superb cioppino and fresh grilled salmon. Klaus serves spaetzel with many of his entrees, a delicious change from potatoes or rice. We thought his wine list was modestly priced and reflected an emphasis on Sonoma County wines . . . and that's a plus in my estimation.

How to get there: Jenner is on State Highway One just minutes north of Bodega Bay and 12 miles south of the reconstructed Fort Ross.

olive Metcalf

Huckleberry Springs
Country Inn
Monte Rio, California
95462

Innkeeper: Suzanne Greene
Address/Telephone: 8105 Old Beedle Road (mailing address: P.O. Box 400);
  (707) 865–2683 or (800) 822–2683
Rooms: 4 cottages, plus The Conference Center with 3 bedrooms and
  kitchen; all with private bath, wood stove, deck. Smoking only in des-
  ignated outdoor areas. Wheelchair access.
Rates: $140, single occupancy, cottage, $175, double occupancy; $550 for
  entire Conference Center; includes breakfast and dinner. Wedding and
  conference rates available.
Open: All year.
Facilities and activities: Dinner served nightly; wines and beers available.
  Swimming pool, Japanese-style spa. Facilities for weddings and business conferences include television, VCR, fax, two telephone lines.
  Nearby: more than fifty local wineries along Russian River Wine Road;
  hiking; canoeing.

Huckleberry Springs is a spectacular 60-acre rural site above the
Russian River that answers the desires of a wide range of inn lovers.
If it's a romantic getaway you want, the combination of privacy and
pampering available here should encourage even dying embers.

Many of us are simply always on the lookout for that country-
quiet spot (with great amenities) to read a book. These secluded

comfortable cottages are perfect, cozy inside with wood-burning stoves, and decks to sit on outside. But there is so much more.

Maybe you need the therapeutic luxury of a pool and spa. In this Japanese-style spa, you can soak while you gaze out at forested hills. Massage therapy and enzyme baths are also available.

Perhaps you want to gather a group for a wedding, a family reunion, a meeting, or a seminar. The architecturally designed Conference Center features a dramatic two-story interior space, three bedrooms, and an equipped kitchen if you care to prepare some of your own meals. Two phone lines, VCR, television, and a fax machine leave no excuses for not getting business accomplished.

But topping the list of good reasons to wind your way up Old Beedle Road in Monte Rio and get acquainted with Huckleberry Springs is *food*. Whatever you're doing—out visiting wineries, hiking through the countryside, conducting a meeting, or just sitting on a deck watching hawks circle the Sonoma hills—owner Suzanne Green will be in the kitchen tending to the gourmet cooking she loves and at which she is skilled.

Suzanne has studied the cooking techniques of various cultures from Thai to French, studying with the famous Jacques Pèpin. Finding this kind of sophisticated approach to food on a mountaintop in Sonoma, combined with the bounty of the local countryside's glorious fresh ingredients, adds up to a wonderful discovery for guests.

A sample of her dinners might be a black bean soup followed by mixed Sonoma greens with a Bosc pear, goat cheese, and a raspberry vinaigrette. Entrees could be angel hair pasta with smoked salmon, snow peas, and shiitake mushrooms in a white wine, tarragon cream sauce; or sauteed pork loin served with ginger-curry carrots and fresh beets. Dessert might be a chocolate cake with a fresh raspberry mousse sauce.

How to get there: Less than two hours from the Golden Gate Bridge. From Highway 101 North, exit west on River Road through Guerneville to the fork in Highway 116 in Monte Rio. Take left fork; make left turn across bridge and then immediate right turn onto Tyrone Road. Continue to second uphill fork on the right (Old Beedle Road) to first right-hand drive.

J: *Suzanne designed her inn to reflect, among other things, the spirit of the* ryokans *of Japan, where the natural beauty provides pleasure to the mind as well as comfort to the body.*

olive Metcalf

Beazley House
Napa, California
94559

Innkeepers: Carol and Jim Beazley
Address/Telephone: 1910 First Street; (707) 257–1649
Rooms: 10; all with private bath and air conditioning, 5 with two-person spa and fireplace, 1 with wheelchair facilities. Smoking only in the gardens.
Rates: $105 to $175, double occupancy, full breakfast.
Open: All year.
Facilities and activities: Beer and wines available. Facilities for weddings, small meetings; beautiful gardens. Nearby: wine touring, hot mineral baths, ballooning, bicycling; shopping, restaurants.

The blue-and-white striped awnings take your eye immediately. They give this chocolate brown, shingled Colonial Revival the look of a grand English vacation house. It is an old Napa landmark and sits on half an acre of lawns and gardens within walking distance of the town's shopping area.

The solid-looking house is beautifully symmetrical, with an especially wide staircase at its center. A beveled- and stained-glass doorway opens to the entry and music room. To the right is a formal dining room; to the left is a long, gracious living room with polished inlaid wood floors and large bay windows at either end, one with a padded window seat. Brightly upholstered sofas and chairs are arranged in several groupings. There are a fireplace, bookcases, and a basket of Napa restaurant menus to peruse. A tea cart arranged with china cups and saucers, tea, coffee, and sherry looks very civilized and Edwardian.

Halfway up the stairway is a window seat and a spectacular half-round stained-glass window. The bedrooms are pleasantly spacious. Carol has made many of the comforter covers herself in big English floral prints with matching draperies. The Master Room up here, with its own fireplace, is the largest accommodation in the main house.

At the back of the property, the old carriage house has been rebuilt from the ground up, modeled after the original barn. These beautiful rooms have fireplaces, high ceilings, and two-person spas. The fresh scent of cedar comes from the bathrooms, which are lined with tongue and groove cedar paneling.

The Beazleys set out a generous breakfast on the dining-room buffet for guests to help themselves and make return trips. Carol is proud that seven of her muffin recipes are included in a recently published collection of country-inn recipes. A typical breakfast has large platters of sliced fresh fruit, yogurt, one of a variety of crustless quiches she makes, and homemade breads and muffins.

How to get there: From San Francisco, drive north on Highway 101 to 37 east, then north on 121 to 121 east; follow to Highway 29. Proceed north to the First Street/Central Napa exit. Follow exit all the way to the end; then turn left at Second Street. Continue ³/₁₀ mile to Warren Street. Turn left to the inn on corner of First and Warren.

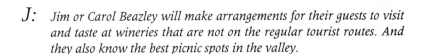

J: *Jim or Carol Beazley will make arrangements for their guests to visit and taste at wineries that are not on the regular tourist routes. And they also know the best picnic spots in the valley.*

Olive Metcalf

Country Garden Inn
Napa, California
94558

Innkeepers: Lisa and George Smith

Address/Telephone: 1815 Silverado Trail; (707) 255–1197, or fax (707) 255–3112

Rooms: 8; all with private bath, including 6 with Jacuzzi, all with air conditioning, most with fireplace. No smoking inn.

Rates: $110 to $175, December through March; $115 to $180, April through November, double occupancy, full champagne breakfast and early-evening hors d'oeuvres and wine. Lowest rates Sunday through Thursday. Two-night minimum on weekends.

Open: All year.

Facilities and activities: Aviary. Badminton/volleyball court. Horseshoes. Gardens, deck, riverbank setting. Nearby: winery tours, hiking, bicycling, hot-air ballooning, picnics, mud baths; fine restaurants all around.

If you're one who is smitten with everything English (as I am), you will be charmed with this "very English Inn," as its owners describe it. It sits, not on the Thames, but on wooded riverside land in the Napa Valley. British innkeepers Janet and Geoffrey Villiers, who formerly owned Old World Inn in Napa, have launched an American innkeeping tradition by putting daughter Lisa and son-in-law George in charge of this hostelry.

The house was built in the 1850s as a coach stop, and it still gives you a sense of "safe haven" when you pull off the road into the acre-and-a-half wooded setting. It sits right on the bank of the

Napa River, almost overrun with trees and what I call a typical British-style haphazard abundance of flora and fauna. Now that Geoffrey Villiers has more time to tend the gardens, that "haphazard" quality seems to be disappearing. The rose garden and lily pond, a little bridge over the creek, and new stone steps down to the lower lawn all show the pleasure the entire family finds in working on their lovely property. There are pathways surrounding a shaded terrace, a deck overlooking the river, and a profusion of flowers and vines and Scottie dogs. On the July day I visited, fat roses in every imaginable color made a dazzling display from a formal circular rose garden.

The common rooms have an English feeling with beamed ceilings and handsome wood mantels over the fireplaces. An assortment of easy chairs and chintz-covered sofas are arranged for conversation; there are British magazines and guide books on the tables.

This is a place to enjoy fair weather or foul. I like the idea of afternoon tea and cookies before the fire, or wine and a cheese board before going out to dinner. When you return, sweetmeats and dessert wines are set out. Those British! They do know how to pause and refresh, don't they?

There are romantically decorated bedrooms in soft colors with antiques, some canopied beds, and many Jacuzzis. One large room has a sitting area between two walls of beveled-glass windows. One has a private deck right over the river.

Breakfast is quite special, served at tables covered with long chintz skirts and top cloths. Champagne or mimosas are poured while you have fruit and coffee cakes, eggs Benedict, or perhaps English bangers and omelets. In lovely weather—and since this is the Napa Valley, not England, there's plenty of it—you can eat on the deck if you like.

How to get there: From Highway 29 in Napa, take Trancas Street east to fork in the road. Bear right (signed 121 to Napa). The inn is ⁷/₁₀ mile on the right.

J: How did they ever lose the Empire when they're so dashedly civilized!

Olive Metcalf

La Residence
Napa, California
94558

Innkeepers: David Jackson and Craig Claussen
Address/Telephone: 4066 St. Helena Highway North; (707) 253–0337
Rooms: 20 in Mansion and French barn; 18 with private bath. Air conditioning; wheelchair access. Smoking outdoors only.
Rates: $75 to $175, double occupancy, full breakfast and afternoon wine social.
Open: All year.
Facilities and activities: Spa, heated pool, tennis; elegant dining room available for parties, catered dinners, concierge service for all area activities. Nearby: wine tours, ballooning, bicycling; fine restaurants, shopping.

The two buildings that together are La Residence are different, but both are so delightful that it is hard to decide which to choose. The inn began with the Gothic Revival mansion Harry C. Parker built in 1870 when he moved to Napa County to farm. He was a river pilot from New Orleans, and the house shows a distinctive Southern character, with all the winning features of a fine Victorian home.

If you ever visited this picturesque farmhouse in earlier years, you should see why its new owners now call it "The Mansion." The graceful architecture has been splendidly renovated and rooms inside elegantly decorated with American antiques, plantation shutters, the finest linens, and coordinated fabrics and wall coverings.

When you see period charm restored with this degree of taste and eye for comfort, you have something special. There are newly added private baths, fireplaces, and a small kitchen where you can keep your wine chilled.

Across the yard is a much newer building, a handsome shingled structure built in the style of a French barn. I say "barn," but I assure you the only animals roaming these elegant rooms are a few porcelain geese decorating the dining room. It's actually called "Cabernet Hall," probably a prudent move on the part of the innkeepers. Claussen, who is from Iowa, says he could imagine giving a telephone description of the accommodations and getting a response, "A barn? I'm not paying good money to sleep in a barn!" Each of the eleven rooms here has a sitting area, fireplace, and French doors opening onto a patio or balcony. Furnishings are English and French country pine, queen-sized beds, and Laura Ashley fabrics.

The two acres of beautiful grounds now have a Jacuzzi spa and a heated pool surrounded by brick patios, gazebos, trellis, and gardens, all shaded by 200-year-old oaks and acacias.

A beautifully presented full breakfast is served in the dining room of Cabernet Hall, sometimes before a blazing fire, and always with fresh flowers and the morning papers. This is an innkeeper production with David cooking and Craig serving. First course is a fresh-fruit plate, followed by an egg entree with home-baked breads or cinnamon rolls.

How to get there: Take Highway 29 through Napa; pass Salvador Avenue and look for the inn sign on the right.

J: *When I heard this inn I admired had new owners and was enlarging, I feared another casualty of charming inn into slick corporate facility. It's good to see La Residence being run with the warmth and personal attention that always separate innkeepers from strictly bottomliners.*

Olive Metcalf

Auberge du Soleil
Rutherford, California
94573

Innkeepers: George A. Goeggel; Phillipa Perry, general manager
Address/Telephone: 180 Rutherford Hill Road; (707) 963–1211
Rooms: 48; all with private bath, fireplace, television, deck or patio, individual temperature control. Wheelchair access.
Rates: $275, double room, to $650 for 2-bedroom suites; continental breakfast, fruit basket upon arrival, choice of daily newspaper, and use of tennis, spa, and swimming facilities.
Open: All year.
Facilities and activities: Lunch, dinner, bar (reservations advised). Wedding and conference facilities. Swimming pool, Jacuzzi, masseuse, steam rooms, tennis courts, bikes for rent. Nearby: wineries, picnicking, hot springs, restaurants, shops.

First, there was the prestigious Auberge du Soleil Restaurant; then it expanded into a chic country inn composed of ten two-story and one three-story Mediterranean-style villas. The entire resort is nestled into thirty-three acres of olive groves spread over a hillside looking down on the Napa Valley.

The atmosphere here is quite simply . . . luxury. Oh, it may be understated and unfussy, but this is *major* luxury. On each level of the villas are two bedrooms, two baths, two fireplaces, and a large living room with a stocked refrigerator—liquors, champagne, wine, and aged cheeses in addition to chocolates and a basket full of crackers and cookies. Just to keep body and soul together, don't you know. Each suite converts to a one-bedroom unit and a one-bedroom suite keeping the amenities. From each private deck is a perfect view of the Napa Valley with the Silverado Trail winding through.

The decor is a blend of European sophistication and California informality—sort of an earthy elegance. Floors are covered with Mexican tiles, and furniture is kept to a minimum, but much of it is bold, like Mexican pigskin chairs and concrete stone-roller lamps. Walls are the same rough, adobe-colored plaster as in the restaurant, with white-framed French glass doors and casement windows with heavy, white louvered doors and inside shutters. The only splash of color comes from fresh flowers and oversized pillows on sofas and chairs. Sheets are percale, towels the thickest; and bathrooms are big enough for small meetings.

One look at the elegant dining room and terrace overlooking the valley tells you this is *not* the place to order anything you ever cook at home . . . not that you're going to find meat loaf on the menu. Liberate your plastic card and wallow in the chic California cuisine. Try salad of duck with mangoes, curry-and-lemon linguine, or braised pheasant with crayfish and truffles. The wine list is a catalog of California's finest. Some of the grapes came from the very valley you look over.

Facilities for weddings or small business meetings are exceptional. There is an intimate dining room with a skylight ceiling that accommodates up to thirty people and a state-of-the-art boardroom for up to fifty.

How to get there: From San Francisco, take Highway 80 northeast to connect with Highway 37, then Highway 29. From Highway 29 in Napa Valley, follow any of the cross-valley roads west to the Silverado Trail; continue north to Rutherford. The inn sits above the trail. Fly-in: Napa County Airport.

olive Metcalf

Rancho Caymus Inn
Rutherford, California
94573

Innkeepers: Tony Prince, owner; John Komes
Address/Telephone: Rutherford Road (mailing address: Box 78); (707)
   963–1777 or (800) 845–1777; fax (707) 963–5387
Rooms: 26 suites; all with private bath, air conditioning, color television, wet
   bar and refrigerator, most with fireplace, some rooms handicapped
   equipped.
Rates: $115 to $275, double occupancy, continental breakfast. Two-night
   minimum for weekends April through November and some holiday
   weekends.
Open: All year.
Facilities and activities: The Garden Grill open daily for breakfast, lunch, Sunday brunch. Nearby: wine touring; easy bicycling, hot-air ballooning;
   interesting restaurants, shops.

    This luxurious inn with red-tiled roofs and rough stucco walls
captures the feeling of early California. It's a two-story building
with colonnades and open balconies, shaped around a central garden court in the Spanish style. Each room has a sitting area with
either a wet bar or a complete kitchen; bed and bath are up two
steps to another level. Most have fireplaces and private patios or
balconies. Hand-hewn beams and planking from an old barn give
the rooms a warm, Western feeling.
    The concept of a handcrafted hacienda was a five-year labor of
love for original owner Mary Tilden Morton. She also designed

Rutherford Square, a dining-entertainment complex next door to the inn. Morton made the inn a showplace for artisans and carpenters. Sausalito artists made the hand-thrown stoneware basins that sit in counters made from slabs of black walnut. Parota-wood chairs and matching dressers were carved in Guadalajara. A Napa artist created the stained-glass-window murals behind the Jacuzzi tubs in the bathrooms of the four master suites.

Much of the inn's character comes from the handcrafted furnishings and appointments done by Ecuadoran artists: hand-carved black walnut queen-sized beds and wrought-iron lamps, vibrantly colored bedspreads, rugs, and wall hangings dyed and woven by South American Indians.

The Garden Grill serves breakfast and lunch in a beautiful dining room with a cathedral ceiling and huge stone fireplace. Given the valley's wonderful weather, you can often eat outside on the terrace and tree-shaded courtyard. Your continental breakfast can be brought to your room or served in the garden. Lunch features a range of salads, sandwiches, grilled items, and pastas.

Sampling all the many superb dinner places in the valley is a gourmet adventure. One of them in Yountville is Mustard's, one of the great restaurants in the country—innovative, fresh, and fun! It's also popular, so be sure to ask the innkeeper to make your reservation.

How to get there: On Highway 29 through the Napa Valley, turn east at the crossroads of 29 and Highway 128, south of St. Helena. The inn is on the left, just past Rutherford Square complex.

J: *Highway 29 is the busiest route through the Napa Valley . . . there's no escaping that fact. The good thing about this location is that you are within five minutes of dozens of the world's most famous wineries, some within walking distance.*

Olive Metcalf

Wine Country Inn
St. Helena, California
94574

Innkeeper: Jim Smith
Address/Telephone: 1152 Lodi Lane; (707) 963–7077
Rooms: 25; all with private bath. Wheelchair access.
Rates: $106 to $181, double occupancy, continental breakfast.
Open: All year.
Facilities and activities: Swimming pool. Nearby: country lanes, tennis courts, hot-air balloon rides, mineral baths, many wineries, antiques stores, restaurants.

The Wine Country Inn has grown the past dozen years, along with the tremendous popularity of the Napa Valley. It has added buildings, patios, and, most recently, a swimming pool and spa, but it is still a family operation. You can hear Jim Smith describing a room to a prospective guest over the telephone, adding, "And my mother made the quilt on the bed."

Unlike many inns in the area, this one was built new from the ground up. The Smiths borrowed ideas from historic buildings in the valley, making their three-story stone-and-wood inn look right at home in the vineyards.

Each room is individually decorated, combining old and new. There are fresh, pretty color combinations, floral wallpapers, carpeting, and modern baths. Most rooms have a fireplace and vineyard view. Patios and intimate little balconies invite you to sit and appreciate the beautiful surrounding hills. Early on weekend mornings, you can usually see vividly colored hot-air balloons wafting their passengers over the vineyards.

Coffee is always ready in the large country-style common room. Make yourself at home in the comfortable sofa or wingback chairs beside an iron stove. Attractive books about wine and the area are all about, along with all the local restaurant menus. In St. Helena, Meadowood has elegant food at lunch and dinner in a beautiful hideaway setting. Within walking distance from the inn, you'll find more casual restaurants.

Guests gather at a long refectory table, or at individual tables throughout the room, for continental breakfast. Along with juice and fruit, the substantial fare includes two nut breads, several pastries, butter, and jams. French doors lead to a deck, which is the best breakfast spot of all with views of vineyards and hills. These are pleasant, relaxed mornings, always with friendly staff there to refill your coffee cup and help you with plans for your day.

How to get there: From Napa, take Highway 29 2 miles past St. Helena. Turn right on Lodi Lane. The inn is on the left.

J: *Take your bikes to St. Helena. If you ride early in the morning on the lanes that wind through still-dewy vineyards, you will begin to understand how the wine country can become a passion.*

Olive Metcalf

The Gables
Santa Rosa, California
95404

Innkeepers: Michael and Judy Ogne
Address/Telephone: 4257 Petaluma Hill Road; (707) 585–7777
Rooms: 6, plus 1 cottage; all with private bath, 3 with wood stove. No smoking inn.
Rates: $95 to $155, double occupancy, full country breakfast and afternoon refreshments.
Open: All year.
Facilities and activities: Sun deck and gardens. Nearby: restaurants, Sonoma and Russian River wineries, Luther Burbank Center for Performing Arts, Burbank home and gardens, Bodega Bay, Russian River, bicycling, tennis, golf, hot-air ballooning.

If you have time to explore only one area of California's wine country, I say choose Sonoma County. This region north of San Francisco has everything—rolling hills and meadows bordered on the west by one of the most spectacular stretches of coastline anywhere; wildflowers, redwoods, colorful historic towns, and through-out the area some of the finest wineries and vineyards in the world.

The Gables is a lodging that does justice to the peaceful feeling of Sonoma. The beautiful rose-painted mansion with burgundy shutters sits on three and one-half acres in a rural setting. It was built in 1877 by one of the few California gold miners who didn't lose his money. Instead, he built this ornate example of High Victorian Gothic architecture with 12-foot ceilings, three Italian marble fireplaces, and a splendid mahogany spiral staircase. The name of the house comes from its most striking detail, the fifteen gables crowning the unusual keyhole-shaped windows.

The house couldn't have a happier fate than being rescued by the Ognes. Every room is invitingly fresh and tastefully decorated in fine fabrics and romantic color schemes. The spacious bedrooms are appointed with lovely antiques (but not so many they clutter the room), private baths, goosedown comforters, freshly cut flowers, and a good selection of books.

William and Mary's Cottage is a separate accommodation next to Taylor Creek. Its sleeping loft, wood stove, and kitchenette make it particularly pleasant for a longer-than-overnight stay.

The atmosphere at this fine country house will invite you to stay around and relax right here. There's a great old (about 150 years) barn on the property with a resident owl family, and a three-holer outhouse . . . strictly for academic inspection. You can stroll through the kitchen gardens, cross the footbridge over Taylor Creek into the meadow, or take a cup of coffee out to the big sun deck and soak in the countryside.

Wonderful restaurants abound in the surrounding area. Michael and Judy are ready to recommend according to your food favorites and will make the necessary reservations at the most "in" places. With your evening meal booked, you can skip lunch and abandon yourself to the big, all-fresh country breakfast the Ognes provide. Besides an ever-changing entree, you always find fresh juice and fruits and freshly baked breads and pastries. Breakfast is served in the dining room at separate tables, or you can join other guests at one long table.

How to get there: About an hour north of San Francisco, exit Highway 101 east at Rohnert Park Expressway to Petaluma Hill Road. Turn north to The Gables on the left. Fly-in: Sonoma County Airport.

J: *I arrived at The Gables and asked to be shown around just as the Ognes were expecting a group of innkeepers and winery association guests for lunch. Being busy didn't diminish their hospitality one whit. They showed the kind of friendly, gracious style that separates real innkeepers from the amateurs.*

Olive Metcalf

Melitta Station Inn
Santa Rosa, California
95409

Innkeepers: Diane Crandon and Vic Amstadter
Address/Telephone: 5850 Melitta Road; (707) 538–7712
Rooms: 6; 5 with private bath.
Rates: $75 to $90, double occupancy, full breakfast and early-evening beverage and cheese.
Open: All year.
Facilities and activities: Piano. Nearby: restaurants, wine touring, Jack London State Historical Monument, Annadel State Park; Spring Lake sailing, fishing; hiking, bicycling, picnics.

Ever heard of the Valley of the Moon? There is such a place in the rolling Sonoma countryside, and it is as poetically beautiful as its name. Jack London called the area "my paradise" and built his famous Wolf House here.

The Melitta Station has been a part of Sonoma's history since the late 1800s as a stagecoach stop, then a railroad depot, a general store, and post office. Diane and Vic are the owners of the turn-of-the-century building, now a bed and breakfast inn. She sold business machines and he was an attorney before coming from Los Angeles to try innkeeping. Now they're so involved with their picturesque inn, Diane is even trying to track down photos of the building from its varied early history. Today, their inn has that winning country charm that magazines love to photograph, but in this instance it is less slick, more genuine, and ever so much more warm.

You step into the sitting room and find a large wood-burning stove, wood floor with colorful rugs, baskets of kindling, and rough beams contrasting with white walls. A local artisan stenciled a border of folk-art designs around the room.

Diane has fresh bouquets around the room, and bundles of drying herbs hang from the rough-beamed high ceiling. A red-and-white quilt hangs on one wall. Furniture is American Country, featuring a mellow pine sideboard and a wicker sofa with bright print pillows. The cozy bedrooms are also furnished with antiques and collectibles.

The Melitta's location wins my heart. It is rural and quiet, but with all the advantages of being in the very center of Sonoma County's abundant attractions. You are surrounded by outstanding wineries, close to the historic town of Sonoma, and near elegant Santa Rosa restaurants. Prospect Park and La Gare are two that are currently very hot.

A hearty breakfast is the only meal served regularly, but everything is homemade, from quiches and tortes to baked apples and muffins. Diane also makes a big, puffy Dutch baby topped with fruit. But this is a very personal inn, and Vic and Diane will arrange just about anything you want: unique luncheons, champagne tours, mud baths and massages, hot-air ballooning, or glider rides. Let the good times roll.

How to get there: From Highway 101, exit at Highway 12 exit and follow signs to Sonoma for 5¹/₂ miles. Cross Calistoga Road; turn right at Melitta Road, first road on the right. Continue about a mile to the inn.

Olive Metcalf

Vintners Inn
Santa Rosa, California
95403

Innkeepers: John Duffy; Cindy Young, manager
Address/Telephone: 4350 Barnes Road; (707) 575–7350; in California, (800) 421–2584
Rooms: 44, including 1- and 2-bedroom suites; all with private bath, vineyard views, air conditioning, television, radio, and telephone, some with fireplace. Facilities for the handicapped.
Rates: $108 to $185, double occupancy, continental breakfast.
Open: All year.
Facilities and activities: John Ash & Co. restaurant serving lunch, dinner, Sunday brunch. Extensive conference facilities, spa and sun deck. Nearby: wine touring; Russian River water sports, fishing.

Four creamy-beige stucco buildings with red-tiled roofs around a plaza complete with fountain make up the splendid Vintners Inn. It rises in the center of a 45-acre vineyard (chardonnay, pinot blanc, sauvignon blanc), the picture of a village (although a new one) in the South of France. Actually, it is just 60 miles north of San Francisco at the crossroads of the Sonoma County wine country.

The European concept was carefully planned by John Duffy when he determined that a luxury country inn was needed in the Sonoma County wine country. "I tried to design it to be the way I like things when I travel," says Duffy. He went to Europe and studied Provence villages, plazas, and architectural details, then came home to re-create the feeling in the middle of his own vineyard.

264

The forty-four rooms were individually decorated in French Country fashion after a meticulous search for authentic details. Chairs at writing desks and in the dining room are from a factory in France; outdoor lamps and standards are from a foundry near Brussels that was in business 200 years. The exceptional antique European pine armoires and desks were collected in East Germany, refinished in Antwerp, and then shipped to the United States. The queen-sized pine beds are new, but they were designed by John from sketches made in France and custom-made by a local craftsman.

There are no small rooms. Their airy spaciousness includes sitting areas, dressing rooms, and elegant bathrooms with brass and porcelain fixtures. Most have a fireplace. Provincial wallpapers with matching draperies decorate all the rooms. Pleasing tall arched windows look out at vineyards or the plaza.

A tiled library and a dining room, both with fireplaces and decorated with more old-world accents, are in the common building. Wine-bar receptions featuring local wines are often held here. This is also where a continental breakfast of fresh fruit and home-baked rolls is served.

The addition to the inn of John Ash & Co. restaurant is another indication of Duffy's concept of excellence. Ash is a highly acclaimed chef who blends classic European training with California's bounty. He focuses on local foods—Sonoma's famous cheeses, oysters from Tomales Bay, and produce and chickens from Sonoma ranches. There is also a full-service bar, light and spacious, that looks out on a vineyard.

How to get there: Just north of Santa Rosa, exit Highway 101 on River Road. Follow west to the corner of Barnes Road. Inn is on the left. Fly-in: Sonoma County Airport.

Olive Metcalf

Sonoma Hotel
Sonoma, California
95476

Innkeepers: John and Dorene Musilli
Address/Telephone: 110 West Spain Street; (707) 996–2996; restaurant reservations: (707) 938–0254
Rooms: 17; 5 with private bath, 2 share 1 bath, 10 rooms on third floor share 2 baths at end of hallways.
Rates: $100 to $115, double occupancy with private bath; $70 to $80 with shared bath; continental breakfast.
Open: All year.
Facilities and activities: Lunch, dinner, Sunday champagne brunch, bar. Located on Sonoma's historic plaza with Mission San Francisco de Solano, Sonoma Barracks, boutiques, restaurants, galleries.

My affection for this old hotel stems from the morning I was coming down the steps from my room and recognized (before I saw her) the unmistakably rich voice of Maya Angelou. She was lingering over conversation and coffee with the elderly man on duty at the desk and, as she told me with a smile, delaying the moment when she would have to climb the stairs and begin work in the tiny third-floor room she kept for writing. From that morning on, I've always thought of the colorful 1870s hotel as having an especially authentic, literary atmosphere. Indeed, Room No. 21 on the third floor is the Maya Angelou Room.

Sonoma is a delightful town to explore, with its history as a distant outpost of the Mexican empire, the northernmost of the

California missions, and General Vallejo's barracks and home. At the Sonoma Hotel, you are directly on the historic plaza and can walk to all the attractions in town.

John and Dorene Musilli have restored and refurnished the entire inn so that the authentic early California atmosphere is more fresh and comfortable than ever. Dorene says there is not a reproduction in the place. The furnishings came from private homes, antiques stores, and loans from the Sonoma League for Historic Preservation. You can sleep in a carved rosewood bed from the Vallejo family, in a solid-oak bed inlaid with ebony, or in impressive brass beds.

The ten small rooms on the third floor are the frugal traveler's way to stay in the heart of the wine country, but not spend an arm and a leg. Yes, you climb the stairway, yes you share two baths at the end of the hall, but you're in the same historic building as the other guests and you'll have the same breakfast as they do.

Regina's Sonoma is the attractive restaurant and long bar on the main floor, gleaming with polished wood and beveled glass. Regina (who formerly operated a restaurant in San Francisco's theater district) has been getting raves with a frequently changing menu that is California fresh cuisine with a dash of "Southern." She is setting her own style in trendy wine-country food with surprising items like shrimp fritters, heavenly biscuits, and a to-die-for blackberry cobbler with peach sauce and ice cream.

Continental breakfast specialties like French croissants and superb bran muffins are baking while guests still sleep. They are a pleasant change of taste from the usual excessively sweet breakfast breads. They are served along with fresh juice, coffee, and tea in the hotel lobby.

How to get there: From San Francisco, take Highway 101 north to Ignacio; then take Highway 37 east to Highway 21, which leads to Sonoma Plaza. The hotel faces the plaza.

olive Metcalf

Timberhill Ranch
Timbercove, California
95421

Innkeepers: Barbara Farrell, Frank Watson, Tarran McDaid, Michael Riordan
Address/Telephone: 35755 Hauser Bridge Road, Cazadero 95421; (707) 847-3258
Rooms: 10 secluded cottages; all with private bath, fireplace, minibar. Handicapped access. Smoking restricted to designated areas.
Rates: $350, double occupancy, Friday, Saturday, Sunday; $325, double occupancy, weekdays; breakfast and six-course dinner included.
Open: All year.
Facilities and activities: Lunch. World-class tennis courts, swimming pool, outdoor Jacuzzi, hiking. Nearby: 4 miles to ocean beach; Salt Point State Park, Fort Ross, The Sea Ranch public golf course.

When your stress level hits an octave above high C and you can't bear making one more earth-shaking decision . . . when you want to seclude yourself with nature (and a close, close friend) for some spiritual renewal . . . when you demand the best in fine food, service, and amenities . . . then head for Timberhill Ranch.

This classy resort on a very intimate scale is off the beaten track, perched high in the hills above the Sonoma coast. Once you've checked in at the reception and dining area, you're shuttled to your cottage in a golf cart, and not a telephone or a discouraging word will ruffle your brow until you grudgingly conclude it's time to go home.

Sonoma's fabulous climate, rugged beauty, unspoiled high meadows, and redwoods are undisputed. What's surprising is to find an inn with such luxury blending into these surroundings. All credit must be given to the two innkeeping couples who planned and built 80 percent of the resort themselves. Their vision accounts for keeping the ranch an underdeveloped oasis of tranquility; for only ten cottages, despite eighty acres of land; for building their world-class tennis courts far from the swimming pool, because "when you're lounging quietly by the water you don't want to hear tennis chatter."

The spacious, cedar-scented cottages are situated for maximum privacy. Each has a stocked mini-bar, a fire laid, a well-appointed tile bath, handmade quilt on the queen-sized bed, comfortable chairs, good lights, and a radio. In the morning, breakfast is delivered to your door to enjoy on your private deck as you look out at a stunning view.

What more? Superb food served beautifully in an intimate dining room with windows overlooking hills and forest—but without reservations, hurry, hassle, or check to interrupt. (Breakfast and dinner are included in the rate.) The six-course dinners, for inn guests only, are what you might expect in one of San Francisco's finest restaurants. Here's a sample of one recent night: chilled artichoke with lemon mayonnaise, beef barley soup, salad with hearts of palm, raspberry sorbet, loin of lamb with red-pepper butter (among five other entree choices), and a dessert selection including puff pastry blackberry torte.

The four owners are hands-on innkeepers, always giving a level of personal attention far removed from a slick resort atmosphere. One told me, "We really like taking care of people and giving them the kind of service and privacy *we* looked for when *we* used to get away." As I watched the reluctant farewell of one couple, the hugs and promises to be back soon, I decided that Timberhill has all the right stuff, including a warm heart.

How to get there: From Highway One north of Fort Ross, turn east on Timber Cove Road. Follow to Sea View Ridge Road. Turn left, follow to Hauser Bridge Road and inn sign on the right.

Olive Metcalf

The Inn at Valley Ford
Valley Ford, California
94972

Innkeepers: Sandra Nicholls and Nicholas Balashov

Address/Telephone: 14395 Highway One (mailing address: Box 439); (707) 876–3182

Rooms: 4 share 2 baths; the W. Somerset Maugham Cottage shares a bath. No smoking inn.

Rates: $55 to $74, double occupancy; $84 for cottage; includes tax, full breakfast, afternoon tea.

Open: All year.

Facilities and activities: Bicycles, sun deck, good bird watching. Nearby: Bodega Bay fishing, boating, beach walking; historic towns, art galleries, antiques, restaurants.

In this age of specialization, here's an inn for lovers of literature. Innkeeper Sandra Nicholls is a romantic with a keen interest in English literature and an inn to indulge her fantasies.

Her guest rooms are named for Virginia Woolf, Colette, and Molly Bloom; the fourth is "a room for the muse." Each is decorated in a style that reflects the writer or character for whom it's named, and stocked with a collection of the author's work.

The house is late-1860s vintage and retains that era's feeling, even with the architectural changes that the innkeepers have made. Rooms are decorated with flair—beautiful fabrics, lace, big puffy comforters, and wicker. The two bathrooms—one with a claw-footed tub, the other with an enormous sunken shower—are as efficient as one could ask.

The wallpaper in the light-filled dining-room sitting area is wonderful. It has a black background with big colorful flowers blooming over it, reminiscent of a gaudy English chintz. You'll have a Sandra-style breakfast here: fruit compote, fresh juice, and just-ground coffee. You'll also see something made with the farm-fresh eggs she gets, and when it's berry time (as it was during our visit), she just *has* to do a "little something" with them . . . perhaps cobbler or coffee cake.

The cheerful dining room looks into a dream of a kitchen. Outside a broad deck overlooks an English-style flower garden with a gazebo, an arbor, and the W. Somerset Maugham Cottage. It's a perfect spot to read. Beyond the garden the view is of the Sonoma countryside.

Merely the address of Highway One tells you that this is beautiful, peaceful territory. A hundred years ago, Valley Ford had 126 people living here; 126 people live here today—reportedly not the same people. Only ten minutes away by car are restaurants and pubs in Bodega Bay.

How to get there: From San Francisco, follow Highway One north to Valley Ford, 5 miles past Tomales. The inn is on the left.

J: *Attention, English majors of ages past: When did you last have a serious conversation about literature? There is every possibility that the atmosphere at this inn could start one.*

Magnolia Hotel

Olive Metcalf

Yountville, California
94599

Innkeepers: Bruce and Bonnie Locken
Address/Telephone: 6529 Yount Street (mailing address: P.O. Drawer M); (707) 944–2056 or (800) 788–0369
Rooms: 12; all with private bath and air conditioning, some with fireplace. No smoking inn.
Rates: $89 to $169, double occupancy, full breakfast. No credit cards.
Open: All year.
Facilities and activities: Swimming pool, Jacuzzi spa. Nearby: Yountville shops, restaurants, galleries; wine tours, hot-air ballooning, picnics.

In the '70s, before the Napa Valley became a bigger tourist attraction than Disneyland, "quaint lodgings" meant the Magnolia Hotel. The first time I stayed there, our party booked the entire hotel—all four rooms—for a birthday celebration. Some of us were enchanted with the old stone building behind an iron gate entwined with roses, but others in the party failed to see any charm in small rooms and doors that didn't lock. The experience was an early indication of which of us would become country inn fans and which would settle only for efficiency.

The valley has grown, and so has the Magnolia (now three buildings surrounded by flower gardens), but the outside appearance is as picturesque as ever. Now there are twelve antiques-decorated rooms (the innkeepers want you to know that all their doors lock), ranging from tiny to spacious, all with a private bath, and some with fireplace, sitting area, and king-sized bed. Second- and third-floor rooms have views and access to several balconies and sun decks.

Only breakfast is served in the little dining room where once were served fine dinners. The innkeepers say that most people come to the valley looking forward to trying some of its famous restaurants; therefore, they would rather concentrate on feeding guests a good breakfast. A ringing bell alerts guests at 9 A.M. to gather for a full, cooked breakfast served family style. The menu changes each day you stay.

For dinner, you're in great luck to be in Yountville. You can walk to half a dozen choices, including The Diner, Mama Nina's (Italian), or the elegant French Laundry.

Through the back courtyard, past the pool and spa, are many interesting shops. Around the corner is Washington Street and Vintage 1870, a brick complex of restaurants, unique shops, and galleries.

How to get there: Follow Highway 29 through the Napa Valley to the Yountville exit. You will see the red brick and flags of Vintage 1870. The inn is opposite the complex, one street farther east on Yount Street.

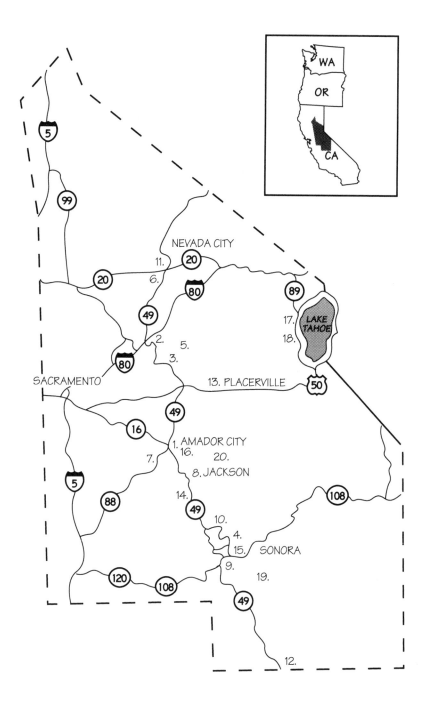

WA

OR

CA

NEVADA CITY

11.

6.

LAKE TAHOE

17.

18.

SACRAMENTO

13. PLACERVILLE

2.

5.

3.

1. AMADOR CITY

16.

20.

7.

8. JACKSON

14.

10.

4.

15. SONORA

9.

19.

12.

California: The Mother Lode and Sierras

Numbers on map refer to towns numbered below.

Olive Metcalf

Imperial Hotel
Amador City, California
95601

Innkeepers: Bruce Sherrill and Dale Martin
Address/Telephone: Highway 49 (mailing address: P.O. Box 195); (209) 267–9172
Rooms: 6, all with private bath, air conditioning. No smoking in rooms.
Rates: $60 to $90, double occupancy, continental breakfast. Two-night minimum when Saturday is involved. Singles deduct $5.
Open: All year.
Facilities and activities: Full bar, restaurant; Sunday brunch and dinner every night. Wheelchair access to dining room. Nearby: antiques and specialty shops in town; attractive opportunities for photographers in town and nearby mines; many wineries; seasonal events include fall Miwok Big Time Days at Indian Grinding Rock State Park, Daffodil Hill's spring blooms, Amador City's Calico Christmas.

I am smitten with this new addition to gold-country lodgings. The 1879 red-brick building with a painted white balcony stretching across the top story sits at the end of the main street running through tiny Amador City, population about 179 citizens. The entire scene reeks of Western nostalgia—it's old, authentic, and romantic.

The outside of this venerable hotel is thoroughly old-fashioned, but inside you'll find it has been stylishly renovated with all the modern amenities and a first-class restaurant. First stop should be the beautiful, old full bar, not a reproduction but the real McCoy. In addition to the usual spirits, they stock a large selection of beers and California wines. The friendly service you find here is indicative of the atmosphere throughout the hotel.

The dining room has a certain touch of elegance with high ceilings, white tablecloths, and fresh flowers, yet it is welcoming and casual. The intimate room (seats fifty-five) has a changing display of local artwork that stands out beautifully against white walls. Dine in your traveling clothes, by all means, but you won't feel out of place if you want to dress for a special occasion, either.

The dinner chefs offer a menu that is both continental and California fresh. The appetizers are so good that it takes careful planning to save room for the entree. Roasted garlic with Brie and Polenta Crostini topped with prosciutto were the two we chose. The main event was a roast pork loin in prune sauce followed by an excellent salad with a house dressing I wish I could duplicate. The pastry chef had several hard-to-pass offerings and after all her work, how could we skip a poppy-seed butter-cream tart with fresh raspberries? Eating it seemed the only kind thing to do.

Six bedrooms upstairs are not large, but unexpectedly comfortable and whimsically decorated. One has an Art Deco feeling with Maxfield Parrish prints and a ceiling fan. One has a vivid hand-painted headboard over the king bed and bright folk art on the walls. Rooms One and Two are slightly larger than the others and open onto the front balcony. (The traffic going by *does* fade away by 10:30 or 11:00.) Each room has a radio and a sparkling white tile bathroom that sports a hair dryer and heated towel bar.

Two balconies are upstairs, one at the back and one at the front of the hotel. A small library is at one end of the hall, with a desk, telephone, and door opening out to the balcony.

In the morning the innkeepers place coffee and newspapers in the hallway outside the guest rooms for early risers. Breakfast is a full, fresh meal prepared with the same skill as the dinner menu. Guests have the option of eating in their rooms, the second floor balcony, or downstairs in the dining room.

How to get there: Amador City is $2^1/_2$ hours from San Francisco on Highway 49.

olive Metcalf

Power's Mansion Inn
Auburn, California
95603

Innkeeper: Tony Verhaart, resident manager
Address/Telephone: 164 Cleveland Avenue; (916) 885–1166
Rooms: 13, including 1 suite; all with private bath, telephone, air condition-
  ing. Wheelchair access. Television available on request. Smoking only
  in patio area.
Rates: $75 to $160, double occupancy, full breakfast.
Open: All year.
Facilities and activities: Nearby: downtown Auburn restaurants, shops, Old
  Town historic area; hills offer facilities for fishing, boating, swimming,
  hiking, horseback riding, snow and water skiing.

The Power's Mansion is a rambling, impressive Victorian with
landscaped grounds and fills a full city block. Yet I heard of one
guest at the door making a return visit calling out, "Hi! I'm home."

Is that any way to act in an imposing place like this? Apparent-
ly it's directly due to the kind of tender loving care you get at this
local landmark, now home away from home for a lot of Auburn
visitors. When we arrived on a drizzly April day, a fire was glowing
in the parlor fireplace, fresh flowers were in every room, and a
plate of home-baked cookies and coffee waited on the dining room
buffet for arriving guests in need of immediate sustenance.

The downstairs entry, parlor, and cozy sitting room (there's a
television here) are elegantly decorated with fine Victorian pieces,

including a beauty of an old pump organ that is in fine working order. Individual round tables are well spaced in the dining room, and a big sunny bay window makes it a cheerful place for breakfast.

Since my last visit, Tony Verhaart has taken over as innkeeper and given up managing Hilton Hotels all over the world. He was opening one in China when the student rebellion began. Auburn may be less exotic, but Tony says he's happy redecorating and managing the Power's Mansion. He's researched its original colors for a soft pink paint job on the exterior and new wallpaper in several rooms.

The comfortable guest rooms are both on the main floor and upstairs. Six of them are actually in a new wing, built so cleverly you can scarcely tell they aren't the same vintage as the 1901 house. They're all pretty, with queen-sized beds and English antique furniture. The Anniversary Room and the Honeymoon Suite are both more lavishly decorated—one in pale lavender, one in peach—and have fireplaces. The Honeymoon Suite also has a major bathroom with a sunken, heart-shaped Jacuzzi tub for two.

There are eighteen historic landmarks in the Auburn area. And even though it has its quaint Old Town district, Auburn is not a sleepy gold-country town; it is the hub of busy recreational, tourist, and forestry businesses. Many travelers in town on business are finding the mansion a comfortable alternative to their usual motel, with an all-the-comforts-of-home atmosphere. Tony cheerfully accommodates breakfast times, clears a dining-room table for someone who wants to work there, lends an ironing board, and is always ready with a pot of tea and cookies to take to your room. Pretty nice treatment.

Breakfast menus vary, but granola and yogurt, juice, homemade muffins, and a strata, quiche, or oven-baked French toast are typical items. Tony recommends Butterworth's for dinner, a fine restaurant in a Victorian house nearby, or the Hummingbird (continental menu), within walking distance of the inn.

How to get there: From I—80 exit on Elm; turn back toward Old Auburn. Turn right on High Street ¹/₂ block to Cleveland Avenue and the inn.

Olive Metcalf

Coloma Country Inn
Coloma, California
95613

Innkeepers: Alan and Cindi Ehrgott
Address/Telephone: 2 High Street (mailing address: P.O. Box 502); (916)
622–6919
Rooms: 5; 3 with private bath, all with air conditioning. No smoking inn.
Rates: $79 to $99, double occupancy, expanded continental breakfast. Package rates available for raft trips and ballooning. No credit cards. Advance notice requested for children.
Open: All year.
Facilities and activities: Hot-air ballooning and raft trips arranged by innkeeper; facilities for weddings, Victorian teas, and small parties; canoeing. Nearby: surrounded by Gold Discovery State Park; historic Coloma; south fork of American River; annual Coloma Christmas celebration, spring Heritage Home Tour, wine tasting, fall apple picking.

Here's Norman Rockwell charm. This old-fashioned house on a country road is so appealing I stopped before I even knew it was an inn. The spic-and-span two-story yellow-and-white house sits on five green acres with a pond, big shade trees, flowers, white wicker on a long front porch, and a gazebo. Sounds almost too adorable?

To the innkeepers' credit, they've not overplayed their treasure of an 1852 house. The long beamed-ceiling living room is fresh and uncluttered. Colorful early American art objects stand out against white walls, old crocks flank the hearth, and a bright quilt hangs on the wall. A vivid oriental rug and easy furniture before the fireplace are inviting.

The Ehrgotts serve breakfast in the dining room, which has a view of the old pond in back. There is always a variety of fresh fruit, home-baked muffins, breads, and good coffee. You can also arrange for a picnic basket if you intend to ramble during the day.

Guest rooms are decorated with antique queen and double beds and pretty quilts, touches of lace here, a stained-glass window there. Each has a sitting area and always fresh-cut flowers. Take a look at a wonderful Eastlake-style bedroom set in a room up the hand-stenciled stairway. The separate Carriage House quarters offer two bedrooms, living room, kitchen, and bath.

Alan is a commercial hot-air balloon pilot and offers flights on request. He also arranges white-water rafting trips. The inn has bicycles, and down at the pond there are ducks to feed and a canoe. I vote for lemonade and a good book on the front porch.

Situated in the middle of the 300-acre Gold Discovery State Park, the inn is surrounded by history. Sutter's Mill in Coloma was the site of the first California gold discovery in 1848, and there are many old structures and points of interest within easy walking distance.

How to get there: From Placerville, take Highway 49 north 8 miles to Gold Discovery State Park. Cross the intersection of 49 and Cold Springs Road and turn onto Church Street. One block down, turn right onto High Street. Inn is on the right.

J: *Dream on this: From a picturesque old church down the road, you arrive in a horse-drawn buggy at the inn for a reception around the gazebo. I'll bet someone would take a snapshot of that.*

olive Metcalf

City Hotel
Columbia, California
95310

Innkeeper: Tom Bender
Address/Telephone: Box 1870; (209) 532–1479
Rooms: 9; all with private half-bath, share showers down the hall.
Rates: Balcony rooms, $85; parlor and hall rooms, $65 to $75; double occupancy; continental breakfast. Theater and lodging packages. Ski package in season.
Open: All year.
Facilities and activities: Lunch, dinner, What Cheer Saloon; Saturday and Sunday brunch. Nearby: town with restored buildings, working weavers, blacksmith, harness, and saddle shops, stagecoach rides, Fallon House Theatre; Fire Muster in May; old-fashioned Fourth of July Celebration; two-week Miners' Christmas Celebration.

Early one morning in Columbia, I walked alone down Main Street's boardwalk, passed a stagecoach and team standing by the Wells Fargo Office, saw a woman in pioneer costume opening her candy store, and listened to the barber outside his shop playing a tune on a harmonica. This is the heart of gold-rush country, and no town captures that spirit better than Columbia.

In its gold-fever days, Columbia had forty saloons, 150 gambling houses, and eight hotels. Today the entire town is a state park, with tree-shaded Main Street barred to cars during the day to enhance the 1850–1870 atmosphere. But this is no static museum ghost town. Columbia is alive and bustling, and the jewel of the town is the City Hotel.

The two-story red-brick building has an upstairs parlor opening onto a wrought-iron balcony. A continental breakfast is served here each morning. Bedrooms are furnished with unusually impressive antiques, massive Victorian bedsteads, and marble-topped bureaus. Half-baths in each room are restoration additions, but showers down the hall are scarcely a hardship when you're provided with a wicker basket to tuck over your arm holding robe, slippers, and all the essentials.

The handsome, high-ceilinged dining room is an improbable surprise. Gold-rush-country explorers usually don't expect white linen, silver napkin rings, and haute cuisine. Elegant entrees range from grilled rabbit with caper sauce to roasted tenderloin with red pepper sauce, but the menu changes seasonally. For years we always completed a meal here with a divine lemon soufflé. Nowadays the soufflé selection changes nightly, but it still must be ordered ahead, so think dessert first is my advice.

That most necessary of mining-town establishments, the What Cheer Saloon, is the place for a nightcap and the local news.

How to get there: From San Francisco, take Highway 580 to Tracy, then 205 to Manteca. Take Highway 120 east, past Knights Ferry, to Highway 108 intersection. Continue on 108 east to Sonora; then Highway 49 north to Columbia.

J: *The nearby Fallon House Theater (circa 1880) is now open year round. Ask the hotel for a schedule of their productions when you reserve your room.*

clive Metcalf

The American River Inn
Georgetown, California
95634

Innkeepers: Will and Maria Collin and Helene Linney
Address/Telephone: Orleans Street at Main (mailing address: Box 43); (916)
    333–4499 or (800) 245–6566
Rooms: 18; 5 with private bath, 7 additional baths shared. 7 suites; all with
    private bath. Queen Anne House separate from main inn, with 5 bed-
    rooms, bath, living room, and kitchen. Facilities for the handicapped.
    Air conditioning.
Rates: $74 to $83, double occupancy; $93 to $98, suites; full breakfast.
Open: All year.
Facilities and activities: Antiques/gift shop, pool, Jacuzzi, croquet, badminton,
    horseshoes, table tennis; bicycles provided. Nearby: restaurants;
    explore the gold country; rafting, kayaking, fishing on American River,
    hot-air ballooning.

This is upscale, beautiful lodging for the gold country. But
that's only fitting for a town that in 1853 estimated it had mined
two million dollars in gold since the discovery in 1848. Once-rich,
booming Georgetown, which then enjoyed the more picturesque
name of Growlersburg, is now the setting of an impressive inn.
There's no escaping the fact that a lot of money has been spent
restoring the original American Hotel, but the innkeepers have also
lavished love, hard work, and attention to detail on the effort.

Antiques, polished pine floors, and bright provincial fabrics
invite you into the attractive common rooms. In the late afternoon,

the innkeepers serve local wines and hors d'oeuvres in the tasteful parlor. They'll also tell you about restaurants you can stroll to for dinner, or others a short drive away. Tall, handsomely draped windows and antique tables and chairs are in the light-filled dining room. Breakfast here is a full production: fresh fruit (from the inn's own garden), juice, quiche or other egg dishes, Canadian bacon, berry muffins, and freshly ground coffee.

The spacious bedrooms have each been individually decorated and have luxurious bathrooms with thoughtful touches like robes. Rooms that open onto porches are especially pleasant. On a midweek visit, when the town is quiet, these are delightful spots for reading in a comfortable wicker chair.

Besides the fresh mountain air and the clear rivers and lakes, history's footprints are everywhere in these foothills of the Sierra Nevada. Georgetown itself is well worth your time. It's a pleasure to see some of the stately homes built in the '70s and '80s, surrounded by well-tended gardens. Georgetown is one of those gold towns with charm but few tourists . . . always a winning combination.

If you're looking for adventure, the innkeepers will arrange hot-air ballooning, rafting, or kayak trips down the American River. They'll even provide the bicycles and pack you a luxury picnic basket to take along while you explore, and you keep the basket for future trips. But a look at the beautiful natural stone swimming pool or the Jacuzzi could easily persuade you that relaxing right here has a lot of merit.

How to get there: From Sacramento, take I–50 or I–80 to Highway 49 to Highway 193. Follow the signs to Georgetown. The inn is 2 short blocks from the junction of California 193 and Main Street. Fly-in: Georgetown Airport.

J: *Here's a deal: Arrange for their limousine airport pickup, and you have free use of the limo while you're a guest.*

Olive Metcalf

Murphy's Inn
Grass Valley, California
95945

Innkeepers: Tom and Sue Myers
Address/Telephone: 318 Neal Street; (916) 273–6873
Rooms: 8, including 2 suites; all with private bath, 4 with fireplace, all with air conditioning.
Rates: $75 to $130, double occupancy, full breakfast.
Open: All year.
Facilities and activities: Swim-spa, sun deck, airport shuttle, arrangements made for sporting activities, many performing arts events. Nearby: Grass Valley's historic district, restaurants, unique shops, saloons, historic landmarks; minutes from Nevada City.

The Sierra foothills are a sportsman's paradise—fish one day, ski the next. You can golf, pan for gold, go white-water rafting, and hike beautiful trails.

Located in Grass Valley, Murphy's Inn offers not only all the Sierra activities but also a front seat to some of the richest history in California. Its innkeepers are active in the local community theater group and local activities. Give them a chance, and their knowledge will help you enjoy your stay in ways you might never find on your own.

Murphy's Inn is an elegant 1866 home built by one of the gold barons, Edward Coleman, owner of the North Star and Idaho mines. It's immaculately maintained, from the manicured topiary ivy baskets hanging on the wide veranda, to the handsome sitting rooms with fireplaces and sparkling decanters of sherry set out for guests.

Beautiful pine, oak, and mahogany antiques are in every room. Four of the bedrooms have fireplaces, some have private entrances. There are large bathrooms, some with skylights and double shower heads. Two suites across the street in The Donation Day House each consist of a king-sized bed, sitting room, fireplace, television, and private bath.

A big, cheerful kitchen and dining area has been added to the house. Tom and Sue can chat with guests while they make "innkeeper's choice" breakfasts. There's always freshly squeezed juice, fruit, home-baked breads, and then whatever inspires them, maybe eggs Benedict, or sausage and hash browns. The house special is Belgian waffles.

Strangers are pleasantly surprised to hear about the many fine local restaurants. Right in Grass Valley, the Main Street Café and the restaurant at the Holbrooke Hotel (with a California Culinary Academy chef) are two of the best.

Any jet setter's opportunities for good entertainment and fun pale beside the calendar of special events around here. The acclaimed Music in the Mountains series, theater, art shows, dogsled races, house and garden tours, Christmas Fairs—the choice is amazing. But staying at this pleasant inn and lolling on the sun deck or in the swimming pool–Jacuzzi spa isn't a bad choice either.

How to get there: From Highway 49, exit on Colfax (Highway 174), turn left at first stop sign. Turn left at second (two are close together) stoplight on Neal Street. Proceed 3 blocks to inn on right corner of School Street. Fly-in: Nevada County Airport.

❂

J: *The Grass Valley area is rich in gold-country lore. A few of the old residences remain, among them the frame house of the notorious Lola Montez.*

olive Metcalf

The Heirloom Inn
Ione, California
95640

Innkeepers: Patricia Cross and Melisande Hubbs
Address/Telephone: 214 Shakeley Lane (mailing address: Box 322); (209) 274–4468
Rooms: 6; 4 with private bath.
Rates: $55 to $90, double occupancy, generous breakfast. No credit cards.
Open: All year except Thanksgiving and Christmas.
Facilities and activities: Beautiful setting for receptions; croquet. Nearby: walking tour of Ione, antiquing; explore surrounding Mother Lode area, Amador County wineries; good restaurants, championship golf course.

The Heirloom's two innkeepers have a handle on every nuance of hospitality . . . and they dispense it with graciousness so genuine you'll know you've come across the real thing. Their thoughtful touches remain fresh and spontaneous—like appearing with a cold bottle of local white zinfandel and a couple of glasses while you're reading in the garden, or tucking a hot-water bottle in the foot of the bed on a cold night.

Their antebellum brick house with classic white Greek columns sits among towering old trees. It's filled with the innkeepers' personal furniture, china, silver, and antiques, including a splendid rosewood piano, said to have belonged to Lola Montez. The atmosphere is grand enough to be special, but so comfortable

288

that perfect strangers feel quite at ease sitting in robes before the fire in the living room, sipping a late-evening port.

Fireplaces, balconies, and private or shared baths are available in the four bedrooms in the house. In the springtime, we've often enjoyed the room with that name, with its private balcony surrounded by wisteria and magnolia.

A unique cottage with two accommodations is separate from the house. Its rammed-earth construction is as old as the Great Wall of China and as contemporary as environmental concern. All the earth scraped away to make room for the foundation makes up the walls and the sod roof. From the outside, the adobe house blends into its surroundings as if camouflaged. Cedar and redwood left in their natural finishes, skylights, wood-burning stoves, and handcrafted accessories give the inside a warm, tasteful ambience.

Breakfast is the leisurely, elegantly presented event that makes an inn visit memorable. Melisande and Pat, dressed in long skirts and pretty blouses, always look wonderful. They serve on beautiful china and pour from silver pots, and whatever the menu, the food is outstanding. There is always a fresh-fruit plate, homemade breads, muffins, and jams. The main dish might be soufflés, a quiche, or tender crepes filled with cream cheese and topped with fresh strawberries. To breakfast on a summer morning under a huge shade tree in this lovely yard is my idea of inn-heaven.

How to get there: All highways into Ione lead to Main Street. One block north of Main on Highway 104, turn down Shakeley Lane to the Heirloom sign on the left.

✠

J: *Nobody does it better!*

Olive Metcalf

Gate House Inn
Jackson, California
95642

Innkeepers: Stan and Bev Smith

Address/Telephone: 1330 Jackson Gate Road; (209) 223–3500

Rooms: 5, including 2 suites; all with private bath. Air conditioning in the Summerhouse. No smoking inn.

Rates: $75 to $105, double occupancy, two-night stay tied to Saturdays, full breakfast. Extra person $20 in Woodhaven Suite.

Open: All year.

Facilities and attractions: Swimming pool, screened-in barbecue room. Nearby: walk to Kennedy Mine Tailing Wheels; visit Indian Grinding Rock State Monument, Amador County Museum, Roaring Camp, gold-rush towns, and other historic sites around Amador County; wineries, golf courses, skiing at Kirkwood, Claypipers Theater.

When you're in the guidebook game, nothing gives your friends greater pleasure than confronting you with a ghastly experience they've had at one of your recommendations. In cold, unblinking print you've raved about a beautiful house, charming innkeepers, and a bountiful breakfast. But the scene your friends describe sounds more like the Bates Motel with service by the Three Stooges. The Gate House is one of those happy exceptions in which people actually make a point of telling me how much more handsome the house is than they had been led to believe and, most especially, how beautifully maintained it is and what good hosts the

Smiths are. High praise, coming from experienced inn explorers, but deserved.

This buttercup-yellow Victorian epitomizes turn-of-the-century charm with its peaked roof, spacious lawn, rose garden, and wisteria-covered pavilion. The summertime swimming pool and quiet grounds look out on the romantic rolling terrain of gold country—380 acres of it owned by the family who originally built the house.

In an area that abounds in Victorian houses, few are as elegantly decorated as the Gate House or enjoy the impeccable housekeeping that makes staying in an old house comfortable and pleasant rather than "an experience." Through a beveled-glass front door you find an interior that owes much of its grandeur to the original solid-oak parquet floors, Italian marble and tile fireplaces, and an oak staircase. Even some of the superb original wallpapers are still in mint condition. Wonderful period furnishings are throughout the inn, but my eye was first taken by a vivid blue-velvet settee in the parlor.

All five accommodations have queen-sized beds, private baths, and sitting areas. The Woodhaven Suite, a former nursery, is especially cozy, lined from ceiling to floor with pine and furnished with a brass bed. A bank of windows looks out over the garden. A grape arbor in the garden leads to the fifth suite, the Summerhouse. It has a cast-iron, wood-burning stove and an immense cedar-paneled bathroom with a built-in claw-footed tub and stall shower.

Across the lawn is a barbecue area you are welcome to use if you tire of Jackson's Italian restaurants. But at breakfast, the atmosphere is more luxurious. The formal dining room is warmed by a collection of Country English china and a silver service. A typical menu will include fresh fruits and just-baked muffins with sausage, seasoned fried potatoes, and an oven-baked egg dish or perhaps French toast or Belgian waffles.

How to get there: Driving north on Highway 49, just past the intersection of Highway 88, turn east on Jackson Gate Road. Follow to the inn on the left. Fly in: Amador County Airport 2 miles from the inn.

Olive Metcalf

The Wedgewood Inn
Jackson, California
95642

Innkeepers: Vic and Jeannine Beltz
Address/Telephone: 11941 Narcissus Road; (209) 296–4300; for reservations, (800) WEDGEWD
Rooms: 6; all with private bath, tub, and shower. No smoking inn.
Rates: $80 to $110, double occupancy, full breakfast.
Open: All year.
Facilities and activities: Terraced English garden, gazebo, croquet, horseshoes; walking trails through surrounding wooded area. Nearby: shopping, sightseeing, dining, and special events in nearby Sierra foothill towns.

Vic and Jeannine Beltz are "nesters," collectors, and antiques lovers, crazy for crafts, enthusiastic about their hobbies, and devoted to people. In other words—they *had* to become innkeepers. Their newly built Wedgewood Inn is the culmination of everything they like to do.

When Vic took an early retirement from IBM, he and Jeannine searched for a country property and built their dream house, a finely constructed Victorian replica. Nestled on five wooded acres just 6 miles from Jackson, you nevertheless feel far from the bustle that goes with many foothill towns. As Vic says, "The only thing you hear are pine needles kissing in the wind."

Beginning at the front door's stained-glass inserts made by Vic, the house reflects the couple's many interests: the ambitious gardening he's begun, the grand piano from Austria that Jeannine plays, the Victorian lamp shades she makes (one has portions of heirloom lace from her wedding dress), her cross-stitch pictures and tapestry, and a collection of dolls. Furniture and antiques collected for many years decorate the inn. There are spinning wheels from various countries, European tapestries hanging in the dining room, and accents from their travels around the world.

Whether you appreciate antiques or not, you will find these spacious bedrooms especially comfortable. Since the house is new, old-fashioned appointments like a wood-burning stove, a claw-footed tub, or a pull-chain toilet can be enjoyed without sacrificing a whit of comfort. I found the washstands Vic has made by inserting elegant sinks into antique dressers and chests especially attractive.

Antique car buffs will find a kindred soul in Vic. He'll show you "Henry," his 1921 Model T Ford that resides in the Carriage House.

When you arrive at The Wedgewood, cheese and a beverage refreshment are served in the parlor. Here is where guests who wish to can enjoy evenings of conversation, games, or singing around the piano. Morning brings coffee, ready and waiting for early risers. Later, a full breakfast will typically include Jeannine's homemade muffins, coffee or poppyseed cake along with fruit compote, and an egg and meat entree. It's all served on bone china.

How to get there: Take Highway 88 east from Jackson 6 miles to 2,000-FOOT ELEVATION sign. Turn right on Irishtown/Clinton roads. Immediately turn right on Clinton Road; go ³/₅ mile to Narcissus Road. Turn left and go ¹/₄ mile to the inn on the left.

clive Metcalf

Historic National Hotel
Bed and Breakfast
Jamestown, California
95327

Innkeeper: Steve Willey
Address/Telephone: Main Street (mailing address: Box 502); (209) 984–3446
Rooms: 11; 5 with private bath, 6 with antique washbasins share 2 bathrooms, all with air conditioning. Rollaways, televisions available.
Rates: $45 to $80, double occupancy, generous continental breakfast. Ask about lower midweek and winter rates.
Open: All year.
Facilities and activities: Lunch, dinner, Sunday brunch; full bar; outdoor patio dining. Nearby: explore old gold-rush town, antiques stores; steam-operated Sierra Railroad, Railtown 1897 State Park; cross-country skiing, backpacking trail heads; forty-five minutes to Yosemite National Park entrance; Calaveras Big Trees State Park.

When you reach Jamestown, you get the full flavor of what a Victorian-era gold-rush town was like. Jamestown was one of the boom towns, swarming with a sudden population bent on quick riches. If it looks familiar to you, it's because it's been used in hundreds of feature films, including *Butch Cassidy and the Sundance Kid*, and, more recently, *Back to the Future III*. Our romantic attraction to those old towns continues, partly because of the picturesque buildings that remain and partly because of the natural loveliness of the Sierra foothills.

Like all gold towns, Jamestown has burned countless times, but the Historic National Hotel is one of its survivors, operating since 1859. The Willey brothers have been working on its gradual restoration for over a decade, matching the facade to photos from the 1800s. Happily, it still looks much like the typical Old West hotel we've seen in movies—two stories with a balcony overlooking Main Street and a wooden sidewalk.

Inside is a massive, long bar (the original) with a brass rail and a splendid 1882 cash register; two dining rooms, and a stairway up to the bedrooms. The rooms are clean and cheerful with quilts, brass beds, and other antique furnishings. The atmosphere is a combination of nineteenth-century charm—pull-chain toilets—with twentieth-century comfort—modern stall showers.

The dining room serves lunch and dinner to the public—a classical cuisine ranging from escargots and gazpacho to steaks, veal saltimbocca, and lamb chops Dijon. The wine list is exclusively from vineyards in the gold-country region. (The hotel recently won a national award for its wine list.) The continental breakfast is definitely of the "expanded" variety: homemade breads, fresh fruit, assorted cereals, juices, hard-boiled eggs, hot beverages, and morning newspapers. Photographs of the hotel and Jamestown's earlier days decorate the walls. Slow-moving brass fans, lace curtains, candlelight, and fresh flowers add still more to an inviting atmosphere. Adjacent to the dining room is a hundred-year-old grape arbor, a pleasant place for breakfast or for enjoying a bottle of wine after a day of exploring.

How to get there: From the San Francisco Bay area, take Highway 580 to the Manteca turnoff. Continue on Highway 108 past Oakdale 30 miles to Jamestown. You enter on Main Street. Hotel is on the right. Fly-in: Columbia Airport; hotel pickup service by arrangement.

olive Metcalf

Jamestown Hotel
Jamestown, California
95327

Innkeepers: Marcia and Mike Walsh
Address/Telephone: Main Street (mailing address: P.O. Box 539); (209) 984–3902
Rooms: 8, including 7 suites with sitting area; all with private bath with tub and shower.
Rates: $55 to $85, double occupancy, continental breakfast.
Open: All year.
Facilities and activities: Lunch, dinner, Sunday brunch, full bar. Outdoor sun deck pleasant for weddings, private parties. Nearby: historic Jamestown, shops, antiques; Mother Lode exploring, gold-prospecting tours; Sierra Railroad.

Old West buffs come to Jamestown to walk picturesque Main Street and to ride the Sierra Railroad's steam-powered locomotives through the Sierra foothills. The Jamestown Hotel is still another attraction, an absolutely smashing restoration accomplishment.

The Walshes have completely redone the hotel, from the old brick exterior to the flamboyant gold-rush-style interior. A tidy lobby, dining room, and inviting cocktail lounge are on the first floor. Upstairs are eight antiques-decorated bedrooms, all named for personalities associated with the area's past—Jenny Lind, Lotta Crabtree, Black Bart, Joaquin Murietta.

These are quaint Victorian-style rooms (seven are suites with sitting areas) with the distinct advantage of not *smelling* old. They're comfortable and immaculate, qualities that were, until recently, hard to find in the Mother Lode. Marcia has chosen colorful wallpapers as backgrounds for antique furnishings. The beds are kings, queens, and doubles. Black Bart's floral bouquets on black and a black, claw-footed bathtub look particularly Victorian. I liked, too, the big portrait of "our next president," William McKinley, a Victrola, and an old eyeglass-salesman's case, complete with all the glasses.

The handsome dining room's wall covering is a fresh floral print on ivory with matching balloon draperies. Fresh linen, plants, and touches of etched glass fill the room with light at lunchtime; during candlelit dinners, the atmosphere is romantic. The dining room opens onto an attractive lattice-covered patio used for summer dining and special parties.

The hotel's kitchen has earned justly high praise. We started lunch with a basket of hot, puffy sopapillas. (*Try* eating just one!) Seafood salads, fresh poached red snapper in white wine sauce, and spinach pasta with linquica and garlic sauce were the specialties the day I visited.

While this small hotel doesn't have quite the personal touch of an innkeeper's home, the staff is particularly friendly. A small plant-filled sitting room at the end of the upstairs hall opens onto a deck area with umbrellas and tables. This is a pleasant place to sit and sip on a summer evening while watching shadows on the foothills.

How to get there: From the San Francisco Bay Area, take Highway 580 to Manteca turnoff. Continue on Highway 108 30 miles past Oakdale to Jamestown. The hotel is on the right in the center of town.

✳

J: *As you gaze at the foothills surrounding Jamestown, remember: There are those who claim there's still "gold in them thar hills!"*

olive Metcalf

Murphys Hotel
Murphys, California
95247

Innkeeper: Robert Walker
Address/Telephone: Main Street; (mailing address: Box 329); (209) 728–3454
Rooms: 9 historic rooms share 4 baths; 20 separate motel units with private baths and air conditioning.
Rates: $65 to $75, double occupancy, continental breakfast included in historic-room rate.
Open: All year.
Facilities and activities: Breakfast, lunch, dinner, full bar. Nearby: town, museum, surrounding historical towns, Mercer Caves, Calaveras Big Trees, Columbia State Historic Park, many local wineries.

On a cold December morning, a fire burned cheerily in the potbellied stove in Murphys' Victorian lobby. A Christmas tree filled the room with the fresh aroma of pine. In the dining room, platters of sausage and hot bowls of oatmeal were bustled to the tables as waitresses and locals bantered about weather and horses, dogs, pickup trucks, and foaling mares.

On crisp, clear winter days like this, when tourists are back in the city, old gold-rush towns show their true character. If authenticity is your delight, then quiet little Murphys, "Queen of the Mother Lode," is a must. It was once a major stagecoach route. A few old stone buildings survive and stand near the hotel in the center of town. Winding roads leading out to Angels Camp and Sheep

298

Ranch are beautiful mountain drives.

But historic lodgings aren't for everyone. You have to be amused with floors that slant; tolerant of shared facilities; fascinated with walls of old photographs; and fond of stick-to-the-ribs fare instead of California cuisine. The picturesque hotel looks very little different today from the way it did when Ulysses S. Grant, Samuel Clemens, Horatio Alger, Henry Ward Beecher, and Black Bart were guests.

Grandest of all the historic bedrooms is the General Grant Room, with a splendid antique bed and a square piano that has been there as long as anyone can remember. The other bedrooms are smaller and are simply furnished with antique beds, dressers, and quilts.

The saloon and dining room on the main floor remain much as they were originally. Chef Marc Kirby has expanded the no-nonsense menu of prime rib, steaks, liver and onions, and fried chicken to include pasta, a spinach salad, and several fresh fish choices. A continental breakfast delivered to guests (along with the morning paper) in the old historic rooms consists of coffee or tea, juice, and a homemade cinnamon roll.

The Mark Twain Ballroom upstairs opens onto a balcony with the original cast-iron railing. The Victorian room, with flamboyant cranberry red chandeliers, was decorated this day for a Christmas party.

A longtime citizen of the town, Elizabeth Kaler, wrote about the hotel in *Memories of Murphys:* "I think the balcony was the most charming. It has an old world air to it that has helped to make Murphys different. It was a rendezvous for friends both far and near."

How to get there: From Highway 49 east of Stockton, take Highway 4 east at Angels Camp to Murphys.

Olive Metcalf

The Red Castle Inn
Nevada City, California
95959

Innkeepers: Mary Louise and Conley Weaver
Address/Telephone: 109 Prospect; (916) 265–5135
Rooms: 8; 6 with private bath. Third- and fourth-floor rooms air condi-
tioned. Smoking on verandas and in garden.
Rates: $70 to $110, double occupancy, full breakfast and afternoon tea.
Two-night minimum Saturdays April 1–December 31.
Open: All year.
Facilities and activities: Saturday morning carriage rides, historical narratives
and poetry readings, Victorian Christmas dinner and entertainment,
picnic baskets by advance request. Nearby: walking path to downtown
shops, restaurants, antiques; local theater, musical events; swimming
in mountain creek; cross-country skiing twenty minutes away.

Back in 1970, a San Francisco architect and his wife visited
Nevada City and stayed at The Red Castle Inn, one of the first bed
and breakfast inns in California. She fell in love with the Victorian
red-brick mansion, and they continued to visit it through the years.
The thought of ever owning it was mere fantasy, but when at last
the Weavers bought it from the former innkeepers, Mary Louise
says it was a case of a dream coming true.

Hanging on a hillside nestled among dense trees, The Red Castle is an impressive sight from many places around Nevada City.
The Gothic-revival mansion is wrapped in rows of white, painted
verandas and lavished with gingerbread trim at roofline and gables.

From the private parking area, walk around a veranda, with stylish canvas draperies tied back at each pillar, to the front of the house, where you can survey the historic mining town's rooftops and church steeples.

Since it was built in 1857, the castle has had a succession of caring owners who have maintained it without compromising its elegant period character. The Weavers have brought not only their respective professional skills in architecture and design but also some impressive art, including several Bufano sculpture pieces, and fine furniture. Eight guest rooms range over the four floors, each one of them a vibrantly decorated, tasteful delight. Most furnishings are Victorian, but not fragile or frilly. An explosion of color from wallpapers, fabrics, and rugs has an engaging effect in combination with the dramatic architecture. Two garret rooms on the top floor share a sitting room, bath, and balcony. It was from here that the original owner's son used to serenade the town with impromptu trumpet concerts.

A cozy sitting room off the entry hall has cushy upholstered sofas, wingback chairs, and an inviting collection of gold-rush history and art books. We helped ourselves to an elegant tea spread here and took it outside. Three small terraced gardens, one with a fountain and pond, are idyllic sitting and strolling areas. A path through cascading vines leads down to Nevada City's main street.

The Weavers are proud of their vintage inn and are enthusiastic about Nevada City. They'll arrange a horse-drawn carriage tour through the town's historic district. They always have good suggestions for restaurants and local events. Their own Victorian Christmas celebration sounds like a truly memorable feast.

The lavish breakfast buffet is a splendid sight—all of it homemade. Ours was typical, but the menu varies every day: juice, poached pears, glazed fresh strawberries, a baked egg curry with pear chutney, cheese croissants, banana bread, jams, Mary Louise's grandmother's bread pudding (what a treat!) with a pitcher of cream, and, of course, great coffee.

How to get there: From Highway 49 at Nevada City, take Sacramento Street exit to the Exxon station; turn right and immediately left onto Prospect Street. The driveway takes you to the back of the house. Walk around the veranda to the front door.

Olive Metcalf

Ye Olde South Fork Inn
North Fork, California
93643

Innkeepers: Virginia and Darrel Cochran
Address/Telephone: 57665 Road 225 (mailing address: Box 731); (209) 877–7025
Rooms: 9 share 3 baths. Smoking outside only.
Rates: $59 to $70 for family room that sleeps 7; expanded continental breakfast.
Open: All year.
Facilities and activities: Nearby: restaurants, Mono Indian Museum, wildflower farm and nature trail, 8 miles to Bass Lake with all recreational facilities, 28 miles to Yosemite gate, Loggers Jamboree first weekend of July, Indian Fair first weekend of August.

You may well wonder where on earth you are when you wind your way into this out-of-the-way village, but Virginia Cochran can tell you precisely. "We're in the exact center of California," she says. "People sometimes think we're gold-rush country, but we're not. This is the gateway to Yosemite and the Ansel Adams Wilderness Area."

The inn that she and husband Darrel have in this remote area is a dandy place to stop over before you head on to Yosemite Park. Or if you've been out camping for a few days, this is a convenient place to regroup, shower, and have a good night's sleep in a clean, comfortable bed.

By all means, bring the children—this is their kind of relaxed, easy place. The living room has a television and opens into a large common room. When it's not being used for breakfast, all the tables and chairs are handy for games. A piano is here, too, and boxes of toys.

The nine bedrooms accommodate flexible sleeping arrangements for families. The rooms are simple and fresh, with country antiques and ceiling fans.

There's not an acornful of pretension here. It's Western-style comfort, where the beautiful scenery at hand overrides indoor decor. You're not going to find Ye Olde South Fork Inn in *House Beautiful*, but you will find comfortable beds and warm hospitality.

The Cochrans (Darrel is retired Navy) have lived in this foothill community since 1972. They know the area well and are helpful in directing you to mountain attractions you might otherwise miss. Their inn is the beginning of the recently designated National Scenic By-Way, approximately 100 miles through national forest lands. The Mono Wind Flower Farm only a mile away is a nationally known wildflower farm with a self-guided nature trail.

This Sierra foothill community, like so many others, does quite happily without shops or chic, but the local events are rousing. The two biggies are the Loggers Jamboree in July and the Indian Fair in August. Ask Virginia, also, about dates for the Mountain Peddlar's Flea Market.

How to get there: From Highway 99 at Madera, follow Highway 145 to Route 41. From Fresno on Highway 99, take Highway 41 immediately. Continue north toward Yosemite about 30 miles to O'Neals. Follow signs to North Fork. Proceed through village to South Fork. Inn is on the left.

J: *Virginia sells her knitting to boutiques. If you arrive just before she sends off a shipment, as I did, you'll get first pick of some fine hand-made sweaters.*

olive Metcalf

River Rock Inn
Placerville, California
95667

Innkeeper: Dorothy Irvin
Address/Telephone: 1756 Georgetown Drive; (916) 622–7640
Rooms: 4, including 1 suite; 2 with private bath, 2 with half-bath. Television, air conditioning.
Rates: $68 to $80, single or double occupancy, full breakfast. $10 for additional person. No credit cards.
Open: All year.
Facilities and activities: VCR, hot tub on deck, rafting, fishing. Nearby: Marshall State Park, antiques stores, wineries, restaurants, touring gold country.

Some people might *tell* you their inn is on a river, when you can see it only from an upstairs bathroom window; Dorothy Irvin really *means* it. Her contemporary house is situated smack-dab on a glorious section of the American River. And this is central-casting river: sparkling, white water rushing over rocks and roaring in your ears. It's understandable that television film companies like using it, most recently for a commercial.

Three bedrooms and the large deck are on eye level with the river, perfect for uninterrupted viewing. Once down the driveway, gate closed, you'll feel totally removed from the bustle of Placerville tourists. Ease into a large, beautiful hot tub on the deck, or walk down the expansive yard and put your feet into the water.

This is a comfortable, unpretentious house. Rooms are pleasant and nicely furnished, but if you aren't out watching the river, the hub of activity is the kitchen and living room. Some freshly baked treat is usually sitting there tempting you. The living room has a large fireplace, sofa and chairs to snuggle into, books, games, and a television if you're at wits' end.

Breakfast here definitely falls into the category called "full." Dorothy calls it a gold-country breakfast. Typically, it might include fresh juice, apple crepes, eggs Benedict, Dorothy's own baked rolls or baking powder biscuits, homemade jams, and fresh fruit. (Lunch, anyone?) This is served on the deck or in a glassed-in breakfast room that looks out at the river.

If you can tear yourself away from enjoying the river from the deck, Dorothy will help you arrange for one- or two-day raft trips with qualified guides.

It's not surprising that most of Dorothy's guests are repeaters. Some of them settle in for a week or two, leaving only for dinner at one of the nearby restaurants.

How to get there: From Placerville, take Highway 49 (Coloma Road) north to intersection of Highway 193 (Georgetown Road) leading to Chili Bar. Cross the American River and turn left immediately on first road, which leads to the inn.

J: *A stack of books, the American River, and thou.*

Olive Metcalf

The Robin's Nest
San Andreas, California
95249

Innkeepers: George and Carolee Jones

Address/Telephone: 247 East St. Charles Street (Highway 49) (mailing
   address: Box 1408); (209) 754–1076

Rooms: 9; 7 with private bath, all with air conditioning. No smoking inn.

Rates: $55 to $95, double occupancy, full breakfast and afternoon snacks
   and beverages.

Open: All year.

Facilities and activities: Wedding and small-seminar facilities; volleyball, badminton, croquet equipment. Nearby: restaurants, swimming, tennis,
   skiing; central location for exploring entire Mother Lode; year-round
   local events; gold-panning tours.

When the former owner finished restoring this Queen Anne
Victorian, she had the original builder's ninety-year-old daughter as
her first guest and put her in the very same room in which the
woman had been born. The old lady recognized the elegant old
bathtub but insisted that the pull-chain toilet must have been a
recent addition. "Mother said that there are *some* things you just
don't do in the house!"

By those genteel but outdated standards, attractive new bathrooms may be an aesthetic mistake, but for the rest of us they only
add to making The Robin's Nest a comfortable addition to gold-rush
area lodgings.

You can't miss this big blue house as you drive into San

Andreas. It sits high above the street looking ornate and well manicured among a setting of fruit trees and lawn. Its 1895 vintage accounts for two parlors and 12-foot ceilings.

Three of the home's original bedrooms on the main floor have those high ceilings, among them the Snyder Suite, the original master bedroom. It still has its 7-foot bathtub, waiting for you to take a leisurely soak.

Upstairs, many of the rooms have been tucked into the huge attic, giving them wonderful gabled ceilings. They are surprisingly spacious rooms, decorated with a pleasant mixture of antiques. The views from these upstairs rooms are of the yard and the surrounding hills, and the San Andreas Suite overlooks the town. From the Windmill Suite, guests can peer through a large skylight to an antique windmill in the back yard. Two rooms up here are especially good bargains. The Nook and the Cranny, with twin beds, shared bath, and views of the foothills, are only $55. In addition to the modern bathrooms, all the rooms have brass lavatories in the room, polished to a warm sheen.

Carolee and George are new owners and innkeepers, but they're already making one of those small gestures that make guests happy: Coffee and tea are set out, ready for the early risers. (It's usually some disgruntled husband who is up stomping about muttering how much he needs a cup of coffee.) At 9 o'clock a full breakfast is served in the dining room. The first course is often a cold fruit soup—strawberry, plum, mango, or whatever is in season. Next follow some of George's homemade breads and then a main course. It may be eggs Benedict or a soufflé. And always at The Robin's Nest you have fresh fruit salad.

How to get there: San Andreas is on Highway 49 between Angel's Camp and Jackson. The inn is on the west side of the highway at the north end of town; parking in back. Fly-in: Calaveras County Airport.

J: *Craft fairs, fiddle festivals, jumping frog contests, and Black Bart Day are just a few of the area's activities. Ask the innkeepers what's going on when you reserve a room.*

Olive Metcalf

La Casa Inglesa
Sonora, California
95370

Innkeepers: Mary and John Monser
Address/Telephone: 18047 Lime Kiln Road; (209) 532–5822
Rooms: 5, including 1 suite with whirlpool tub; all with private bath. No smoking inn.
Rates: $75 to $100, double occupancy, tax included, full breakfast.
Open: All year.
Facilities and activities: Hot tub; pond on grounds; old gold-mine area to explore. Nearby: gold-rush towns, antiques shops, restaurants; fishing, 18-hole golf course, water sports; Dodge Ridge skiing 30 miles.

What a surprise to see a grand English-style country house in the wooded foothills of the Sierras. La Casa Inglesa is one of the Mother Lode's newest inns and is on its way to becoming one of the most elegant. Mary Monser's Hispanic background accounts for the inn's name and its unique blending of two cultures.

The Monsers built their home on the Kincaid Flat, the site of the former Kincaid Gold Mine. The old mine shaft lies sunken near the center of a 2-acre pond on the property. The day we arrived gardeners were planting a large flower garden in the front lawn; Mary said it would be the variegated English kind. Another lower garden is down by the pond.

I like the feeling of the fine oak paneling in the entryway and throughout the formal dining room. It's impressive but still welcoming. A large, comfortable but somewhat formal living room with a fireplace is for guests to use.

The spacious guest rooms upstairs embrace you with the charm of pitched ceilings. Decorated with appealing wallpapers and quality fabrics, they're fresh and airy and have queen-sized beds and wonderful bathrooms. The grand suite is the largest and has an opulent bath with a whirlpool-spa. I was smitten with another room that looked very English to me. It might be the white-and-green floral wallpaper, or maybe the iron bed, but it's probably the grand oak bathtub sitting in a bay that stroked my Anglophile tendencies. For one mad moment, I fantasized Alistair Cooke soaking there. A patio and hot tub are on this upper level of the house.

You don't go B&Bing to hang around someone else's kitchen, but this one will knock your socks off. Mary says people do tend to wander in . . . and stay. Brick and blue tiles are the background and accent color for all the finest culinary appointments, the star being a handsome wood-burning cook-stove in an arched brick enclosure. And if kitchens don't turn you on, the gourmet breakfast that comes out of it will: fresh fruits of the season, a variety of Mary's homemade breads and jams, and a main-course specialty.

How to get there: Take Highway 49 south through Sonora. At the intersection with Highway 108 just before the Safeway store, bear right onto Lime Kiln Road. Continue 2^1/$_2$ miles to the inn on the left. Fly-in: Columbia Airport 4 miles north of Sonora.

olive Metcalf

Lavender Hill
Sonora, California
95370

Innkeepers: Alice Byrnes and Carole Williams
Address/Telephone: 683 South Barretta; (209) 532–9024
Rooms: 4; 2 with private bath.
Rates: $65 to $75, double occupancy, full breakfast. No credit cards.
Open: All year.
Facilities and activities: Nearby: downtown Sonora restaurants, shops; historic
gold-rush towns; two repertory theaters; Columbia State Park; Dodge
Ridge ski area; good stop for Yosemite trip.

The gold country has long lured California history buffs to
explore its beautiful countryside and colorful towns. You could
always find lodgings rich with authentic ambience and history—
qualities less sentimental travelers call dusty, musty, and old. But
something new is happening on the scene. Inns are now opening
that are often still in charming old buildings, but they're being
architecturally restored and freshly decorated for comfort.

The Lavender Hill is a premier example of the new trend. It sits
on one of Sonoma's quiet streets above the town, as pretty and
appealing as a sedate Victorian lady. A soft shade of dove gray covers its turn-of-the-century lines, and an immaculate planted yard,
flowers, and trees surround it.

Inside is period charm with polished wood floors, spacious
rooms, and tall ceilings, but all restored and clean. The attractive

310

entryway has a captivating working white iron stove. Opening from here are two elegant parlors and a sunny dining room, all furnished comfortably rather than in prim, hard Victorian. Guests are invited to make themselves at home.

A handsome stairway leads up to the bedrooms. The largest is the Lavender Room, named for its luscious carpet color. A few judiciously chosen antiques and colorful linens make an appealing room. Three of the guest rooms have queen-sized beds and one has twins.

If you come to the gold-rush countryside to relax and perhaps get the feeling of that age, you should try Alice's old-fashioned porch swing. Watching the passersby is a pleasant way to pass the time.

Breakfast is generous here—fresh fruit, perhaps scrambled eggs, and always, says Alice, something fresh from the oven like whole-wheat bread or cinnamon rolls. For other meals, Sonora has a range of restaurants from hearty Italian to the continental Hemingway's. You can walk to many of them. The city of Sonora caters to tourists and has activities scheduled for almost every weekend of the year. I particularly enjoy the two repertory theaters, one in Sonora and one in nearby Columbia.

The house is a lovely setting for a small wedding. However you choose to spend your time, when you see this quiet, tasteful inn sitting above the bustle of downtown Sonora, I think you'll be glad you came.

How to get there: From downtown Sonora, take Highway 108 east out of town. At Safeway store on right, get in center lane; make first left onto South Barretta. Inn is on the right.

Olive Metcalf

The Foxes
Sutter Creek, California
95685

Innkeepers: Pete and Min Fox

Address/Telephone: 77 Main Street (mailing address: Box 159); (209) 267–5882

Rooms: 6 large suites; all with private bath, air conditioning, and queen-sized bed, 3 with cable television, 3 with fireplace. Smoking outside only.

Rates: $95 to $135, double occupancy, full breakfast. Singles deduct $5.

Open: All year.

Facilities and activities: Covered parking. Nearby: walking tour of Sutter Creek historic buildings; restaurants, antiques, specialty stores, art galleries.

The six elegantly decorated suites at The Foxes are the zenith of Mother Lode luxury. When they bought this historic house, realtor Pete Fox and his wife, Min, an antiques dealer, thought they would simply combine their businesses under one roof. But Min's flair for creating beautiful settings meant "good-bye antiques store, hello innkeeping." Pete has since moved his office across the street, and Min spends all her time pampering guests and making every room a picture.

Their name was an easy handle for a symbol. You'll see foxes—fluffy, stuffed, patched, toy, ceramic, funny, and artistic—throughout the house. But Min's lavish decorating goes far beyond a cute theme. Her handsome house is the background for outstanding antiques and her knack for putting things together with great taste.

Three spacious rooms are in the main house, and three are in the carriage house. You can't go wrong with any choice, since every room is not just elegant but comfortable. If you enjoy beautiful rooms, you should try arriving before all guests check in for a chance to see more of them.

The Honeymoon Suite is the only downstairs room and has a private entry. It is an opulent setting, with a large brick fireplace, a latticed-front Austrian armoire, and a demicanopied bed with a Victorian burled walnut headboard. Fabrics are sumptuous in a creamy blue and camel. A crystal chandelier sparkles in the adjoining bathroom with matching wallpaper and balloon window draperies.

Upstairs are Victorian and Anniversary suites. A Louis XIV tapestry in rich burgundy and cream sets the color scheme for the first suite. There's also a 9-foot Victorian headboard and matching dresser; an adjoining room is your breakfast chamber. The Anniversary Room has a cathedral ceiling, a massive Viennese walnut armoire deeply carved in a rose motif, and an old-fashioned tub.

Breakfast is "cooked to order," says Min, so they can cater to any special dietary restrictions. She takes your order the previous night, and Pete turns out beautiful fruit compotes, eggs any style, bacon or ham, sourdough French toast, Swedish pancakes stuffed with fruits and yogurt, and jams. Whatever the menu, it arrives on an impressive silver service and is arranged on the elegantly appointed table in the sitting area of each room. It does feel posh to lounge in your "jammies," pouring coffee from a silver pot and scanning the morning paper that's been delivered to your door.

How to get there: Sutter Creek is on Highway 49, which becomes Main Street in the center of town. The inn is on the west side of the street.

J: *Don't rush it. The longer you're here, the more elegant touches you'll see.*

olive Metcalf

The Gold Quartz Inn
Sutter Creek, California
95685

Innkeepers: Wendy Woolrich, general manager; Glenyce Wilson, concierge
Address/Telephone: 15 Bryson Drive; (209) 267–9155
Rooms: 24; all with private bath, television, telephone, air conditioning, access to sitting porch. Handicapped facilities. No smoking inn.
Rates: $75 to $125, double occupancy, full breakfast and afternoon tea.
Open: All year.
Facilities and activities: Conference, wedding, and banquet facilities; concierge services. Nearby: historic Sutter Creek shops and restaurants, antiquing, picnic spots, wine-tasting tours, gold panning, Indian Grinding Rock, Daffodil Hill, historic town of Volcano; hiking, bicycling, horseback riding, and skiing available.

This handsome new inn was built to blend into the distinctive Mother Lode atmosphere. It has a nineteenth-century look and feeling, but with more comfort and luxury than you would ever expect from strictly authentic gold-rush-era lodgings. If you like warm Victorian decor that is also invitingly fresh, period furniture chosen for comfort as well as style, and commodious rooms instead of overstuffed cubby holes, you'll find this is an elegant place to sample the gold country. Even the hallways are spacious—and there is an elevator. Definitely upscale for a country inn.

With twenty-four rooms, this is obviously more than a Mom-and-Pop operation, so it is likely that one of the abundant staff will check you in, show you your room, and point out some of the pleasures offered. We were shown through the generous main-floor common rooms available to all guests, including a graceful parlor decorated in soft mauve colors, with fireplace, Victorian-style sofas and chairs, and a television hidden in a period cabinet. The atmosphere was of a genteel nineteenth-century room without a hint of stuffiness. Several fresh bouquets added to the inviting aura.

Our bedroom, as do all the rooms, opened onto a sitting porch that wraps around the inn. Inside we had a white-iron king-sized bed dressed in white eyelet comforter and shams, and good reading lights at each side. There was also a small private deck out our back door.

Afternoon tea was the real thing. Set out on the dining room buffet were iced tea, lemonade, tea and coffee, platters of cookies, petits fours, fruit bars, and cake.

One of the advantages of an inn with staff is the accommodation that they make to individual breakfast preferences. Here you can help yourself to an early-morning buffet of cereal, coffee, and juice and enjoy the quiet of the dining room or take in the morning sun on the porch. Later, you can have a full breakfast including fruit, several hot entrees, muffins, and jams.

The dining room is lovely. Tables set for four give you privacy if you want it, but allow for conversation with other guests—and that is, after all, why many people go to country inns. Again you find fresh flowers and attention to pretty details, like an antique sugar bowl. A peek into the kitchen reveals why so many events are catered at The Gold Quartz. They have superb facilities and a staff that knows how to do the job.

Having a concierge on the premises is a great help if you are exploring this area for the first time. It is rich with history, and Glenyce Wilson can suggest some memorable excursions.

How to get there: From the Bay Area, follow Highway 88 toward the Sierras. Turn left onto Highway 49; turn right on Bryson Drive.

Olive Metcalf

The Hanford House
Sutter Creek, California
95685

Innkeepers: Lucille and Jim Jacobus

Address/Telephone: 61 Hanford Street (mailing address: Box 1450); (209) 267–0747

Rooms: 9, including 1 suite; all with private bath, queen-sized bed, air conditioning. Access for the handicapped and special facilities in one room. No smoking inn.

Rates: $75 to $110, double occupancy, expanded continental breakfast. Discount Sunday through Thursday, except holidays.

Open: All year.

Facilities and activities: Innkeeper knows American sign language; midweek small groups and meetings welcomed. Nearby: walking tour of Sutter Creek, historic houses, antiques shops, art galleries, restaurants; golfing, skiing, many local wineries.

Modern comfort in California country ambience is the atmosphere at The Hanford House. A 1930 cottage is at the core of a handsome two-story brick building with ample off-street parking in front. Jim Jacobus calls it "old San Francisco warehouse style," but you must understand that there are some very chic warehouses in that city.

The interior of the cottage at the nucleus of the inn has a Spanish feeling, with soaring whitewashed beams. It consists of a delightful parlor, with brightly slipcovered sofas, antique pine

316

tables, magazines and plants, and some of the many teddy bears that hibernate at the inn.

The newer brick wing has guest rooms with luxurious baths, and they are furnished in a captivating mélange of California country, early American, and nineteenth-century pieces.

On the top floor is a large suite with a fireplace. A common deck up here overlooks the rooftops of Sutter Creek and the foothills. It's a choice spot to take your morning coffee—ready at 7:30 A.M. along with a newspaper.

Breakfast is a relaxed affair served at separate tables between 8:30 and 9:30 A.M. in the dining area. Juice, fresh fruit, and a selection of cheeses, muffins, or sweet rolls make up the continental fare, with your choice of hot beverage.

Jim's past experience as a Bay Area stockbroker and Lucille's former position in a mental-health agency seem remote from life in the Sierra foothills, but now they're both enthusiastic converts to country life. They're eager for guests to know about points of interest and good restaurants around Sutter Creek. Right next door is the Pelargonium Restaurant, which serves elegant California cuisine. Around the corner is The Palace, whose reviews get better and better.

How to get there: Highway 49 runs through the center of Sutter Creek. At the north end of town where the highway divides, turn left. Immediately on your left is the inn.

Olive Metcalf

Sutter Creek Inn
Sutter Creek, California
95685

Innkeeper: Jane Way

Address/Telephone: 75 Main Street (mailing address: Box 385); (209) 267–5606

Rooms: 19; all with private bath, electric blankets, and air conditioning, some with fireplace.

Rates: $45 to $97, double occupancy, full breakfast; 12 percent discount for senior citizens. Two-day minimum on weekends. No credit cards.

Open: All year except Thanksgiving and the day before, Christmas Eve, and Christmas Day.

Facilities and activities: Handwriting analysis and professional massage by appointment; enjoy inn's gardens, hammocks, library, and games. Nearby: good town for walking; art galleries, antiques, historic houses, restaurants.

When the subject is California inns, the talk invariably goes to the Sutter Creek Inn and Jane Way. Jane started the phenomenon of country inns in this state back in the 1960s. In fact, she's become a legend in her own time. Former guests like to swap stories about what she did while *they* were there: Jane captivating her guests with tales of the house ghost; Jane doing handwriting analysis; Jane ladling brandy into your before-breakfast coffee; Jane and the famous swinging beds. Her boundless energy and flair have made the Sutter Creek a prototype for country inns.

On a busy street of shops, restaurants, and overhanging balconies, the Sutter Creek Inn is a charming New England–style residence surrounded by a green lawn, trees, and flower beds. Some bedrooms are in the main house, others in outbuildings in back that Jane has extensively remodeled and decorated with great ingenuity. Their names recall Sutter Creek's gold-rush history—Wood Shed, Lower Wash House, Tool Shed, Miner's Cabin.

Each room is completely different. Nine have fireplaces, some Franklin stoves, some private patios; others open onto the garden. And there are the swinging beds—an idea Jane discovered in Mexico—but not to worry, they can be stabilized if you wish. Room appointments are cozy and comfortable, right down to the selection of magazines and books. During the winter months, guests are welcomed with hot spiced cider and homemade cookies; in summer it's fresh lemonade.

Gathering in the beautiful living room for coffee before breakfast is the quintessential inn experience. Jane holds court, introducing guests and overseeing breakfast. When the breakfast bell rings, you move to four polished pine tables in the large cheerful kitchen.

The meal might include eggs a la Sutter Creek (baked in cream cheese sauce and served on an English muffin) or pancakes full of chopped apples and nuts, served with wild blackberry syrup and ham. Hot biscuits or muffins and fresh fruit and juice put you in a benign glow for the day. Or is it Jane's coffee?

How to get there: Sutter Creek is 4 miles north of Jackson on Highway 49, which runs through the center of town. The inn is on the west side of the street.

J: *Pick up a copy of the* Stroller's Guide to Sutter Creek *at any store along Main Street. It will lead you to the back streets of older buildings and interesting stores.*

Olive Metcalf

Mayfield House
Tahoe City, California
96145

Innkeepers: Cynthia and Bruce Knauss

Address/Telephone: 236 Grove Street (mailing address: Box 5999); (916) 583–1001

Rooms: 5 share 3 baths; 1 suite with private bath. King-, queen-, and twin-sized beds. Wheelchair access.

Rates: $70 to $105, double occupancy, full breakfast and complimentary wine or brandy and cheese.

Open: All year.

Facilities and activities: Nearby: shops, restaurants, tennis courts; free buses to Squaw Valley and Alpine Meadows skiing 10 miles away; hiking, bicycling, boating; all the attractions of Lake Tahoe.

Mayfield House is an agreeable alternative to motel or condo digs while you enjoy the mountain air of Lake Tahoe. The house is a fine example of old Tahoe architecture. It was built in 1932 by Norman Mayfield, one of Lake Tahoe's pioneer contractors. Refurbished in 1979, it is comfortable and traditional in atmosphere, serene rather than chic. It's the kind of place to read and relax in.

All the bedrooms have down pillows, down comforters, and robes. They each have a sitting area, very cozy if you like breakfast served in your room. In the `30s, one room, now called Julia's Room, was always reserved for Julia Morgan, the architect of San Simeon and a personal friend of the owners'. It's a surprisingly feminine, simple room in contrast to many of her projects. She designed several estates along the west shore of Tahoe for which Mayfield was the contractor. Much of her work was done here at his home.

The Mayfield Room is the master suite upstairs. It has a sitting area, dining area, and king-sized bed. One of the bathrooms up here features a 6-foot-long tub installed by the tall owner, who evidently liked to stretch out while he soaked.

On the main floor, the wood-paneled former office of Norman Mayfield is decorated in brown, beige, and rust plaid. With its outside door, it offers easy access for a wheelchair.

The Margaret Carpenter originals on the walls and fresh flowers lend a pleasant feeling to the large living room. With its fireplace and snuggly sofas, it's a cozy place to read and enjoy your complimentary wine in the afternoon.

A full breakfast is served in the dining room, unless you choose the quiet of your bedroom or the patio. There are juice, seasonal fresh fruit, cheeses; entrees like crepes, Portuguese toast, or Finnish pancakes, and homemade pastries along with coffee and teas.

How to get there: From San Francisco, take Highway 80 to Truckee; turn south on Highway 89 to Tahoe City. Turn north on Highway 28 to Grove Street; turn left.

J: *One of the most talked-about restaurants in northern California is here in Tahoe City. Wolfdale's has a small, sophisticated menu of exceptional cuisine that changes frequently. Try a summertime lunch on the deck overlooking the lake.*

Olive Metcalf

The Captain's Alpenhaus
Tahoma, California
96142

Innkeepers: Joel and Phyllis Butler

Address/Telephone: 6941 West Lake Boulevard (mailing address: Box 262); (916) 525–5000

Rooms: 9; 7 with private bath; 6 housekeeping cottages. Some pets welcome.

Rates: $60 to $145, double occupancy, full breakfast. $12 per extra person.

Open: All year.

Facilities and activities: Restaurant, full bar, Basque nights (accordion music) Wednesdays; swimming, spa, hiking, biking, tennis, Ping-Pong, horseshoes, volleyball, badminton. Nearby: Lake Tahoe attractions; 2 miles from downhill skiing at Homewood; ¹/₄ mile from Sugar Pine Point State Park for cross-country.

The fresh invigorating air of this beautiful area can be downright inspiring. As a recreational area it is unrivaled. Tahoma, situated on the west shore of Lake Tahoe, is known for a little more quiet beauty than other parts of the lake. You can quickly get to the nightspots and gambling if the fever strikes, but The Captain's Alpenhaus seems to lure skiers and hikers to its more countrylike atmosphere in the trees.

Most guests were enjoying the pool the hot day I visited, but the inn's Swiss Alpine look is especially appropriate with snow on the roof—and they get plenty of it. Skiers are only minutes away from both Alpine and Nordic skiing.

The cheerful dining room has a rich floral green carpet, and pictures and objects reveal a European touch. It's the scene of three meals a day—big breakfasts, light lunches, and robust dinners. European country specialties are featured—hearty soups, sauerbraten with *spätzli*, fondues, pasta dishes, and fresh seafood.

Basque night is a popular Wednesday night event that really brings people in. Typical, authentic Basque food is served family style in big bowls accompanied by much toasting, accordion music, and—before you know it—singing. You don't leave Basque night a stranger.

Retired Navy Captain Joel Butler and his wife Phyllis bought the inn in 1988 and have redecorated everything. A small lounge area with a stone fireplace and a bar provides a place for guests to get acquainted. It's casual, with a friendly atmosphere you'll feel the minute you walk in. Upstairs, the bedrooms are decorated in warm, romantic country prints, with hand-painted wood furniture and thick comforters for cold mountain nights.

The cottages with living room, fireplace, and kitchen are a good bargain for families. There's nothing like fixing a few of your own meals to make a vacation more affordable. These are well equipped and cozy, with the same country feeling the inn has.

How to get there: From Sacramento, take Highway 80 to Truckee and Highway 89; continue south to Tahoma. Inn is on the right of the highway.

J: *The bike path that circles the West and North Shores begins right here at The Captain's Alpenhaus.*

olive Metcalf

Oak Hill Ranch
Tuolumne, California
95379

Innkeepers: Sanford and Jane Grover
Address/Telephone: 18550 Connally Lane (mailing address: Box 307); (209) 928–4717
Rooms: 4; 2 with private bath and queen-sized beds. 1 cottage (sleeps 5) with private bath, kitchen, fireplace. No smoking inn.
Rates: $67 to $110, double or single, full breakfast. $18 per extra adult. No credit cards; personal checks okay.
Open: All year.
Facilities and activities: Nearby: bicycle or walk beautiful countryside; explore southern Mother Lode; near Dodge Ridge skiing; 63 miles to Yosemite; Sonora restaurants.

Discovering Tuolumne is a delightful experience, but the capper is to follow a country back road another mile past town, then up the lane to this gracious ranch home. The Grovers say their Ranch Victorian was completed in 1980, but it's actually 20 years old. Since they began collecting Victorian building materials and furniture in the 1960s, the house has been their dream.

The house was designed by their architect son in the '70s, but years of stripping old wood (and an understanding contractor) were required before the dream came to life. The result is the period ambience of high ceilings, wide hallways, and authentic wood detailings in an immaculate background of modern kitchen, plumbing, and heating. If you're from condo-land, the generous size of the house alone is a pleasure.

The setting is spectacular, on a wooded hill overlooking miles of rolling terrain with the Sierra range in the distance. On a crisp October morning, the Grovers, in period costume, welcomed me into an inviting living room with a fire burning in the fireplace, fresh flowers, and refreshment. It was downright pastoral ensnarement.

A wonderful floral carpet sets the tone of stylish, uncluttered, Victorian charm. The upstairs and downstairs bedrooms have fetching decors, one with a canopied bed, another opening to a balcony that overlooks pastures and ponds.

Your hosts (retired educators) are naturally hospitable, and they're adamant about always putting their best foot forward. They'll help you choose restaurants in the area and point out some beautiful drives to take as well as the many recreational pursuits to enjoy in Tuolumne County.

Many innkeepers endeavor to make breakfast a special treat, but the Grovers know that it's not just a lot of food that makes the occasion special, it's serving it with style. When guests gather for an Oak Hill breakfast in the impressive dining room (it must be more than 20 feet long), Jane, in long skirt and ruffled cap, and Sandy, in crisp shirt and arm bands, make the morning memorable. The menu may feature quiche, crepes Normandie, baked eggs, or French toast, always freshly made in their large farm kitchen and engagingly served.

How to get there: From Sonora, take Highway 108 to Tuolumne Road; follow to center of Tuolumne. Turn south on Carter Street to the schoolyard, left onto Elm Street, and right on Apple Colony Road. Follow 1/2 mile to Oak Hill sign on left. Fly-in: Columbia Airport; inn pickup.

clive Metcalf

Saint George Hotel
Volcano, California
95689

Innkeepers: Marlene and Charles Inman
Address/Telephone: 2 Main Street (mailing address: Box 9); (209) 296–4458
Rooms: 20; 14 on two floors in hotel share a bath and a half-bath on each floor; 6 separate motel units, all with private bath.
Rates: Rooms start at $62, double occupancy, including full breakfast. Saturday nights approximately $50 per person including dinner and breakfast.
Open: All year except Mondays and Tuesdays and first six weeks of year.
Facilities and activities: Dinner Wednesday through Sunday by reservation; full bar. Facilities for meetings; luncheons arranged for twenty or more. Nearby: town of Volcano; original jail, stone ruins of Wells Fargo, "Old Abe"; other historic gold towns, shopping, antiques, restaurants, Indian Grinding Rock State Park.

Volcano is a highlight of any Mother Lode tour, the most picturesque of all the gold-rush towns. Its enduring charm is that it doesn't change. Located a few miles off Highway 49, it has somehow remained aloof from gentrification, beautification, supermarkets, gas stations, neon, and boutiques!

During its heyday, more than ninety million dollars in gold was taken from the hills and gulches around Volcano and poured into the United States Treasury. It was during the Civil War, and the issue of whether the gold would go to the North or the South was decided by virtue of the abolitionists in town having "Old Abe."

The ancient cannon (which would have been more of a threat had there been any cannonballs to go with it) was never tested. The abolitionists prepared by gathering stones from the riverbed for ammunition, but the outnumbered southern sympathizers retired from the fray.

The Saint George Hotel is *the* can't-miss landmark on Main Street. The modest three-story structure was admittedly looking well worn, but its vine-covered balconies gave it an Old West appeal I couldn't resist. The old balconies have been replaced, but none of the old charm has been lost. Even the turned ballasters have been copied from the original 1862 building. From the balconies, you can look out over the quiet town (population eighty-five) and the rolling hills of the beautiful countryside. The spring wildflower display on nearby Daffodil Hill is one of the wonders of the gold country.

The two upstairs floors contain simple bedrooms, some of them quite large, with shared baths at the end of the hall. Each is decorated with antiques and crocheted bedspreads. A modern annex is available with private baths, but only the hotel has the old-time flavor. On the main floor are the dining room and the lounge, notable for a floor-to-ceiling mirror cracked by what everyone chooses to believe is a bullet hole.

Dinners on weekends offer a single entree: prime ribs of beef on Saturday and spring chicken on Sunday. Hearty soups, breads, and desserts are made at the hotel.

How to get there: Five county roads lead into Volcano, each a winding route through the foothills. Try the road east from Jackson on Highway 88 to Pine Grove, then north on Volcano–Pine Grove Road to Volcano. Beautiful.

✳

J: *Volcano is not exactly life in the fast lane, as evidenced by the posted business hours of the Outhouse Antiques:* Mon. Tues. Wed. Thurs. closed. Fri. Sat. & Sun. open 12–3.

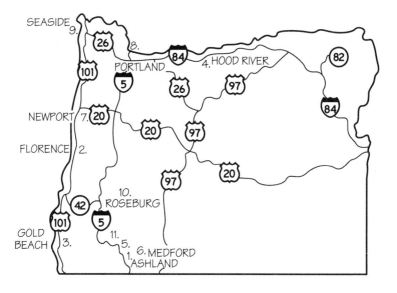

SEASIDE 9.

26

8.

84

4. HOOD RIVER

82

PORTLAND

101

26

97

84

5

NEWPORT 7.

20

20

97

FLORENCE 2.

97

20

10.
ROSEBURG

42

97

GOLD
BEACH 3.

101

5

11.
5.

6. MEDFORD
1. ASHLAND

Oregon

Numbers on map refer to towns numbered below.

Olive Metcalf

Chanticleer Bed and Breakfast Inn
Ashland, Oregon
97520

Innkeepers: Jim and Nancy Beaver
Address/Telephone: 120 Gresham Street; (503) 482–1919
Rooms: 7, including 1 suite with kitchen; all with private bath, air conditioning, and direct-dial telephone.
Rates: $105 to $190, double occupancy, weekends and summer; winter rates lower; full breakfast. $20 each additional person.
Open: All year.
Facilities and activities: Facilities for small business conferences. Nearby: Ashland theaters, restaurants, Lithia Park, shops; Rogue River white-water rafting, Mt. Ashland skiing.

With the success of its Shakespearean festival, Ashland has become a mecca for bed and breakfast inns. I've collected a file of clippings about them, mostly letters written to travel editors from past visitors singing the praises of one particular inn—the Chanticleer. Now that I've been there too, I can appreciate the enthusiastic chorus. It's undoubtedly one of the most attractive, romantic inns in Ashland.

The name comes from Chaucer's tale of Chanticleer and the fox, a European barnyard fable. The feeling here is cozy and European. The country living room has a warm appeal with its blue rug, rock fireplace, and hearth. Comfortable, cushy furniture, books, and an ever-welcome tray of sherry complete the picture. I'm always favorably predisposed toward *any* room that includes these amenities.

Everything about you looks freshly painted and is immaculate. If you're not off to a matinee, it's a pleasure to spend your day at this inn. Some of the rooms overlook Bear Creek Valley and Cascade foothills; others open onto a brick patio and a perfectly lovely rock garden.

The seven cheerful bedrooms are engagingly decorated with crisp linens, cotton slipcovers on puffy goosedown comforters, wallpapers, and fresh flowers. Complimentary toiletries and thick towels appoint your private bath. Several of these rooms accommodate a family of four nicely.

Jim and Nancy think of many ways to be obliging. They're endlessly helpful in choosing where to have dinner and what to see in the area. But most thoughtful, I think, is having in your room copies of most of the current plays running in Ashland's three theaters and a good light to read by. Wonderful for resolving after-the-play discussions.

Everyone who stays here raves about the breakfasts, and with good cause. Even the orange juice and fresh fruit seem tastier than when you prepare them at home. Maybe it's Jim and Nancy's solicitude for everyone's comfort, or perhaps it's the lively conversation with other guests that accounts for this. Of course, the baked pears with orange sauce, blintzes, quiche, or shirred eggs with cream, the hot breads and blueberry muffins, the superb coffee and teas have something to do with it, too.

How to get there: Driving north to Ashland on I-5, take exit 11; proceed along Siskiyou to Iowa Street, and turn left. At Gresham Street, turn right. Inn is on your right.

J: *Hospitality here extends to the house invitation to help yourself to refreshments in the refrigerator and coffee, tea, and cookies any time of day.*

Olive Metcalf

Hersey House
Ashland, Oregon
97520

Innkeepers: Gail E. Orell and K. Lynn Savage

Address/Telephone: 451 North Main Street; (503) 482–4563

Rooms: 4; all with private bath and air conditioning, 2 rooms with daybed accommodate three people; 2-bedroom guest house with kitchen also available. No smoking inn.

Rates: $80 single, low season, to $120, high season, for three persons, full breakfast. No credit cards for advance deposits.

Open: Mid-April through October.

Facilities and activities: Player piano, extensive Oregon book collection, out standing English garden. Nearby: Ashland restaurants, theaters, shops, Lithia Park; biking, golf, tennis, historic mining town of Jacksonville.

No car; no hassle. Those just are two great advantages of Hersey House. It is open almost exclusively for the Ashland theater season, and you couldn't choose a more comfortable or convenient place to nestle in while you see it all.

Ashland's beautiful theaters—including the experimental and conventional as well as the outdoor Elizabethan Stagehouse—are as highly regarded as the talent they draw. But what makes Ashland pure pleasure for theater lovers is the low-key atmosphere and the easy way you can take it all in. A few days of first-rate theater in the beautiful setting of the Rogue Valley can easily diminish the allure of more high-powered metropolitan theater seasons.

At graceful Hersey House, Ashland's abundant charms are only a short walk away, but don't rush. This is a house where you'll enjoy lingering. Begin with the English garden that has been photographed and included in several gardening books. Then take in the view of the Rogue Valley while you relax or read on the big front porch. You're invited to join your hosts and other guests for a social hour in the main parlor.

The house was built in 1904, and five generations of the Hersey family lived there. When the present owners converted it into an inn, they were careful to keep the Victorian charm while they entirely updated and refurbished it. They evidently succeeded, even in the eyes of Hersey family members, who have lent the inn some grand family portraits of the first Herseys to live in the house. The portraits now hang in the stairway.

There are only four guest rooms, but each one is a beauty, tastefully decorated in airy floral prints, several with matching wallpaper, a queen-sized bed, and tiled bath. The Sunshine Terrace Room has a private balcony and a view overlooking the Cascade foothills; the Eastlake Room has a view of Mt. Ashland.

Breakfast in a theater town inn is especially congenial because the conversation has an immediate hook: What did you see? . . . What did you think of it? . . . Where did you have dinner? The innkeepers stoke the talk with freshly brewed coffee and herbal teas, fresh juice and fruit, and home-cooked delights that change daily, like orange nut bread, Eggs Hersey, or gingerbread pancakes with lemon curd.

How to get there: From I–5, take exit 11 into Ashland. Proceed north along Siskiyou, which becomes Lithia Way, then North Main Street. Inn is on the left.

J: *One of the biggest points separating a fine inn from one that is just so-so is having the innkeeper around. At Hersey House, either Gail or Lynn is always on-site.*

olive Metcalf

The Morical House
Ashland, Oregon
97520

Innkeepers: Pat and Peter Dahl
Address/Telephone: 668 North Main Street; (503) 482–2254
Rooms: 5; all with private bath and air conditioning. No smoking inn.
Rates: $85 to $115, double occupancy; $10 less for single; November–
February, $70; full breakfast.
Open: All year except January 15–31 and December 24–25.
Facilities and activities: Putting green, croquet, badminton. Nearby: wineries,
biking, fishing, river rafting, skiing; 1-mile walk to Ashland restau-
rants, theaters, shops.

Theater is the main reason people from all over the world flock
to Ashland. The Oregon Shakespearean Festival performs a three-
play repertory from June through September in the outdoor Elizabethan Stagehouse and a season of other plays from late February
through October in the two indoor theaters.

But gorgeous scenery has always been Oregon's primary
attraction for travelers, and Morical House offers some of the best.
The 1880s house is surrounded by an acre of lawns, rocks, rose gardens, and more than a hundred varieties of trees and shrubs, and it
looks out on a panoramic view of Bear Creek Valley and the Cascade Mountains.

When the Dahls decided they wanted to own "the perfect
B&B," they left their Marin County, California, home and began a

search that led them to Ashland and The Morical House.

The house was completely restored in 1982 with tasteful attention to its period charms such as stained-glass windows and detailed woodwork. The traditional nineteenth-century house had undergone many additions during the years in a way that makes the downstairs floor plan unconventional but entirely pleasing. Several light-filled sitting rooms, with comfortable sofas and chairs and well-stocked bookshelves, call you in to enjoy them. An ice machine and a ready tea kettle help make this an inviting house to nestle in.

To take full advantage of the inn's vista, a glassed-in porch was added across the back of the house. Eating one of the house breakfast treats, like Dutch pancakes, here, with the sweeping view before you, is a splendid beginning to the day. Pat also likes to try new recipes for her more health-oriented guests. She's enjoying all the fresh local produce and Oregon's special bounty of blueberries, raspberries, Marionberries, and Red Haven peaches.

Beautifully decorated bedrooms are upstairs, with mountain views and non-Victorian comforts of private baths, air conditioning, and soundproofed walls. The very private third-floor room is a favorite. What bliss to soak in a grand old claw-footed tub and read a play you'll see performed that night.

How to get there: Driving north on Highway 5, take exit 19 at Ashland. Follow to the inn on the left.

J: *Real Ashland theater buffs go to both matinee and evening performances. But this pleasant inn gives you a ticket to such a scene-stealing panorama of sky and land that it could easily become your matinee performance choice.*

Olive Metcalf

Mt. Ashland Inn
Ashland, Oregon
97520

Innkeepers: Jerry and Elaine Shanafelt
Address/Telephone: 550 Mt. Ashland Road; (503) 482–8707
Rooms: 5, including 1 suite with Jacuzzi for two; all with private bath, queen- or king-sized bed, and individual thermostat. No smoking inn.
Rates: $80 to $130, double occupancy, full breakfast and beverages. Special rates November through April, excluding holidays and weekends.
Open: All year.
Facilities and activities: Meeting room for small gatherings with sitting area and audiovisual equipment, VCR for guests. Light suppers available in winter by prior arrangement for additional charge. Hiking, sledding, cross-country and downhill skiing. Nearby: river rafting, Ashland Shakespeare Festival February through October, Britt Music Festival June to September in Jacksonville.

A late April snow was falling as I drove up the road to Mt. Ashland, making the passing scenery all the more breathtaking. At 5,500 feet, just 3 miles from the summit, the beautiful Mt. Ashland Inn sits nestled in the Siskiyou Mountains 16 miles south of Ashland, a snug haven of outstanding craftmanship and hospitality.

The cedar log structure was handcrafted by the Shanafelts from lumber cut and milled on the surrounding property. But don't picture a cottage in the woods improvised by a couple with some land and a chain saw. Jerry's remarkable design and woodworking skills are apparent everywhere your eyes rest—in hand-carved

mountain scenes on the doors, the decorative deck railing, log arch-
ways, stained-glass windows, and a unique log-slab circular staircase. Most amazing to me were the twelve Windsor chairs he made
one winter, each one a smooth, perfect piece of art.

The peeled log walls of a common room draw you in with the
warmth of cushy furniture, brilliant oriental rugs, mellowed
antiques, and a stone fireplace. Can you imagine how the fire,
music playing softly, and hot spiced cider hit me on this cold afternoon? Right. It was sleepy time in the mountains.

Each of the guest rooms upstairs has a view toward Mt. Shasta,
Mt. McLoughlin, or some part of the Cascades. The Sky Lakes Suite
on the ground floor has a Jacuzzi for two, a rock wall with trickling
waterfall (operated by the guests), a rock patio, a wet bar, and a
view of Mt. McLoughlin.

When I looked out the window in the morning, the fir trees
were thickly frosted with snow, and I felt like Heidi in Oregon. But
pretending I was roughing it in the wilderness just wouldn't fly in
the face of all the comforts: big chairs with reading lights by the
windows, a queen-sized bed topped with a handmade quilt, and the
woodsy aroma of cedar filling the air.

Breakfast in the dining room was fresh juice and fruit and a
tasty entree of puffy orange French toast. Daffodils on the table
were picked that morning as they popped through the snow.

If you must stir from this comforting cocoon, a cross-country
skiing path that ties into old logging roads is out the back door.
Three miles up the road, Mt. Ashland offers fairly demanding
downhill skiing. For hikers, the Pacific Crest trail passes right
through the property. The premier attractions in the area are the
Ashland theaters, about a twenty-five-minute drive (to good restaurants, also) from here.

A bonus of being up the mountain is that when Ashland is
covered in clouds and fog, you're often in a pocket of sunshine
here.

How to get there: North on Highway 5 take Mt. Ashland exit 6; turn right
under the highway. At stop sign turn left, parallel highway ½ mile. Turn
right on Mt. Ashland Road to ski area. Inn is 6 miles from the highway.

olive Metcalf

The Winchester Inn
Ashland, Oregon
97520

Innkeepers: Michael and Laurie Gibbs
Address/Telephone: 35 South Second Street; (503) 488–1113
Rooms: 7; all with private bath, direct-dial phone, and air conditioning.
Rates: $79 to $115, double occupancy, spring and summer, full breakfast.
 Reduced winter rates.
Open: All year.
Facilities and activities: Dinner, Sunday brunch; Dickens Christmas Feast; special wine-maker dinners. Winter murder mystery weekends. Nearby: Ashland theaters, Lithia Park, shops, restaurants, river rafting, skiing.

 West Coast inns that offer meals are few and far between. The Winchester Inn is the only one in Ashland that serves dinner to the public as well as to inn guests.

 This inn is a graceful Queen Anne Victorian in Ashland's downtown historic district. It was first a private home; then it was Oregon's first hospital. White and stately, with a broad front porch, it looks engaging from the outside, and once you enter the handsome double doors, you'll not be disappointed inside, either. Pale-rose carpeting runs from the entry, through the impressive parlor with leaded-glass windows, and up the stairs to the bedrooms.

 I was there for Sunday brunch and thoroughly enjoyed the atmosphere in the glassed-in dining room. A Vivaldi tape was being played in the background, and my view of the colorful terraced gardens provided a delightful setting. Warm-weather breakfasts are served on an inviting patio decorated with clusters of potted flowers, where you can sit at umbrella tables under the trees.

Champagne, orange juice, and a coffee cup kept refilled soothe you while you study the menu. As you sip away enjoying the music and flowers, you're served hot scones with the house nut-butter and marmalade.

Entree choices that morning were eggs Benedict, sausage omelet, or stir-fried fresh vegetables and chicken. Attacks of desire for California-style cuisine grip me periodically when I get out of state, and this fresh stir-fry filled the bill.

Upstairs are the fresh, attractive bedrooms with high ceilings, antique beds, and green plants. Each one is decorated in a different pastel color—pale raspberry, lavender, blue—with comforters to match. Room treats cover all tastes—fresh flowers for the sentimental guest, a different chocolate treat each day for the sweets lover, and a crystal decanter of Spanish sherry for philosophers.

For theatergoers—and almost every visitor to Ashland is one—the Winchester's location is a great convenience. From the patio, you can hear the trumpets summoning players and audience to the outdoor Shakespearean theater. Forsooth . . . take thine umbrella.

How to get there: On I–5 driving north, take the first Ashland exit; it becomes Main Street. Continue to center of town; turn left at Second Street, and go 2 blocks. The inn is on the right corner of Hargadine Street.

Olive Metcalf

The Johnson House
Florence, Oregon
97439

Innkeepers: Jayne and Ronald Fraese
Address/Telephone: 216 Maple Street (mailing address: Box 1892); (503) 997–8000
Rooms: 6, including The Rose Cottage; 3 with private bath. Limited wheelchair access. No smoking inn.
Rates: $75 to $85 with shared bath, $95 to $105 with private bath, double occupancy, full breakfast.
Open: All year.
Facilities and activities: Nearby: waterfront of Siuslaw River; shops, restaurants, antiques in Old Town Florence; lake fishing; Oregon Dunes Recreation Area; clamming, crabbing, beachcombing, bird watching.

    The coastal town of Florence could be one of your most enjoyable discoveries on a driving trip from California to Vancouver, B.C. It is the halfway point from San Francisco, just off Highway 101 and situated on the northern edge of the National Sand Dunes Recreation Area. This fabulous stretch of coast has beige-colored dunes higher than those of the Sahara, their contours constantly being changed by sand washed ashore and by the wind. They are wonderful to drive along or walk. Sometimes the coast lupines, strawberries, sand verbenas, and monkey flowers will be in bloom on the fore-dunes or on the open sand.
    The historic community nestles at the mouth of the wide Siuslaw River. The Johnson House is the oldest house in town, and

Jayne and Ronald have restored it and the house next door with an eye for original structure and details that give every room the atmosphere of warm Oregon coast living a century ago.

From the snow-white picket fence around the outside of The Johnson House and The Rose Cottage to the beautiful bed linens and puffy comforters inside, everything here looks fresh, clean, and light. It is a homey, comfortable atmosphere without frills. There are sinks in the rooms that share baths, tall ceilings, antiques, and lace curtains. A living room and a cozy sitting area at the stairway landing are inviting places to curl up and browse through the book collection.

Count on a hearty breakfast that varies daily. Menus include homemade breads, fresh fruits, and a variety of soufflés, omelets *aux fines herbes,* or crepes with fresh salmon.

For other meals, there is no need to get back in the car. A walk 1 block to the waterfront of Old Town Florence will introduce you to a colorful pioneer fishing village with small restaurants and coffee shops. The village is an appealing blend of old and new, with a small fishing fleet, antiques shops, and boutiques. Stop in the Siuslaw Pioneer Museum to see the logging and sailing artifacts from the glory days of the sailing schooners.

How to get there: From Highway 101, Florence is 1¹/₂ blocks east. The inn is on the left.

olive Metcalf

Tu Tú Tun Lodge
Gold Beach, Oregon
97444

Innkeepers: Dirk and Laurie Van Zante
Address/Telephone: 96550 North Bank Rogue; (503) 247–6664
Rooms: 16, including 2 suites each accommodating 6; all with private bath.
   Wheelchair access.
Rates: $115 to $155 for river-view rooms, $159 to $169 for suites, $189 for
   garden cottage, double occupancy, meals extra. $10 extra person.
   Daily rate for two including dinner and breakfast: $190 to $200.
Open: April 27 to October 27. Two suites with kitchens available all year.
Facilities and activities: Breakfast, lunch, dinner for guests or by reservation,
   full bar. Swimming pool, 4-hole putting green; jet boat white-water
   Rogue River trips; salmon and steelhead fishing, seasoned guides available. Nearby: scenic flights over Siskiyou Mountains, hiking, beach-
   combing, scenic drives, legalized gambling in Gold Beach.

In case you have the mistaken notion that the Northwest con-
sists only of fir trees and lumberjacks, consider the motto of Tu Tú
Tun Lodge: "Casual elegance in the wilderness on the famous
Rogue River."

That's summing it up modestly, for this is a very special blend
of sophistication and an outdoors-lover's paradise. Top-notch
accommodations and superb food are those of a classy resort, but
the young owners create a friendly atmosphere that's more like that
of a country inn.

Guest rooms are situated in a two-story building adjacent to the lodge. Each has comfortable easy chairs, extra-long beds, a dressing area, and a bath with tub and shower. Special touches that make wilderness life civilized aren't forgotten—fresh flowers, good reading lamps, and up-to-date magazines. Two recently redecorated rooms now have Japanese-style soaking tubs in their outdoor area. The suites can accommodate up to six persons each. No telephone or television intrudes as you watch the changing colors of the Rogue's waters at sunset from your private balcony or patio.

A bell at 6:30 P.M. calls guests to the lodge for cocktails and hors d'oeuvres. Dirk and Laurie introduce everyone, and by the time they seat you for dinner at round tables set for eight, you'll feel you're dining with friends. The set entree dinner they serve is outstanding. It always features regional specialties, frequently grilled over mesquite. Fresh chinook salmon, a soup, crisp salad made from locally grown greens, freshly baked bread or rolls, and a raspberry sorbet is a typical dinner.

After dinner, guests usually gather around the two fire pits on the terrace overlooking the river to enjoy an after-dinner drink, inhale the scent of jasmine, and take in the beauty all around. There's much to talk about as you share ideas for the next day's plans. If those plans call for an early-morning rising for fishing, a river trip, or hiking, breakfast and lunch baskets will be ready for you.

One adventure almost every visitor to the lodge tries is the exciting 104-mile white-water round trip up (and down) the river. Jet boats stop at the lodge's dock to pick up passengers in the morning.

How to get there: Driving north on Highway 101, pass through Gold Beach, cross bridge, and watch for signs on right to Rogue River Tavern. Turn right and drive 4 miles to tavern; follow signs another 3 miles to lodge on the right.

J: *The name comes from the Tu Tú Tun Indians who lived in a village on the very site of the Lodge. "Tunne" meant "people"; "Tu Tú Tunne" were "people close to the river."*

olive Metcalf

Columbia Gorge Hotel
Hood River, Oregon
97031

Innkeeper: Lynne La Fountaine
Address/Telephone: 4000 Westcliff Drive; (800) 345–1921
Rooms: 46, including 2 fireplace suites; all with private bath. Wheelchair
access.
Rates: $175 to $225, double occupancy, enormous farm breakfast. $35 for
each additional person in room. Ask about special package rates during
winter months.
Open: All year.
Facilities and activities: Breakfast, lunch, dinner. Valentino Lounge with
nightly entertainment, gift shop, beautiful grounds and gardens; facilities and arrangements made for weddings, business meetings. Nearby:
golf courses, Maryhill Museum, river rafting, skiing, hiking; stern-
wheeler excursion trips on Columbia River; sailboarding capital of "the
planet!"

When you're imposing, venerable, and have the word "hotel"
in your title, you're not exactly a country inn, but the Columbia
Gorge Hotel is too spectacular a setting to miss. Besides, they serve
one of the all-time great breakfasts *anywhere,* included in your room
rate.

Many people fondly remember the famous breakfast that origi-
nated at Snoqualmie Falls Lodge more than twenty-five years ago.
I'll never forget the wide-eyed wonder of three little boys when the
honey was swirled and poured with a flourish from high above the

table. The whole happening has been transplanted to the grander surroundings of the Columbia Gorge Hotel with all the important elements still in place. You'll read with astonishment a menu that warns, "It's not a choice; you'll get it all." And get it you do: fruits and apple fritters, old-fashioned oatmeal, sausages, pancakes, eggs, and the pièce de résistance, baking powder biscuits with apple blossom honey "poured from the sky." It's show biz—but so good!

Just an hour east of Portland, the red tile–roofed hotel sits high above the mighty Columbia on the edge of a deep canyon with sweeping vistas of Mt. Hood and Wah-Gwin-Gwin Falls, a 206-foot cascade that tumbles into the river just behind the hotel. It was built in 1921 by timber baron Simon Benson. The elegantly appointed large public rooms, massive plastered beams, and decor still have a nostalgic '20s feeling, even though everything has recently been redecorated and modernized. Valentino and Clara Bow are two Jazz Era names who supposedly were guests. The Valentino Cocktail Lounge off the lobby (containing a fireplace and grand piano) is named for him.

Only two rooms have a fireplace, but each room is individually decorated, simply and comfortably. You can have garden or river views. About thirteen acres surround the hotel, grounds that have most visitors walking among the gardens with a camera in hand. From April to mid-November, it's a picture of thousands of blooming plants.

You should know that the hotel is frequently the location for business meetings where participants hold meetings and wear name tags. But celebrities are common among the guests here, also, Doc Severinson and Burt and Loni among them. July is one of the most exciting times to be here. That's when the international competition in sailboarding takes place. Quite a sight on the Columbia.

How to get there: Driving east along the Oregon side of Columbia River, take exit 62, off I–84 in Hood River. Fly-in: Hood River County Airport just minutes away.

Olive Metcalf

Jacksonville Inn
Jacksonville, Oregon
97530

Innkeepers: Jerry and Linda Evans

Address/Telephone: 175 East California Street (mailing address: P.O. Box 359); (503) 899–1900

Rooms: 9, including historic cottage; all with private bath, air conditioning, and television.

Rates: $80 to $100, double occupancy; $175 for cottage, full breakfast.

Open: All year.

Facilities and activities: Dinner, Sunday brunch. Lounge, wine and gift shop. Nearby: historic Jacksonville's restored homes, museum, art galleries, shops; Britt Music and Art Festival June through August; 15-mile drive to Ashland theaters.

Jacksonville is a wonderful discovery, the oldest town in southern Oregon. It began in 1851 with the discovery of gold in Rich Gulch, but, unlike so many mining boomtowns, it didn't become a ghost town when the gold ran out; quartz mining was to follow.

Exploring an old mining town is always a history of tragedies, and Jacksonville has survived its share. A smallpox epidemic in 1868 killed many of the original settlers; a flood in 1869 swept tons of mud and rock through the center of town; and fires destroyed most of the town's original frame buildings.

The inn is one of Jacksonville's early permanent structures—a two-story brick building erected in 1861. The walls of the dining room and lounge were built of sandstone quarried locally, and specks of gold are visible in the mortar. The eight bedrooms over the restaurant, lounge, and gift shop are up a stairway at the side of the building. They are not large, but each has a private bath and is individually decorated. The look is refreshingly uncluttered, attractively furnished rooms with antiques from the area: brass beds, rockers, and oak highboys with beveled mirrors.

A full breakfast is served between 8:00 and 10:00 A.M. in the dining room: fresh-fruit plate followed by your choice from an enticing menu. A few items offered on a recent morning were fresh poached fish with a tomato caper relish, spinach and mushroom gâteau with Mornay sauce, brioche French toast, Belgian waffle with fresh berries, and homemade granola with fresh fruit. Dinner offerings are pasta, prime rib, veal, and specialties such as fresh salmon and razor clams in season. The Evanses are proud of their cellar of more than 500 wines.

This old town abounds with things for the tourist to do. They range from soaking up historical atmosphere in the cemetery (any fancier of headstone inscriptions will relish some of them here, like HANGED FOR A KILLING) to a banquet of cultural events and attractions in the area. The Britt Music Festival June through August is an outstanding music series featuring international musicians giving nightly concerts running the gamut from jazz to country to classical in the beautiful setting of the Britt Gardens. To enjoy the full flavor of a concert under the stars, ask the inn to prepare a picnic basket for you, then walk up the street to the Gardens. This is what summer nights are made for.

How to get there: From Highway 5 between Phoenix and Grants Pass take any of these roads west into town: South Stage Road, Highway 238, or Hanley Road; take Applegate Road or Old Stage Road leading south into town. All roads lead to the town's main street, California, and the inn.

❀

J: *If you want to know what's playing at the Britt Festival and to get ticket information, call (800) 88–BRITT.*

olive Metcalf

Under the Greenwood Tree
Medford, Oregon
97501

Innkeeper: Renate Ellam

Address/Telephone: 3045 Bellinger Lane; (503) 776–0000

Rooms: 4; all with private bath with tub and hand-held shower. Smoking on porches only.

Rates: $85 to $105, double occupancy, lavish breakfast and high tea. Single rate $5 less.

Open: All year.

Facilities and activities: Bicycles, paddock facilities, accommodates weddings and private parties. Nearby: restaurants, historic Jacksonville and Britt Music Festival June–September, Ashland Shakespeare Festival, Mt. Ashland skiing, Rogue River rafting, antiquing in Medford, short trips to Crater Lake, Oregon Caves National Monument.

No matter how delicious the food at an inn may be, sometimes you have to speak first of the innkeeper. So it is at Under the Greenwood Tree, owned, inspired, cherished, decorated, and directed by Renate Ellam and indelibly stamped with her ebullient personality.

She brings an abundance of experience (she was a San Francisco designer) and skills (she's a Cordon Bleu graduate cook) to the art of innkeeping. And art is what she makes it. If that sounds like grandiose praise for a four-room bed-and-breakfast inn, try it before you judge.

Her 125-year-old farmhouse sits on ten acres with old apple, pear, cedar, and black walnut trees. Renate was directing the construction of a gazebo when I arrived, and she pointed out sixty-five recently planted rose bushes. There is nostalgic appeal to this land and old farm buildings, some dating from 1861. The granary and weigh station are possibly the oldest in Oregon.

In the house, a first glance tells you it's been decorated by a professional; a second look tells you the rugs are real Persian; the quilts museum quality; and fabrics, wallpaper, antiques, and art objects are quite special. But is it comfortable, you ask? True, the rooms are not large, but with lovely decor, a private bath, top-of-the-line mattresses, and elegant linens, you don't belong at an inn if you have a complaint here.

The heart of Renate's style is the joy she seems to get from nurturing people. It begins with a warm welcome and a 4:30 P.M. high tea. At night she turns down the bed and leaves a handmade European truffle with a copy of the lines about the Greenwood tree from *As You Like It*. Nothing pleases her more than doing something special for an anniversary or a celebration like a garden wedding around her unique gazebo. One season she noticed guests returning downcast from performances of *Macbeth* in Ashland and decided a dessert repast was needed to send them off to bed more cheerfully.

Renate serves a full gourmet breakfast by an old parlor stove in a sunny dining room overlooking acres of lawns. The scene may be country charm, but the table service is sterling silver and Rosenthal china, the tables are hand-carved, and the chairs upholstered in velvet. The menu springs fresh every day from the best local ingredients available and Renate's inspiration. This day there were raspberries picked that morning, homemade muffins and nut bread, white grape and cranberry juices, a soufflé with Oregon cheese, and a dessert course extravaganza.

How to get there: From I–5 driving north, exit at ramp 27, Barnett Road, turn left onto overpass; at first signal turn left on Stewart. Follow approximately 3 miles until it becomes Hull. Continue 1 block; turn right on Bellinger Lane. Inn is on the left.

olive Metcalf

The Sylvia Beach Hotel
Newport, Oregon
97365

Innkeeper: Goody Cable
Address/Telephone: 267 N.W. Cliff; (503) 265–5428
Rooms: 20; all with private bath, some with ocean view, fireplace, patio or
deck. No smoking inn.
Rates: $45 single to $125 double, breakfast and hot spiced wine in library at
10:00 P.M. Two-night minimum on Saturday.
Open: All year.
Facilities and activities: Tables of Content Restaurant serves breakfast and din-
ner; wine and beer available. Gift shop, ocean-view library. Nearby:
miles of shoreline to explore.

There are two kinds of people in this world: those who rarely
pick up a book once they escape school, and we other enlightened,
productive, noble souls who believe books, not bread, are the staff
of life. If you are among the latter, read on, for here is an inn to
delight you.

The hotel is named for the owner of the Paris bookstore
Shakespeare and Co., the well-known patron, booster, publisher,
and soft touch for so many of the Lost Generation, that glamorous
group of writers of the '20s and '30s. This is a literary lodging, with
all the trappings and every nuance contributing to that atmosphere.
The large, four-story dark green wooden structure with a red roof
stands on a bluff overlooking the surf. (It would add to the atmo-

sphere if you could arrange to arrive on a dark and stormy night. We arrived on a sunny summer afternoon, but never mind.) A large painting of Sylvia Beach and James Joyce opposite the check-in desk sets the tone immediately. Even here in the lobby/common room, some guests who were bicycling the coast rested their back-packs and sat reading. Others browsed the gift shop area with its small but interesting inventory of new books and a wonderful collection of photographs and drawings of every literary light you've ever heard of.

Each bedroom is named for an author and has an appropriate theme decor. There are three categories of accommodation: Classics, Best Sellers, and Novels. Classics (oceanfront with fireplace and deck) include Agatha Christie on the first floor, Mark Twain and Colette on the second. Best Sellers–Hemingway, E. B. White, and Alice Walker among them–all have an ocean view. Emily Dickinson and Tennessee Williams are an unlikely duo sharing the second floor with Dr. Seuss and others. Novels are without an ocean view, but two have patios. A dormitory-style room is provided for the children of guests.

Choose your author-named room carefully, according to your taste. They range from a hilariously macabre Edgar Allen Poe room (with black wallpaper, a raven on the nightstand, and a pendulum over the bed) to an opulent Agatha Christie suite with clues from Christie mysteries hidden somewhere in the room. A perfectly wonderful second-floor library fronts the ocean and ascends to the attic. This sprawling room with fireplace, sofas, and comfortable chairs is lined with photographs of authors. Here is where you'll have hot spiced wine served at 10:00 P.M.

Tables of Content is the name of the restaurant on the lower floor where meals are served family style. This is not just ordinary hotel fare—this is excellent cuisine specializing in fresh local seafood and all-homemade breads and desserts.

It seems to me, the reason for seeking out inns is to find something different and have an experience you're unlikely to find in a motel. For that reason alone, The Sylvia Beach is truly a trip.

How to get there: From Highway 101 in downtown Newport, turn west on Northwest Third and follow it down to the beach where it meets Cliff. The hotel is located right on the ocean.

olive Metcalf

General Hooker's B&B
Portland, Oregon
97201

Innkeeper: Lori Hall

Address/Telephone: 125 S.W. Hooker; (503) 222–4435 (phone and fax); (800) 745–4135

Rooms: 4; 1 with private bath, 3 rooms share 2 baths; all with air conditioning, cable television, and VCR. No smoking inn.

Rates: $60 to $95, single occupancy; double occupancy usually $10 more; generous vegetarian continental breakfast and afternoon beverage.

Open: All year.

Facilities and activities: Library; extensive catalogued taped movie collection for VCRs; pleasant old neighborhood for walking. Nearby: excellent YMCA facilities, public track, parks, tennis courts; walk or public transportation to Pioneer Courthouse Square, PSU, Performing Arts Center, Waterfront Park, shops, restaurants, Oregon Health Science University.

With its gingerbread trim painted prettily, this dainty Victorian house seen from the outside predicts an interior you won't find. Lori Hall has been cheerfully unauthentic in restoring the house in a tree-lined, gentrifying neighborhood at the edge of Portland's downtown. Inside you find an atmosphere that is not nineteenth-century at all; the feeling is light, open, and contemporary. Lori calls it "neo-Victorian." I call it comfortable.

She has blended a few massive antique pieces with her fascinating collection of modern art and books and set it all against a background of white, touches of navy and tan, and neutral-color textured fabrics. A small parlor/sitting room is as interesting as it is comfortable.

On the landing of the stairway up to the bedrooms is an impressive mirror, old and enormous. At the top of the steps in the hallway is a refrigerator stocked with wine and soft drinks. My room was the Iris. It has a private entry via a roof deck with a glamorous view at night of downtown Portland. The room was sleek and cheerful: a comfortable daybed extended to double bed size, a desk, a built-in buffet for wine glasses, books, television, and VCR. (The film collection is downstairs.) The Victorian element was a handsome armoire. Combined with the Daisy, these two rooms make a suite for three or four with private bath and entry.

The largest room is the Rose, with a 7-foot-long bed, private bath, and skylight view. This room, as they all do, has access to the roof deck. Colors are bone white and navy, a beautiful batik patchwork comforter is on the bed, and touches of rattan are around the room.

It wasn't surprising to meet a young woman, another guest, traveling alone on business. This is just the kind of secure, relaxed atmosphere that increasing numbers of businesswomen are discovering as an alternative to a confining motel room. We talked around the breakfast table in the morning, enjoying the fresh fruit, homemade granola, hot muffins, and good coffee. Lori Hall is a fourth-generation Portlander who really knows and loves her city.

I know you're bored with tales of ubiquitous inn cats, but mention must be made of the Hooker B&B cat. She's named Happy, of course, and she even gets her own mail. This velvety Abyssinian thinks she is a dog and races up and down the steps playing fetch. Hilarious? Maybe you have to be there.

How to get there: Hooker Street is in the downtown area between Southwest First and Second Avenue, 1½ blocks east of Barbur Boulevard. Coming from downtown, get on First Avenue at the Marriott Hotel and go south for ¾ mile to Hooker. Turn right to the inn with its lamppost on the right side.

Olive Metcalf

Portland's White House
Portland, Oregon
97212

Innkeepers: Larry and Mary Hough
Address/Telephone: 1914 N.E. Twenty-second Avenue; (503) 287–7131
Rooms: 6, including 1 carriage house suite; all with private bath, TV upon request. No smoking inn.
Rates: $88 to $104, suite $135, double occupancy, full breakfast and afternoon tea.
Open: All year.
Facilities and activities: Grand setting and facilities for weddings, receptions, private parties, business meetings. TV in ballroom. Nearby: Portland's shops, Saturday Market, restored waterfront area, restaurants.

How do you feel about the White House as a B&B? When you go to Portland, you'll have a chance to try an inn that looks remarkably similar to the Washington, D.C., lodging.

At the Portland White House, stately Greek columns, circular driveway, fountains, and landscaped grounds are a pleasant alternative to big-city accommodations. What's more, the rates are less than a downtown hotel, and you have the advantages of staying in a pleasant area to walk, with plenty of free parking and a full breakfast elegantly served.

This big white house in a quiet residential neighborhood is what you would expect of a lumber baron's home: pretty impressive. Through the mahogany front doors is a large entry hall with its original hand-painted murals and oak inlaid floors. At one side is a formal parlor, its French windows draped in lace, which is quite inviting as a sitting room for guests. At the other end of the hall, the formal dining room is a blend of mahogany, crystal chandeliers, and a lace-covered dining table. A hearty full breakfast is served here, on the patio, or in your room.

A sweeping central staircase leads to six guest rooms on the second floor. They are sweetly old-fashioned with a mixture of antiques and old favorites. All the rooms have queen-sized beds, and three of these are canopy beds. The Balcony Room affords the opportunity to fantasize about the roaring crowds below yelling for your victory . . . or maybe your neck.

When you watch Larry and Mary Hough work together as afternoon guests begin arriving, you would have to agree they're a perfect team. "We've found our niche," says Mary. Her mother ran a boardinghouse in England, so she comes from a legacy of innkeeping. Mary, who is Irish, used to buy and sell antiques, but taking on this 1912 mansion (with forty-three leaks in the roof) was a big leap. They seem to thrive on it.

The Houghs make a strong bid for hosting special events. The house lends itself well to weddings, parties, and business meetings. If the word I hear is correct, that cocktail parties are coming back into fashion, this would be a grand place to have one.

No one who lives here agreed with me, but I found Portland confusing and difficult to drive around. In addition to the directions below, get some backup detail from the Houghs when you make your reservation.

How to get there: Driving south on I-5, take the Lloyd Center–Coliseum exit to the second stoplight. Turn right on Wilder. Continue to Twenty-second Avenue and turn right; continue 3 blocks to the inn. Driving north on I-5, take the Lloyd Center exit to the first stoplight. Turn right on Wilder and continue as above.

J: *The doorbell doesn't play "Hail To the Chief" (personally, I think it would be a nice touch), but the Houghs do keep George Bush in a cage. He's the house bird.*

olive Metcalf

The Boarding House
Seaside, Oregon
97138

Innkeepers: Dick and Barb Edwards
Address/Telephone: 208 North Holladay Drive; (503) 738–9055
Rooms: 6, plus 1 cottage; all with private bath and television. No smoking inn.
Rates: $55 to $95, double occupancy, breakfast. Deduct $5 for single; add $10 for each additional person. Children under 3 are free.
Open: All year.
Facilities and activities: Piano, Victrola, fireplace in parlor. Nearby: biking, kite flying, beach, clam digging, swimming, fishing on Necanicum River; Seaside shops, restaurants; annual Yuletide in Seaside, volleyball tournaments, Dixieland jazz festivals.

THIS OLD HOUSE SERVES COMFORT is the motto posted at the door. The rustic 1898 Victorian boardinghouse on the Necanicum River keeps that promise, and at a refreshingly modest price. It was once a house where railroad workers and travelers new to the area came and went. Built entirely of fir tongue-and-groove lumber, with beamed ceilings and paneling throughout, the house has been completely restored. Modern comforts include private baths, color televisions, and a private side entrance. Brass and white iron beds, down quilts, antiques, and wicker add a country touch.

There is a delightful paneled parlor for relaxing with a piano, comfortable sofa and chairs, and a window seat. One feature sure to please those intrepid souls who travel with children is that this inn actually welcomes little ones. Barb Edwards says "This is a family-oriented inn, so we have it fairly childproof. We also have high chairs, playpens, and daybeds."

Behind the house is a 100-year-old cottage sitting right on the river. It has been renovated and is a wonderful family accommodation sleeping six. Children will love the sleeping loft. Parents will appreciate that it is self-contained with a microwave. The river is also great for entertainment, watching the ducks and heron, or taking out one of the paddle boats available for rent.

Breakfast is served in a sunny, paneled dining room with beamed ceilings, a built-in buffet, touches of stained glass, and another big window seat. Tables are covered to the floor with blue-and-white cloths. You can also take your breakfast outside to a wraparound porch.

The Edwardses' menu is a full one with juices, lots of fresh fruit, and something like a fancy French toast with fresh berry sauce and whipped cream or a special egg dish and rich coffee cake as typical entrees.

The town of Seaside is in the extreme northwest corner of Oregon in an area called the North Coast. This marks the end of the Lewis and Clark Trail and encompasses the oldest settlement in the West: Astoria.

One of the joys of being in a quaint seaside town is to forget the car and walk to all the attractions. From the Boarding House, you are 4 blocks from the ocean and 2 blocks from downtown. The nearly 2-mile beach promenade is lined with charming old houses. You can rent horses, or dig for clams, or surf fish. The resort-atmosphere town has small shops and a variety of restaurants. Dick and Barb will point you in the direction of your interest.

How to get there: Exit Highway 101 at Seaside and follow signs to City Center; the street becomes Holladay Drive. Inn is on the right.

J: *That thirty-pound chinook salmon that's been eluding you just might be here off the banks of the Necanicum.*

olive Metcalf

Gilbert Inn
Seaside, Oregon
97138

Innkeepers: Dick and Carole Rees
Address/Telephone: 341 Beach Drive; (503) 738–9770
Rooms: 10, including 2 suites; all with private bath with tub and shower; color television. No smoking inn.
Rates: $65 to $85, October through March 30; $70 to $90, April through September; double occupancy, full breakfast.
Open: All year except January.
Facilities and activities: Nearby: 1 block to the beach, 1 block to main street shops, restaurants, other attractions; Quatat Marine Park, Seaside Museum, Tillamook Head Trail, Fort Stevens State Park, Cannon Beach.

Dick and Carole Rees cut their innkeeping teeth as owners of The Boarding House, another inn in Seaside. With the purchase of the Gilbert Inn, they found an exceptionally attractive building worthy of their considerable talents for turning a house into an inn.

This Queen Anne Victorian was built by Alexander Gilbert in 1892. It must have been the most beautiful house in town then, but today, after the Reeses' lavish attentions, it is the very picture of a seaside inn—a yellow-and-white stunner with turret, porches, flagpole, gardens, and white picket fence. The parlor you enter signals the refreshing style of these innkeepers. They have a century-old house but have opted for traditional comfort and contemporary good taste rather than quaint clutter. The big fireplace in the center of the room and the natural fir tongue-and-groove ceilings and walls throughout the house contribute a cozy warmth and appealing period charm. But the dazzling green rug and fresh floral covering on sofas and chairs are fashionable and lively.

Each of the eight bedrooms and two suites is distinct and decorated so engagingly that I couldn't choose one over another. The thick carpeting, down comforters, linens, and pillows are all fine quality. Again, Carole has decorated captivating, pretty rooms but without clutter. The Turret Room is popular with its tall four-poster bed, old fir ceilings and walls, and the turret window. The Garret constitutes the entire third floor and has a queen and two twin beds.

Breakfast is served on a restored side porch that looks out on a flower garden. Pink walls, white iron tables and chairs, pink-and-white oriental rugs, and lots of green plants make the setting one of the prettiest places you'll ever linger over breakfast. I wonder how the Reeses ever get their guests to move on. Breakfast menus include a wide variety of Rees specialties, but one recipe is an especially big hit—French toast with a filling of cream cheese and walnuts, baked and served with an apricot sauce.

But Seaside is a popular and historic town and there are things to see. Many of the town's attractions are within walking distance of the inn. The Turnaround, at the end of Broadway (the main street) is the official end of the Lewis and Clark trail. This is a spot to watch the sun set over the Pacific.

How to get there: Driving north, exit Highway 101 at the city center on Holiday Drive. Continue to a flashing red light, Avenue A; turn left and proceed to the beach. Inn is on the left corner at A and Beach. Driving south, exit 101 at North Broadway. Proceed 2 blocks past Broadway to Avenue B. Turn right to the ocean. Inn is on the left.

J: *As of this writing, the standards of quality and comfort to be found at Gilbert Inn make it one of the best bargains I found on the Oregon Coast.*

olive Metcalf

Steamboat Inn
Steamboat, Oregon
97447–9703

Innkeepers: Sharon and Jim Van Loan; Patricia Lee, manager

Address/Telephone: Located on the North Umpqua River; (503) 496–3495 or 498–2411; fax (503) 498–2411*2

Rooms: 8 cabins, 5 cottages, 2 river suites; all with private bath; cottages and suites with fireplace, living room, minikitchen, and soaking tub. Limited wheelchair access.

Rates: Cabins, $85; cottages, $125; river suites, $195; double occupancy, breakfast extra. Addtional adults, $20.

Open: All year.

Facilities and activities: Breakfast, lunch, dinner daily; special Fisherman's Dinner ($30) for inn guests or by reservation, weekends only during winter season; wine and beer bar; no smoking in restaurant. Nearby: steelhead fishing, swimming, nature trails, downhill and cross-country skiing, vineyards.

After a twisting 38-mile drive along the North Umpqua River, in a downpour that never slowed, the welcome at Steamboat Inn was underwhelming. I was looking for a cup of coffee and good cheer. Instead, I entered a room pungent with gloom. Seated morosely around a 20-foot-long pine table were a dozen fishermen.

They eyed this intruder sourly and went back to staring bleakly out the windows. The frustrated group, I learned, were angling fanatics from all over the world, who come to this extraordinary 39-mile stretch of white water reserved strictly for fly fishing and who feel very proprietary about it. Only destiny and the inn's gastronomical reputation had brought us together.

Pat Lee, who doubles as chef and angling guide, rescued me with coffee and a tour that was cheering. This may be "the greatest stretch of summer steelhead water in the United States," as Jack Hemingway says, but it's also an idyllic spot for readers and loafers.

The rustic main room with a huge rock fireplace opens onto a glass-enclosed sun porch where meals are served. Beyond the flowers and trees are eight cabins sitting right on the river, connected by a long deck. You needn't be a fisherman to have a visceral reponse to the majestic setting of tall fir trees and white water tumbling past. The cabins are unexpectedly well appointed: paneled and carpeted, furnished comfortably, all with modern baths, good beds, and reading lights. And each room opens onto the deck. Cottages, in a wooded setting one-half mile from the inn, and two new river suites have more luxurious amenities—fireplace, living room, soaking tub, and minikitchen.

All day, the kitchen serves hearty breakfasts, fast lunches, and early dinners to distracted anglers. But come evening, the restaurant closes, and the inn assumes a different identity. Out come linens, silver, candles, and it's haute cuisine on the North Umpqua: The Fisherman's Dinner.

In deference to fishermen who can't quit until dark, wine is poured and hors d'oeuvres are set out half an hour *after* sunset. Sharon Van Loan and Pat do the classy cooking that has won compliments from *Fly Fisherman* to *Gourmet*. A typical entree might be a pork loin in lemon-basil marinade, sauced with a tomato, thyme, and applejack combination; perfectly braised carrots with hints of mustard and mint; then a watercress salad with hazelnuts, followed by freshly ground coffee and perhaps a Bavarian chocolate torte.

Do real fishermen deserve less?

How to get there: From Roseburg, take Highway 138 east for 38 scenic miles along the North Umpqua River. Inn is on the right.

olive Metcalf

Wolf Creek Tavern
Wolf Creek, Oregon
97497

Innkeepers: Joy and Mike Carter
Address/Telephone: 100 Front Street (mailing address: P.O. Box 97); (503) 866–2474
Rooms: 8; all with private bath and air conditioning. Wheelchair access.
Rates: $45, double occupancy; $60 for Parlor Chamber; continental breakfast $3 extra.
Open: All year except Christmas Day and first two weeks in January.
Facilities and activities: Breakfast, lunch, dinner, Sunday brunch; wine and beer bar; small seminar and wedding facilities. Nearby: 20 miles to Grants Pass headquarters for Rogue River fishing and boating guides; U.S. Forest Service Office for maps, information about 40-mile Rogue hiking trail.

Looking for all the world just like a stagecoach stop ought to look, the Wolf Creek Tavern looms up unexpectedly among dense trees along Highway 5. The imposing two-story white building was once a way station for stages that stopped on the six-day trip between Portland and Sacramento.

Wolf Creek Tavern's history is surrounded by legendary romantic—and largely unauthenticated—events, but records indicate that it was built around 1857. The State Parks and Recreation Division acquired it in 1975 and leases it to the Carters to operate as an inn.

Today the tavern is providing good food and beverages, comfortable beds, and old-fashioned hospitality for the traveling public, but with some modern conveniences. They include heating, air conditioning, and a bath for every room. These are unpretentious rooms, clean, plain, and simple. Furnishings in the first-floor rooms represent pieces from the early 1900s to the 1930s, but one of the rooms upstairs has been furnished as an 1870s chamber. Another special bit of history preserved upstairs is a tiny room with a single bed where Jack London used to stay.

On the first floor, a central stair and hallway divide the ladies' parlor from the men's sitting room—the taproom. Original paint colors were researched and have been reproduced on walls, woodwork, and chimneys. The tavern and dining room have pine floors and rustic tables with burgundy and blue cloths. Waitresses dress in period costume.

At dinner, as I listened to the banter between the staff and familiar locals who had stopped in for the innkeepers' good cooking, I wondered where they had come from. Driving in a few hours earlier, it seemed as though this was practically a wilderness, and now the sounds of friendly travelers having a good time filled the tavern.

Entree choices included Athenian scampi, scallops in sauce Suisse, and weekend tavern specialties such as prime rib. I planned ahead for the night's special dessert: fresh peach-and-apple crisp . . . a la mode. Good thinking. Homey old dishes like this made with fresh fruit from the garden are so soul-satisfying.

How to get there: Leave I-5 about 20 miles north of Grants Pass at exit 76. Follow the signs to Wolf Creek.

෧

J: *This remote stop gives you a feeling for what it must have meant to earlier travelers to find good cheer and hospitality after hours of bouncing in a stagecoach.*

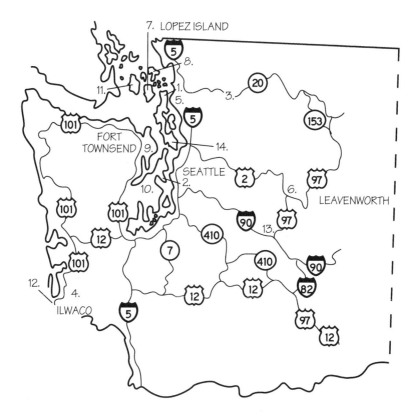

7. LOPEZ ISLAND

8.

11.

1.

3.

20

153

101

FORT
TOWNSEND

9.

5.

5.

14.

SEATTLE

2.

2

6.

97

LEAVENWORTH

10.

101

101

12

90

13.

97

410

7

410

90

12.

101

12

12

82

4.

97

ILWACO

5

12

Washington

Numbers on map refer to towns numbered below.

Olive Metcalf

The Channel House
Anacortes, Washington
98221

Innkeepers: Pat and Dennis McIntyre
Address/Telephone: 2902 Oakes Avenue; (206) 293–9382
Rooms: 6; 4 with private bath. No smoking inn.
Rates: $69 to $89, double occupancy, breakfast and evening snack.
Open: All year.
Facilities and activities: Hot tub. Nearby: restaurants, ferry docks leading to San Juan Islands, British Columbia; explore Deception Pass, Washington Park, Mt. Erie.

A bedroom off the library was mine when I first stayed in this 1902 Victorian. It's a pretty room with a brass bed, a log-cabin quilt made by Dennis's mother, and other antique appointments. From the bathroom you can see the Guemes Channel and the San Juan Islands. Two guest rooms have recently been added in Rose Cottage, behind the main house. Each has a private bath with whirlpool tub, a fireplace, and a queen-sized bed. The inn's facilities are not well suited to children under twelve.

The library itself is a fine place to spend time—a good stereo, comfortable furniture, and interesting books and magazines. Making yourself at home for an evening among another person's books is almost as personal as moving into his or her bedroom. In the case of the McIntyres, the library reflects Pat's English background, a love of spy novels, mysteries, current fiction, and the history and biography that Dennis reads.

Pat's decorating is fun—not an all-Victorian theme or mood, but rather a collection of interesting pieces: an elegant antique here, a romantic chaise there, enlivened with something amusing like stuffed sheep (on the stairs) she brought back from Scotland.

Two bedrooms upstairs have the best view in the house—from the claw-footed tub in the common bathroom. An elegant dining room with French doors going out to the garden is downstairs from the living room. Breakfast here consists of especially fine coffee (made from a blend of fresh beans), fresh fruit, a variety of hot entrees like stuffed French toast, and homemade muffins with several spreads.

"Doing" the islands is one of the main reasons one comes to Anacortes, but trying to figure out the least expensive route while stopping at all the towns you want to see can loom as a complex undertaking. The McIntyres are thoughtful hosts who will help you make sense of the ferry schedule and even volunteer breakfast at a time convenient to the ferry you want to catch. This is the kind of treatment that gives innkeeping a good name.

How to get there: From Seattle, take I–5 north to junction with State 20 past Mt. Vernon. Follow 20 west to Anacortes. Remain on 20 through town. The name changes to Commercial, then Oakes. Inn is on the right. Fly-in: Anacortes airport.

J: *Here's a suggestion for touring the islands that makes sense: Buy cheap walk-on tickets for the ferry, returning at night to Channel House as home base. The savings when you don't take a car are significant, and you can always rent bikes or mopeds for exploring during the day.*

Olive Metcalf

The Bombay House
Bainbridge Island, Washington
98110

Innkeepers: Bunny Cameron and Roger Kanchuk
Address/Telephone: 8490 N.E. Beck Road; (206) 842–3926
Rooms: 5, including 1 suite; suite and 2 on first floor with private bath, all with air conditioning. No smoking inn.
Rates: $55 to $95, double occupancy, expanded continental breakfast.
Open: All year.
Facilities and activities: Nearby: an island to bicycle; Fort Worden State Park, Eagle Harbor Waterfront Park, Indian battlegrounds, picnic areas, tennis courts, golf; shopping, restaurants in Winslow.

At Bombay House, you can sit at the breakfast table enjoying muffins, homemade granola, and fresh fruits and watch the big white ferries gliding through Rich Passage. All the ships bound for the Bremerton Navy Yards go through, too. In the daytime, it is endlessly fascinating; at night, the lighted ferries look like ocean liners in the dark waters.

"Unlikely" is the way the big house strikes me. Part Victorian, part nautical, and part just the independent ideas of the master shipbuilder who built it in 1907. The house sits on a half acre of green lawn, a hilltop location with marine views and wonderful unstructured gardens. It's a delightful place for a country-style wedding—there is even a rustic, rough cedar gazebo. During my May visit, a big American flag was flapping in the breeze, the flowers were glorious, and twisted old apple trees looked romantic.

If you have visited the inn before, you will surely remember the unexpected sight of a full-size rabbit named James Brown snoozing on the brick open-hearth fireplace. Poor James passed on to that great bunny patch in the sky Thanksgiving 1989. He has been replaced as necessary "cute" inn animal with Rex, the cat. Rex is quite the hunter and entertains guests at the breakfast table with bird-watching alerts.

The bedrooms are all roomy, except for the cozy Crows Nest, which has one of the best views from the house—but you have to be in bed to see it. The Captain's Suite is the spacious master bedroom upstairs. You have good views from here, a sitting area with a wood stove, small refrigerator, game table, and sleeper couch. The bathroom facilities feature a claw-footed tub and a shower. The first-floor King Room has a unique blue-tin soaking tub in the room. The Red Room has a brass bed, a sitting area, and a tub and shower across the hall.

This is an informal house with a casual kind of atmosphere. The morning meal is served in the kitchen, not a formal dining room, and the innkeepers have a young child. Bunny says that at Christmas they have custom decorations that are great.

How to get there: From Seattle, take Winslow Ferry to Bainbridge. Proceed left on Winslow Way, right on Madison, left on Wyatt. Turn right at the Y in the road. Past the elementary school on your left, bear to the right down the hill. Turn right on Beck. The inn is on the corner.

✳

J: *On a scale of one to ten, the thirty-minute ferry ride from Seattle Harbor to Bainbridge Island rates a ten: a glorious panorama of that city's skyline and the romantic fun of heading for an island!*

olive Metcolf

Cascade Mountain Inn
Birdsview-Concrete, Washington
98237

Innkeepers: Ingrid and Gerhard Meyer
Address/Telephone: 3840 Pioneer Lane; (206) 826–4333
Rooms: 6; all with private bath. No smoking inn.
Rates: $70 to $90, double occupancy, full breakfast.
Open: May 15 to October 15.
Facilities and activities: Dinners arranged if one party books entire inn; spectacular setting. Nearby: restaurants; nature hikes, biking, fishing, Skagit River boat launch, North Cascades National Park.

Snoqualmie, Snohomish, Klickitat, Quinault. Colorful place names are indigenous to Washington state, so why my enthusiasm for a placed called Concrete? Merely because it's a region of such startling natural beauty it leaves you tongue-tied; a little-known area of rich green meadows, deep river valleys, lush forests, and, towering over all, the amazing, always snowcapped Cascade Range. Besides, the town name has recently acquired a hyphenated upgrade to Birdsview-Concrete.

Sitting on ten acres of meadowland bordered by the North Cascades is the handsomely designed new (1985) Cascade Mountain Inn. The Meyers had been coming here for years with their sons to fish. When Gerhard Meyer retired after thirty years of international corporate life, he and his wife, Ingrid, chose this remote spot to build an inn from Ingrid's design.

Having been all over the world, the Meyers have a collection of furniture and art from each place they lived that now makes their inn a kind of international house. Eiderdown quilts and pillows, furniture, and porcelain plates decorate the German room. Bamboo, shells, lace, and oil paintings from the Philippines depict that region. The Peruvian room in warm brown has handwoven bedspreads, a duo of handsome leather chairs, and smaller Peruvian articles like hats, calabashes, and money bags. American and Scottish rooms are also in the main house. In addition to their interesting decor, these are spacious rooms, comfortable and immaculately maintained. The sixth room is a large studio over the garage decorated with tiles and wall hangings from the Meyers' hometown, Bremen. With a separate entrance, minikitchen, and nonstop views, this is a very private snuggery.

Ingrid gives a European flavor to her efficient kitchen style. She makes and serves six different kinds of bread and jam. There's her European granola (müesli) and yogurt mixed with fresh fruit or, in winter, blueberries and raspberries she has frozen. These and more keep guests happy at breakfast while she does the hot dish, maybe quiche or German pancakes, served at a big table in a cheerful glassed-in breakfast room looking out at the meadow or on the patio.

Few people are familiar with this scenic region, but the Meyers are, and they take great delight in sharing suggestions for activities at every time of year. Day-trip possibilities abound. They'll pack and label breakfast and lunch for hikers who want to start out early. They know where to point you when the salmon and steelhead are running, or what programs or classes might be available from the North Cascades Institute. In the winter you're welcome to sit around the fireplace in the living room (a television is here), and in summer, there's often a campfire outside. Warm hospitality is a part of the package with the Meyers . . . it's their natural way.

How to get there: From I–5 north of Burlington, drive 24 miles east on Highway 20 to a sign reading LODGING, NEXT RIGHT. Turn right on Wild Road ¹/₄ mile to Pioneer Lane. Turn right.

The Inn at Ilwaco
Ilwaco, Washington
98624–0922

Innkeeper: Laurie Blancher
Address/Telephone: 120 Williams Street N.E. (mailing address: P.O. Box 922); (206) 642–8686
Rooms: 9; 7 with private bath, cots available. No smoking inn.
Rates: $55 to $75, double occupancy, breakfast. $15 additional person.
Open: All year.
Facilities and activities: Frequent plays and concert productions at The Playhouse; customized arrangements for meetings, weddings, family gatherings; mystery weekends for twelve to eighteen people. Nearby: restaurants; Fort Canby, Fort Columbia State Parks; Lewis and Clark Interpretive Center; North Head and Cape Disappointment lighthouses; two 9-hole golf courses; miles of ocean beaches; charter-boat salmon fishing.

I smiled when Ginger Brewer, one of the Ilwaco inn's owners, described the town enthusiastically as a "great destination point." One thing is sure, you have to *want* to go to Ilwaco to get there.

The funny thing is—Ginger is quite right about this off-the-beaten-track town. It lies at the extreme southern end of the Long Beach Peninsula, where the Columbia River meets the ocean. It's that rare find, a coastal town that escapes cuteness, where the streets aren't jammed with tourists and you won't find a single T-shirt shop selling "World Famous Ilwaco" souvenirs. You'll find the Port of Ilwaco, a library, a city park, tennis courts, shops, and restaurants. A little farther afield is the Coast Guard station and two picturesque lighthouses, Cape Disappointment and North Head. Climb the trail to the Fort Canby Interpretive Center and see the ocean as Lewis and Clark saw it.

The inn itself is one of the best sights in Ilwaco. The gray-shingled building began life as a Presbyterian church in 1928 before being rescued and restored by four otherwise occupied people: Ginger, a public relations entrepreneur; her husband, Glenn Brewer, an architect; her sister Dolores, a decorator; and Dolores's husband, Bob Blancher, a dentist and handy with a hammer. (Ouch!) Together they transformed the old Sunday school classrooms into uncluttered bedrooms and the spacious church coffee room into a parlor/breakfast room/lounge.

But here's the most innovative part of their renovation: They've turned the heart of the church, the sanctuary, into The Playhouse, a 120-seat theater. In addition to drama, The Playhouse hosts concerts, classes, meetings, and weddings and is one of the locations used for the inn's Mystery Weekends. The local Peninsula Players were fortunate to find this inviting space and innkeepers who have ambitious plans for turning their wonderful building into a regional center for the performing arts. Make your reservations to include The Playhouse. I want to be there especially to hear the old bell in the church tower ring out, calling all to the play. Ginger let me climb up and ring it, and it sounded great.

The family-style breakfast served in the parlor might include eggs Florentine, oatmeal and walnut pancakes with orange sauce or a soufflé, homemade breads, and juice and fresh fruit. Several of the finest restaurants in Washington are in easy driving distance, including the Ark at Nahcotta and The Sanctuary (another transformed church) in Chinook.

How to get there: Highway 101 goes directly through Ilwaco. Turn right off Spruce Street as you come into town from the east.

J: *Many would say the peninsula is at its best in winter. Try some winter storm watching from the clifftop bunkers near the fort and lighthouses, then nip back to the inn for tea and a snooze.*

Olive Metcalf

Downey House
La Conner, Washington
98257

Innkeepers: Jim and Kay Frey
Address/Telephone: 1880 Chilberg Road; (206) 466–3207
Rooms: 5; 3 with private bath. Wheelchair access. No smoking inn.
Rates: $75 to $95, double occupancy, full breakfast.
Open: All year.
Facilities and activities: Hot tub. Nearby: minutes from La Conner's unusual
    shops, restaurants, waterfront; April tulip festival.

Downey House is a big, beautiful, 1904 farmhouse sitting on the outskirts of one of Washington's most picturesque towns. It has the kind of roadside appeal that people pull off the road to photograph—broad green lawn, flower beds, and old trees. When I visited the last week of April, acres of tulips were ablaze in the surrounding countryside, and Mt. Baker loomed majestically over the valley.

This is a house of memories and roots deep in the Skagit Valley. The Freys acquired and moved the house (surprising for a house this large) to this site in the mid-1960s. They raised their family here and in 1986 began sharing it as an inn.

If you love the history of families who remained together and part of the land through several generations, the old photographs here will delight you. A few lucky guests with roots in the area have picked out relatives in some of the threshing scenes and old school groups.

The good news for all guests is that nostalgia and antiques are dished out in updated comfort. There's not a whit of musty-dusty atmosphere. These personal objects collected from both Kay and Jim's families are refinished, polished, and lovingly cared for—treasures like the pump organ, a china cupboard, and a huge old-fashioned dining-room table where breakfast is served.

The bedrooms are roomy and decorated with fresh, light fabrics and handsome Victorian pieces—an elegant chair here, a fine old chest there, and several big walnut beds. The fifth bedroom is separate from the house: the Downey Room, a suite with its own bath. It's a warm contemporary room in rich green and beige—even the ceiling beams are green—and decorated with a collection of David Hagerbaumer's watercolors of wildlife scenes.

Kay and Jim are innkeepers who genuinely enjoy their guests. You're welcome in the big country kitchen, and, after breakfast is served, they like to join everyone at the table with a cup of coffee. That breakfast often includes their own potato sausage, and always fruit, juice, and an egg dish or crepes.

How to get there: Driving south on I–5, take exit 230 to La Conner. Turn left at Best Road, which becomes Chilberg Road 5 miles from Highway 20. Inn is on the right. Driving north, take exit 221 to La Conner and Conway. Continue on Fir Island Road west, crossing a bridge. Road becomes Chilberg Road. After crossing a second bridge, the inn is 1 mile ahead on the left.

❁

J: *The charms of La Conner, sitting on Swinomish Channel at the edge of the Skagit River Delta and bordered by mountains and islands, are obvious. And in late April, when great rippling fields of tulips are in bloom, it can take your breath away. But alas, the busloads of tourists arrive then, too.*

olive Metcalf

La Conner Country Inn
La Conner, Washington
98257

Innkeepers: Rick and Reinhild Thompson
Address/Telephone: Old Town; (206) 466–3101
Rooms: 28; all with private bath, fireplace, television.
Rates: $69, single, to $93, double occupancy, continental breakfast. Children 12 and under share room with parents at no charge.
Open: All year.
Facilities and activities: Lunch, dinner, Sunday brunch, full bar, conference facilities. Nearby: explore La Conner Historic District, galleries, shops, restaurants, waterfront; biking, boating, fishing; Swinomish Indian Village.

La Conner just has to face the music—it's too picturesque to escape its destiny of becoming the perfect getaway weekend place, and only an hour and a half from Seattle. One citizen, unhappy with his town's increasing popularity, suggested in the local paper that signs on Interstate 5 be swapped with those of another town. I could have told him that is an old ploy that merely adds a maverick appeal to the town. Bolinas, California, has become famous, not for swapping, but *removing* signs to their town.

One main street of unique shops, restaurants, and commercial buildings dating from the late 1800s runs along the Swinomish Channel. This protected waterway is lively with commercial and pleasure crafts, and tugboats with rafts of chained-together logs in tow. The bustle of lumbering and fishing and the pastoral beauty of the surrounding countryside are both part of daily life here. Artists Mark Tobey and Morris Graves, among others, have been attracted to this little fishing community in the fertile Skagit Valley, with nearby mountains visible on the horizon.

The La Conner Inn is in the heart of the town, just a few steps from the waterfront. It is a contemporary inn with attractive, weathered cedarwood rooms and fireplaces. Some antique appointments like brass beds are used, but modern comfort is the tone, with private baths, and with televisions hidden in pine armoires. A large common room called the library is where continental breakfast is served—juice, coffee, tea, and hot chocolate, and large cinnamon rolls.

The restaurant adjacent to the inn is good news. Its specialty is local seafood, of course. But it also takes advantage of the fresh local fruits and vegetables—and prepares them beautifully. Try the tortellini primavera and, for dessert, the fresh raspberry tart. Another dessert specialty that guests come back for is called Queen Mother's Cake. It's a dense chocolate cake made with pulverized almonds instead of flour.

How to get there: Driving north from Seattle, leave I–5 at Conway; follow signs west to La Conner. From Whidbey Island, go east on Highway 20 to signs for La Conner.

J:　*Check out a shop across the street called Chez La Zoom. It has some extraordinary handmade clothing.*

Olive Metcalf

Haus Rohrbach Pension
Leavenworth, Washington
98826

Innkeepers: Kathryn and Bob Harrild

Address/Telephone: 12882 Ranger Road; (509) 548–7024

Rooms: 10 in main lodge; 6 with private bath, all with air conditioning and adjoining balconies; plus 2 luxury suites in The Chalet, each with fireplace, private bath, whirlpool tub for two, microwave, and sink. Wheelchair access. No smoking inn.

Rates: $70 to $165, double occupancy; $10 less for single occupancy; $98, The Chalet; full country breakfast for all rooms; occupants of The Chalet may have extravagent continental breakfast served in room. $15 additional person; $10 for children 12 and under.

Open: All year.

Facilities and activities: Heated pool, hot tub, sledding, two mountain bikes for rent, snowshoeing in front meadow. Nearby: Bavarian-style village of Leavenworth; restaurants; spring Mai Fest, Chirstmas Lighting Festival, January Ice Festival, white-water rafting, winter skiing, tobogganing, year-round fishing, hiking.

Forget about the high price of getting to Europe and take yourself to the country byways of central Washington's Eastern Cascade Mountains. In the Swiss-looking Tumwater Valley, you'll discover an entire town that has adopted the image of a Bavarian village. Believe it or not, it works.

Similar gimmicks imposed on a town by the local merchants can sometimes have grotesque results, but in this instance, the natural setting is so perfect that the effect is quite pleasing. There are several streets of Alpine-decorated shops and restaurants, with hanging baskets of brilliant flowers in every doorway.

Haus Rohrbach is a country inn nestled among the foothills overlooking the entire valley. The three-story lodge has wide balconies adjoining every room, overflowing flower boxes, and views of meadow and mountains, cows, geese, and gardens.

A comfortably furnished common room and an adjoining deck overlooking the valley are where guests gather. The decor has a European country feeling. After a day of outdoor fun, it's inviting to relax around the fire for conversation.

The most recent addition is The Chalet, a separate structure from the main house, with two wonderfully warm, attractive suites. Pine paneled cathedral ceilings, tiled baths, gas fireplace faced with floor-to-ceiling river rock, and French doors that open onto a large private deck are some of the features. In the main house, the bedrooms are appealing with pine details and colorful cotton fabrics.

Kathryn serves breakfast on the balcony in good weather— sourdough pancakes, cinnamon rolls, and other delights she bakes while you watch. She'll pack you a picnic, too, for a day of exploring the beautiful countryside.

The Terrace Bistro is *the* place to go in town for fine dining. The Harrilds agree the chef is world-class, but I advise you to come back to the pension for your "afters." Get into something with a stretchy waistband and cast your eyes over the variety of desserts available every night: old-fashioned sundaes and shakes; apple, peach, blueberry, and (oh, joy!) peanut butter pies; rhubarb crisps; a white chocolate mousse cake; and Schwarzwalder Kirsch Torte. Courage. Your bed is just up the steps.

How to get there: Going east on Highway 2 after Stevens Pass, turn left on Ski Hill Drive at entrance to Leavenworth. Go 1 mile; turn left on Ranger Road. You'll see the inn on the hillside.

J: *If you can look at valley and mountains from the balcony here without attempting to sing an exuberant chorus from* The Sound of Music, *you've more restraint than I. The cows didn't seem to mind.*

olive Metcalf

Mountain Home Lodge
Leavenworth, Washington
98826

Innkeepers: Chris Clark and Charlie Brooks

Address/Telephone: Mountain Home Road (mailing address: Box 687); (509) 548–7077

Rooms: 9; all with private bath and air conditioning.

Rates: Summer: $78 to $108, weekdays; $88 to $118, weekends; double occupancy, meals extra. Winter: $148 to $178, weekdays; $168 to $198, weekends; double occupancy, all meals and complimentary wine.

Open: All year.

Facilities and activities: Breakfast, lunch, dinner. Pool, hot tub, winter tennis, television, VCR. Nearby: hiking trails, snowmobiling, sledding, cross-country ski trails, fishing, golf, horseback riding.

Mountain Home Lodge was an unexpected discovery while I was traveling through central Washington—and one of the most memorable. This outstanding full-service country inn in the Wanatchee Valley (apple country) combines the luxury facilities of a resort with the intimate atmosphere of an inn.

Although it's only 3 miles above Leavenworth, getting there is an adventure. As the innkeeper warns you over the phone, it is on a "primitive gravel road" that winds up the mountain. When you emerge into the meadow surrounding the inn, you'll feel intrepidly off the beaten track. During winter, the inn's heated snowcat picks you up at the bottom of the road.

The contemporary cedar and redwood house with a broad deck surveys a spectacular Cascade Mountain setting. The greeting is a warm one. These innkeepers spare nothing in seeing that you feel at home and have any service that you require. One of them— usually Charlie—is always there.

The common-room decor suits the spacious mountain feeling, like the massive Attila the Hun–style sofas in sheepskin and burled redwood. Not the thing for your condo, but they look terrific flanking the stone fireplace. Carpeted bedrooms have fine tiled bathrooms (with an abundance of thick towels), colorful bed linens, and good reading lights.

The outdoor pool and hot tub (with fabulous views) are open Memorial Day to Labor Day. There is a 1,700-foot toboggan run and miles of cross-country ski trails, right from the back door. Since this is not a designated ski area, you can enjoy the quiet beauty in rare solitude.

In the late afternoon, I sat on the deck with other guests, sipping wine and watching the sun set over the Cascades. Hunger finally brought us inside to an Italian feast beginning with melon and finger-size pizza for hors d'oeuvres, then on to homemade ravioli *and* lasagna. We sat in one end of the living room looking out at the panorama of sunset and mountains. Soft music played, and deer grazed in the meadow below. The only flaw was the thought of having to leave.

How to get there: From Highway 2 just east of Leavenworth, turn south on Duncan Road (by the Duncan Orchard); it becomes Mountain Home Road. Follow to the inn.

olive Metcalf

Edenwild Inn
Lopez Island, Washington
98261

Innkeeper: Susan Aran

Address/Telephone: Lopez Road (mailing address: P.O. Box 271); (206) 468–3238

Rooms: 7, all with private bath, some with fireplace; garden and water views. Handicapped facilities. No smoking inn.

Rates: $90 to $140, double occupancy, full breakfast and afternoon aperitif. Ask about winter rates November through April.

Open: All year.

Facilities and activities: Facilities for small weddings and small conferences. During winter season, lunches and Saturday night ethnic dinners by reservation. Nearby: Lopez Village shops, hiking, bicycling.

When your request for a reservation is answered with a map of an island, a ferry schedule, and the assurance that ferry landing, sea plane, and airport pick-up is available, I say you're on your way to an adventure. The Edenwild Inn on Lopez Island is such a place. Just getting there is a romantic adventure.

The island slopes gently up from the ferry landing to reveal rural nature at its most picturesque. Pasture, fields, and farms are interspersed with dense woodland, and the shoreline is notched with bays and coves.

The recently built inn is about 4¹/₂ miles from the ferry landing. A broad porch dotted with chairs wraps around three sides of the large house, giving it an inviting, traditional look. Dozens of antique rose bushes and a green lawn brighten a brick patio and pergola to the parking area. Inside is a spacious, casually elegant country house with pale oak floors and fresh bouquets. Bright fabrics cover sofas and chairs grouped before the fireplace. An old upright piano sits here, and the work of some wonderful local artists is displayed here and all through the inn. Breakfast and other meals are served in the adjoining dining room.

Each one of the seven bedrooms appeals to me. It could be because they are new and fresh, or perhaps it is the comfortable built-in beds, or the terrific looking black-and-white tile bathrooms, or the views—Fisherman's Bay, garden, or San Juan Channel. From Room 5, we thought our view of the main garden and the channel the best in the house . . . until we watched a magnificent sunset that beat them both.

In addition to a full, family-style breakfast for house guests, Susan offers wintertime island visitors (November through April) her version of a soup kitchen. Her collection of great soup recipes is the source for lunches of a bowl or cup of homemade soup, freshly baked bread from an island bakery, and desserts. Susan is also having fun during the winter months with Saturday-night ethnic dinners—anything from Chinese to Cajun. The only thing certain is that you'll need a reservation. This energetic innkeeper and her staff will see that you eat well and have a good time.

An unexpected bit of excitement occurred as we were packing the car to leave. An awfully attractive man helped put our bags in the trunk and then blushed becomingly when we recognized his well-known face. When he's at the inn, this first-rate actor is strictly Susan's husband.

How to get there: From the Lopez Island Ferry Landing, proceed 4¹/₂ miles to Lopez Village Road. Turn right.

J: *Can you imagine what this usually quiet inn must have been like when Jonathan Winters was a guest for a few days? Susan says no one stopped laughing the entire time.*

Olive Metcalf

MacKaye Harbor Inn
Lopez Island, Washington
98261

Innkeepers: Mike and Robin Bergstrom
Address/Telephone: Route 1; (mailing address: P.O. Box 1940); (206) 468–2253
Rooms: 6, including 2 suites; 4 rooms share 3 baths, 1 suite with private bath. No smoking inn.
Rates: $69 to $105, double occupancy, full breakfast.
Open: All year.
Facilities and activities: Bicycles, guided kayak tours. Light-meal kitchen privileges. Nearby: MacKaye Harbor (your front yard), beachcombing, rowing, fishing, kayaking, sailboarding, bicycling, small village, shops, museum.

This is a great getaway, beginning with the adventure going to an island always holds. The hour-long ferry trip from Anacortes to the San Juans stops first at Lopez Island. Depending on the weather, it can be a misty surrealistic glide through the islands when you can turn up your raincoat collar and feel mysterious, or a stunning, too-brief voyage of picture postcard scenes of the snowcapped Cascades, forested islands, and water.

A 12-mile drive to the other end of the island brings you to MacKaye Harbor and the inn, the only one on the island so easily accessible to the beach. The restored Victorian, unpretentious but comfortable, sits directly across the road from the low-bank, sandy beach. A waterfront-view sitting room offers an ever-ready pot of coffee and baked treats to enjoy by the fireplace. Sofas and easy chairs, magazines and games appoint the room.

The Captain's Suite is on the first floor. Three other bedrooms are on the second floor, including the Harbor Suite with a fireplace and private sun deck.

Across the road is the beach, a quiet, clean stretch of sand and rock, fun to play on or to simply sit and watch the activity all around—otters, seals, eagles, and deer. The inn has kayaks and a 12-foot rowboat for guests to use. The harbor is an especially good spot for sailboarding and kayaking.

Think about asking the innkeepers to pack you a picnic lunch to take exploring. A must is a walk to Agate Beach, where you can watch the activity around the boat docks and the salmon fleets, July through September. Lopez is a low-key kind of island, not chic, no quaint streets of boutiques, no tarted-up storefronts. It's about 17 miles from end to end and 7 miles at its widest, with a tiny village, a few shops, and a museum.

If you spot a delicatessen called Gail's, stop in. It has a fresh perky atmosphere and food to match. Wildflower's is another spot for good food or to pick up a few things to have as your own special dinner for two back at the inn. They will set a fine table for you, and the surroundings couldn't be more pleasant.

The island is a bicycling heaven. The inn keeps bikes on hand, and even if you haven't ridden for years, you won't have any difficulties managing these flat roads and lanes. When I was there in late April, few people were around, but the tulips and azaleas were blooming in profusion.

How to get there: Leave the ferry and proceed south on Center Road about 10 miles to a T in the road. Turn left on Mud Bay Road to the fire station. If you pass a service station, you've gone too far. Turn right on MacKaye Harbor Road; proceed to the inn on your left.

Olive Metcalf

Orcas Hotel
Orcas Island, Washington
98280

Innkeepers: Craig Sanders and Cindy Morgan

Address/Telephone: Orcas Ferry Landing (mailing address: Box 155); (206) 376–4300

Rooms: 12; 2 with private bath and Jacuzzi tub, some with toilet and sink in room. Wheelchair access.

Rates: $65 to $170, double occupancy; $10 less for single; full breakfast. $15 for rollaway.

Open: All year.

Facilities and activities: Lunch, dinner, Sunday brunch buffet; full bar. Nearby: all water sports including kayaking, boat charters, bicycle and moped rentals, tours to Yellow Islands and outer islands, hiking trails, horseback riding, Moran State Park, Mt. Constitution.

When you leave the Orcas Island ferry and gaze up at the ornate red-roofed hotel with white picket fence perched on a rocky knoll, you're going to be awfully pleased if you have reservations. It is quite captivating. The three-story Victorian with flowers lining the steps up to the long front veranda looks the very picture of a quaint old inn, which it is.

Built between 1900 and 1904, the Orcas Hotel has the requisite checkered past to legitimately be called "colorful." It is on the National Register of Historic Places and was extensively restored in 1985.

It was lunchtime when I went through the handsome front

doors with their brass hardware and hand-painted glass panels. There was a cheerful buzz emanating from the cocktail lounge, and a steady parade of customers passed through the parlor to the dining room. The old-fashioned Victorian parlor is pretty, but some wonderful photographs of Orcas almost a hundred years ago and the hotel with the original owners were what made me linger.

It's a country, seaside atmosphere in the dining room. There is a big rock fireplace, and you have a view of the harbor from one side of the room. Some of the kitchen's recipes date from the early days of the hotel, but the beautiful salads and entrees I saw came from a thoroughly modern kitchen. Fresh fish from the island's waters are a specialty, of course.

The feeling in the twelve bedrooms is Victorian. The two largest, Blue Heron Room and Kittlebrew Lake Room, have private baths with Jacuzzi garden tubs and French doors opening onto a sun deck. There are antiques, modern queen-sized beds with quilts custom-stitched by Orcas quilters, and wonderful water views of Harney Channel, Shaw Island, and Blind Bay with its sentinel rocks.

Orcas Island's 56 square miles and 125 miles of coastline are enormously popular with hikers, boaters, and nature lovers. Lots of Northwest families have been coming here for summer vacations for generations. If at all possible, avoid your discovery trip during the peak of summer. Spring and fall are lovely times here with sprays of colors and a slower pace. If you're a writer, misanthrope, a Greta Garbo type, or just hiding out, the winter months will give you a blue-and-green landscape, soft rains with an occasional drencher, and plenty of quiet.

How to get there: From Anacortes, take the San Juan Islands ferry to Orcas Island—about a forty-five-minute trip. You may leave your car in the ferry parking lot at Anacortes and buy a "walk-on" ticket if you don't want to bring your car with you. The inn is directly above the ferry landing. Fly-in: Eastsound Airport. Boat moorage free for Orcas Hotel guests.

Olive Metcalf

Turtleback Farm
Orcas Island, Washington
98245

Innkeepers: Bill and Susan Fletcher

Address/Telephone: Crow Valley Road, (mailing address: Route 1, Box 650, Eastsound); (206) 376–4914

Rooms: 7; all with private bath, king- or queen-sized or double beds, and individual heat control. Wheelchair access. No smoking inn.

Rates: $65 to $135, winter; $65 to $155, May 1 to November 1; double occupancy; full breakfast and afternoon beverage.

Open: All year.

Facilities and activities: Farm; pond stocked with trout. Nearby: hiking trails in Moran State Park; bicycle and moped rentals; swim, picnic at Lake Cascade; fishing, kayaking, sailing; good restaurants.

Set back from a country road, Turtleback Farm looks like an attractive, well-kept old farmhouse, a big green two-story clapboard building. But it's been featured in numerous articles, and, despite a remote location, it is usually booked months in advance. This may well be the gem lodging of Orcas Island.

The reasons are clear once you settle in. This is a first-rate, impeccably maintained inn. It delivers the quiet country charm that so captivates inngoers but with all the comforts you could ask for.

The inn was once an abandoned farmhouse being used to store hay, now restored from the ground up. There are seven guest rooms, a parlor, dining room, and a tree-shaded deck that runs the length of the house. This is a wonderful place to sit on a warm day and enjoy looking out at acres of meadow with mountains beyond. We're talking idyllic, tranquil setting.

Even if the weather turns dismal, the comforts of this house will keep you charmed. The decor is tasteful and nonfussy, with muted colors and mellow wood trim and floors, and open-beam ceilings. Each guest room has a modern bath appointed with antique fixtures, claw-footed tub, pull-chain toilet, and wall shower. The pedestal sinks came from the Empress Hotel in Victoria. There's a cozy parlor where you can curl up and read before a fire. (The custom here is, "If you find a book you can't put down, take it with you and just return it when you finish.")

The dining room is still another place to enjoy the view and have a cup of tea or a glass of sherry. An outstanding breakfast is served here, course by course at individual tables on bone china. The menus change, but a typical morning would see juices, local berries, granola, an omelet with ham, and English muffin. Seconds are always offered.

What do you do on an 80-acre farm if you're fresh from the city? If you're smart, you settle yourself on the deck with a blade of grass between your teeth, a big hat tipped down over your nose, and think things over—very, very slowly. Then there are the exhausting demands of critter watchin'. There are ducks and blue heron, sheep, chickens, a rambunctious brown ram named Oscar, and visiting Canada geese. You're welcome to fish the large pond by the main house—it's stocked with trout. If you're a picnic fan, the paths leading to private little spots will be irresistible. The Fletchers make every effort to acquaint you with all that the island offers. They'll make arrangements for you to charter a boat, rent a moped, play golf, or whatever sounds good to you.

How to get there: From Orcas Island ferry landing proceed straight ahead on Horseshoe Highway to first left turn; follow to Crow Valley Road. Turn right and continue to the inn, 6 miles from ferry landing. Fly-in: Eastsound Airport.

olive Metcalf

James House
Port Townsend, Washington
98368

Innkeepers: Carol McGough and Anne Tiernan

Address/Telephone: 1238 Washington Street; (206) 385–1238

Rooms: 12, including 2 garden suites and 1 cottage; 4 with private bath, 3 with fireplace. Limited wheelchair access. No smoking inn.

Rates: $52, single, to $135, double occupancy for Bridal Suite; full breakfast. Reduced rate November through February.

Open: All year.

Facilities and activities: Nearby: downtown Port Townsend waterfront attractions, shopping, restaurants; tour Victorian homes; museum in City Hall; convenient base for touring Olympic Peninsula.

Francis Wilcox James was a man who evidently believed in thinking big. During the 1890s, when a fine, large house could easily be built for $4,000, he spent $10,000 building James House for his retirement. The parquet floors are made of oak, walnut, and cherry woods. The newel posts, spindles, and banisters are fashioned from native wild cherry from Virginia. James had the logs brought around Cape Horn, and the carving was done in the house.

Well, why not? He was probably the richest man in Port Townsend. In an 1890 *City Directory*, he lists himself simply as "Capitalist." What a solid, reliable ring it has. Why didn't I major in that at college?

His splendid Queen Anne extravaganza sits on a bluff above

the town's waterfront and business district. It's now on the National Register of Historic Places and is one of the town's premier inns—the first bed and breakfast in the northwest.

Most of the twelve spacious guest rooms are furnished with massive antique furniture—the kinds of pieces that look right only in huge, high-ceilinged rooms like these. The Gardener's Cottage and Garden suite have some fine wicker pieces. These rooms will sleep three and four people; they're comfortable accommodations for parents traveling with children over twelve.

The Bridal Suite is the most luxurious of the accommodations. It has parquet flooring, a small, elaborate, mirrored fireplace, a balcony, and an anteroom with a cranberry-red Victorian fainting couch. The enormous antique bed is perfectly at home here. A wicker settee, coffee table, and rocker sit in a four-window bay looking out at Port Townsend's waterfront and the mountains, snowcapped most of the year.

On the main floor are two elegant parlors with fireplaces and a formal dining room. A full breakfast, featuring wonderful home-made scones and muffins, and quiche or other hot dishes, is served in the dining room and around the oak kitchen table next to the wood cookstove.

How to get there: Three ferries serve the area: from Mukilteo to Clinton; from Seattle to Winslow; from Edmonds to Kingston. The latter two both lead to Hood Canal Bridge. Proceed to junction with Highway 20; follow to Port Townsend. After the first stoplight, take Washington Street off to the left, past the Port Townsend Motel. Inn is at top of the hill on the left next to the post office.

J: *Summer visitors to the peninsula are often frustrated by the complexities of the ferries and the long lines to get on them. Summer travelers are well advised to take the ferry routes that allow advance reservations rather than just line up. Washington State Ferry information (within Washington only): (800) 542–6400; outside Washington, (206) 464–6400.*

olive Metcalf

Old Consulate Inn
Port Townsend, Washington
98368

Innkeepers: Joanna and Rob Jackson
Address/Telephone: 313 Walker Street; (206) 385–3553
Rooms: 8, including 1 tower suite; all with private bath, king-sized bed, and
air conditioning. 1 with fireplace. No smoking inn.
Rates: $59 to $155, double occupancy, full breakfast and afternoon tea.
Reduced rate November through March.
Open: All year.
Facilities and activities: Facilities and catering for weddings and small business
meetings; billiard room, television, fireplace. Nearby: restaurants, ten-
nis courts across street, Victorian homes of Port Townsend, ferry, mari-
na.

Things have changed at the Old Consulate, starting with its
name. You might have known this Queen Anne inn as Hastings
House, but the story now is new owners, modern construction,
fresh decor, and a comfortable atmosphere.

In a town of fine Victorians, this one is a premier survivor.
Like all the really big houses in Port Townsend, it sits on a bluff
high above the town with commanding views of water and mountains. Frank Hastings, the son of the town's founder, built it in
1889. The Jacksons believe that this was the first house in Port
Townsend to have electricity. It was once a consulate, which is how
its present name came about.

Some of the mansion's outstanding features are a front parlor with its original chandelier, formed in the shape of big, green bunches of grapes, and a fireplace framed with Italian tile that was ordered in a kit. It must have been one of the first. Newel posts on the stairway are quite remarkable: an iron nymph on the main floor, and upstairs a Tiffany design. Even the hinges on some of the doors are intricate pieces of art. A handsomely designed new stairway is well worth a trip to the third floor just for the view looking down.

Every bedroom is decorated with fresh, light fabrics and colors that contrast with the Jacksons' collections of antique dishes, dolls, and furniture. Unless you make reservations well ahead, you'll miss the Tower Suite, but do take a look, at least. There's a padded, circular window seat in the tower, and, of course, the view of the harbor is splendid.

Joanna has opened a study on the main floor that will ease the frustrations of the many men who are talked into a Victorian B&B by their wives and can't find a single spot to relax and be comfortable. It has big overstuffed sofas, a television, and magazines. Rob has recently completed a garden-level billiard room that makes a pleasant addition to the inn. In addition to the grand Victorian billiard table, you'll find television, a fireplace, games, and comfortable sitting area down here.

Guests gather in the ornate dining room for a multicourse breakfast, family style. Joanna does all her own baking. She's the kind of openhanded innkeeper that always keeps snacks around. There's never a KEEP OUT sign on this kitchen. The coffeepot is always on, and you help yourself. The Jackson motto is, "Your room is just a bedroom; the house is yours to enjoy."

How to get there: Driving into Port Townsend on Highway 20, take Washington Street exit to the left, just past signs for Worden State Park. Inn is at top of hill on the left corner.

※

J: *The open stairway running four flights is an architectural stunner. In a town of beautiful views, this one rates high.*

Olive Metcalf

Ravenscroft Inn
Port Townsend, Washington
98368

Innkeepers: Leah Hammer, John Ranney, and Papa Sam
Address/Telephone: 533 Quincy Street; (206) 385–2784; fax, (206) 385–6724
Rooms: 8; all with private bath, 2 with fireplace. No smoking inn.
Rates: $65 to $160, double occupancy, full breakfast.
Open: All year.
Facilities and activities: Steinway grand; monthly events (call for specifics); massage available; facilities for weddings, private parties, small business seminars; fax, personal computer. Nearby: neighborhood of historic homes, walk to waterfront, shops, galleries, restaurants.

A refreshing alternative to Victorian lodgings is now available for visitors to Port Townsend. Ravenscroft Inn has elegant, contemporary comforts in a classic historical design that blends gracefully into a neighborhood of nineteenth-century houses.

Leah, John, and Leah's father, Papa Sam, are new owners of the inn but longtime fans of both the architecture and the culture of the early Colonial period. The two-story house, called a Charleston Single design, is authentically placed on the lot as Colonial houses were, facing the water. An upstairs deck (strictly speaking, a piazza) runs the length of the house and offers wonderful views of the Olympic Mountains and Mt. Baker. You can watch the waterfront activity, follow the Puget Sound shipping lanes, and see the big white ferries gliding in and out.

A large common room called The Great Room is a favorite gathering spot for guests, especially when one of the innkeepers treats them to an impromptu concert on the Steinway. Other musical events are frequently scheduled at the inn.

Eight spacious guest rooms are well decorated with imported fabrics, queen-sized beds, and wingback chairs. Some rooms have a fireplace and French doors opening to the piazza. If you're tired of inns with "authentic" bathrooms, these modern tile ones will look especially welcome.

The elegant and open (and huge) kitchen is striking in white and colonial blue—maybe it's dapple gray. Both John and Leah enjoy creating new dishes here for their gourmet breakfasts. No matter what the hot entree may be, one favorite they often serve first is a Morning Sunday consisting of fresh granola topped with yogurt, fresh fruit, then another sprinkle of granola and crowned with a strawberry fan. The coffee, Ravenscroft's own blend, is ground fresh, of course, usually served with a morning concert.

Innkeeping is the latest in a number of fulfilling careers for these innkeepers. They have all had other pursuits. John, an accomplished musician, has been on the faculty of the University of Southern California School of Music and Loyola Marymount. All three are enthusiastic about innkeeping and enjoy musical events and holiday celebrations at this beautiful inn. Catch this act while they're hot.

How to get there: Proceed along the waterfront to the end of Water Street at City Hall. Turn left up Monroe Street 2 blocks to Clay; turn left. Continue 2 blocks to Quincy Street. Inn is on the left.

ò

J: *The UIC (ubiquitous inn cat) on duty here is Claudé. Petting is permitted.*

Clive Metcalf

Manor Farm Inn
Poulsbo, Washington
98370

Innkeepers: Jill and Robin Hughes

Address/Telephone: 26069 Big Valley Road N.E.; (206) 779–4628

Rooms: 7 rooms, all with private bath; Farm Cottage with 2 bedrooms, 1 bath; Beach House with 2 bedrooms, 2 baths. No smoking inn.

Rates: $100 (November through April) to $170 (regular season), double occupancy; Farm Cottage, $170 or $190 in season; Beach House, $195 (off-season) or $245. $35 each additional person in Cottage or Beach House. Included in rates: juice and scones delivered to room; full breakfast and 3:30 P.M. tea service.

Open: All year.

Facilities and activities: Dinner by reservation. Facilities for small (up to fifty people) conferences, telephone, VCR hookup; wedding facilities; hot tub, fishing pond, farm animals. Nearby: countryside walks, cycling.

Track down Poulsbo, Washington, on a map and you might well wonder, "Why would I ever go to the interior of the Kitsap Peninsula?" Don't say I didn't alert you. Here is merely everything a country inn ought to be: a tranquil, pastoral atmosphere, completely insulated with fine decor and superior food and drink.

Jill and Robin Hughes are the young couple who have shaped a clapboard turn-of-the-century farmhouse into a French-style country inn. Robin is English and has skills as an architect, horticulturist, environmentalist, farmer, veterinarian, and gourmet chef. He and Jill exude enthusiasm for their individual outlook on innkeeping—a "hands-on environment" where people can touch and experience country life while enjoying all the civilized comforts. Sheep graze in the soft rolling countryside, and there is even a pond stocked with clever trout to test your fishing skill.

The seven luxurious bedrooms are painted white, with high, peaked ceilings and exposed supporting timbers. French Country antiques—massive pine armoires, mellow pine writing desks— inviting beds with puffy eiderdowns, and a feeling of clean space are first impressions. Each room's welcoming extras include instant hot water for coffee or tea, fruit baskets, and huge baskets of fresh flowers.

Given the luxury of time to settle in for more than a one-day stay, the Farm Cottage or Beach House will ruin you for home— unless you recently decorated with French Country pieces and, as with the Beach House, have a magnificent view of the Olympic Mountains. Fireplace, spa, kitchen, television, and stereo in both these accommodations make it easy to be content.

A morning knock on your door delivers fresh juice, hot scones, and jam, all to fuel you for the walk down the covered veranda to the dining room for a full three-course breakfast. Dinner is a gourmet event. First you join other guests in the drawing room for hot canapés and imported sherry. (It's a lovely room with raspberry-colored sofas and wingback chairs by a fireplace.) You're escorted to the dining room for a leisurely meal on snow-white linen with fresh flowers. A typical menu might include hot sole mousse, green salad with fresh fennel, poached oysters, scallops, shrimp in truffle sauce, rosemary roasted chicken, fettuccine with walnuts, and a choice of sinful desserts (Jill's specialty).

How to get there: From Seattle, take Winslow Ferry; proceed on Highway 305 (about 10 miles) to Bond Road, and turn right. Go to Big Valley Road; turn left, and continue 4¹/₂ miles to inn on the left.

J: *What an ideal setting for a very personal country wedding.*

Clive Metcalf

San Juan Inn
San Juan Island, Washington
98250-0776

Innkeepers: Skip and Annette Metzger
Address/Telephone: Friday Harbor (mailing address: P.O. Box 776); (206) 378–2070
Rooms: 10, 4 with private bath. Rollaway bed available. No smoking inn.
Rates: Summer: $74 to $94, double occupancy, full breakfast. Lower winter rates. $15 each additional person.
Open: All year.
Facilities and activities: Nearby: ferry landing, bike and moped rentals, Friday Harbor shops, restaurants; explore American Camp, English Camp, Whale Museum.

San Juan Island is the second largest in this cluster of 172 islands. Still, it's a rather unlikely place to have once been considered an international tinderbox. The "Pig War" of 1859 is now part of the romantic history of the islands, but at the time it was a full-fledged confrontation between Great Britain and the United States. It started when an American potato farmer shot a pig running through his potato patch. The unfortunate pig belonged to an Englishman, and the incident was the spark that ignited the long-simmering dispute between the two nations. The United States actually had cannons poised, and the British had five warships ready for action when an agreement was reached that eventually made San Juan an American possession.

Historic buildings of both the American and English camps survive, with exhibits and picnic areas. Both historic sites are within easy bicycling distance from the San Juan Inn, which also offers the more contemporary diversions of Friday Harbor's interesting shops and restaurants.

The inn has been around since 1873, but former owners wisely rewired, replumbed, and restored it for comfort. (Mindful that a pig almost started a war, who knows what damage an obstreperous toilet might cause?)

As the inn is only a block from the waterfront, breakfast in the parlor is especially entertaining, with a view of the big white ferries pulling in and out of the harbor and unloading hikers, bikers, and cars. Rigors of the morning watch are sustained with coffee and tea, juice, and hot blueberry and honey bran muffins. This room is pleasant at night, too, with its old iron stove and big chairs from which to watch the harbor lights reflected in the water.

Bedrooms are named after local islands and ferries. They are small and clean, with a Victorian feeling in flowered wallpaper and wicker headboards and chairs. Some rooms have brass beds and pine washstands. A few rooms have harbor or garden views.

A tiny brick patio garden—a cozy spot to sun and watch the ferries or perhaps read up on the Pig War—is adjacent to some interesting craft shops.

How to get there: From Anacortes, take the ferry to Friday Harbor. Inn is ¹/₂ block from landing on your right. Fly-in: Friday Harbor and Roche Harbor airstrips. Marine facilities. Float plane flights from Seattle to Friday Harbor.

◆

J: *This is not major information, but the calico cats used as doorstops are awfully cute.*

Ollie Metcalf

The Shelburne Inn
Seaview, Washington
98644

Innkeepers: David Campiche and Laurie Anderson
Address/Telephone: 4415 Pacific Way (mailing address: Box 250); (206)
   642–2442; fax, (206) 642–8904
Rooms: 15, all with private bath. Wheelchair access.
Rates: $85 to $120; suites $155; double occupancy, full breakfast. $10 additional person.
Open: All year.
Facilities and activities: Lunch, dinner; the Heron and Beaver Pub; wheelchair
   access to dining room. Wedding and small conference facilities. Nearby: beach walks, North Head Lighthouse, charter fishing, clamming;
   drive "World's Longest Beach Drive"; historic Oysterville.

Around the Shelburne breakfast table one recent morning, a
poll of home towns revealed that all the guests except one were
within 75 miles of home. Even people living close by come to stay
here because the Shelburne is a rarity in southwest Washington—a
Victorian inn with authentic period atmosphere *and* an excellent
restaurant.

It was built in 1896 as a boardinghouse, and later joined to
another building with a covered passageway. The present owners
kept the original design in mind as they expanded and refurbished.
Their most outstanding addition is a treasure from Morcambe, England. Art Nouveau stained-glass windows dating from the late
1800s were rescued from an old church that was being demolished

there. These floral-patterned beauties are now in the restaurant wing and pub, looking as though they've been there for the past one hundred years.

The wood-paneled common room is a cozy setting, with an old brick fireplace, and with coffee, current magazines, and newspapers at hand. The innkeepers' country breakfast is served family style at a large table here. Fresh herbs from their garden flavor the egg entrees, the sausage is homemade, and pastries are freshly baked. Pretty civilized fare to find on this wild stretch of seacoast. A sun deck and the Heron and Beaver Pub are popular additions to the inn.

The creaky-floored bedrooms are cheerful with fresh flowers, antique furniture, and bright quilts that set the color scheme. My fancy for "extras" was satisfied with a basket of toiletries and freshly baked homemade cookies in my room.

The restaurant has many fresh fish specialties prepared with skill and sophistication. No batter-fried fish plates here. Salmon in season always heads the list of favorites, but the availability of fresh local oysters and mussels provides wonderful eating. My filet of rockfish was moist and sauced with capers, olives, and fresh tomatoes and accompanied by wild rice with raisins and nuts. The "house salad dressing" is a standout. It involves a sour cream base with Dijon mustard. Homemade desserts, an extensive wine list, and thoughtful service made for a thoroughly pleasant meal.

How to get there: From Seattle, take I–5 through Olympia to Highway 8, then to 101 South. Avoid major detours in Aberdeen by taking Highway 107 or Montesano cutoff before Aberdeen to meet Highway 101. Follow south to Seaview and flashing yellow light. Turn right onto Highway 103; the inn is 5 blocks ahead on the left.

J: *Don't think of leaving without a stroll through the inn's flower and herb garden and then a walk to the beach. It's a particularly secluded stretch.*

Olive Metcalf

The Moore House
South Cle Elum, Washington
98943

Innkeepers: Eric and Cindy Sherwood

Address/Telephone: 526 Marie Avenue (mailing address: P.O. Box 629); (509) 674–5939

Rooms: 12; 10 in main house, 4 with private bath, 6 rooms share 2 large bathrooms, one for men and one for women, each with shower; 2 cabooses in yard, each with private bath, queen bed, 3 twin bunks, color television, refrigerator, and sun deck.

Rates: $33 to $105, double occupancy, full breakfast. Ask about family rates.

Open: All year.

Facilities and activities: Additional meals by arrangement. Hot tub, play ground equipment, paddock facilities, cross-country skiing, sleigh rides from back door; facilities for weddings, small meetings; special events planned by innkeepers. Nearby: old towns to explore, river rafting, floating, hiking, fishing, apple picking.

A bit of railroad history has been salvaged in quiet little South Cle Elum. A 1909 L-shaped building originally used as a crew house for the Chicago, Milwaukee, St. Paul and Pacific Railroad has been turned into a homespun country inn that is now on the National Register of Historic Places. It's an inn that will delight railroad buffs and give visitors a taste of once-thriving railroad days.

Who wouldn't get a kick out of sleeping in a real caboose? These two each have a queen-sized bed, private bath, television, fridge, and coffeemaker. They are mounted on rails and sit in a landscaped area surrounding the inn. They also have single bunks, so the entire family can enjoy the fun.

In the main house, what were once twenty-eight bare-essential rooms for a group of rugged men have been turned into ten cheerful guest rooms, many with brass beds, quilts, and antique wardrobes. Each one has a small brass plaque on the door bearing the name of one of the men who actually worked the Milwaukee and stayed at the crew house. Outside the two-story colonial-blue building are several railroad breaker signals, and inside is a steadily growing collection of that era's memorabilia.

The original inn's owners researched that time period and the building, even tracing men on the crews, some of whom became interested and involved in the restoration. Many have contributed wonderful photographs of their railroad days, now displayed on the inn's walls. There are also letters from the time, a conductor's uniform, even china from the dining car.

You'll find an unpretentious, relaxed atmosphere in the dining room and sitting area that opens through French doors to a deck and hot tub. It's a house furnished for casual comfort, conversation, and children. There is an upright piano, games, books, and a large wooden train that younger children love to ride. While I visited, children played games on the big dining room table, enjoyed the hot tub, and downed platters of blueberry pancakes.

How to get there: From Seattle on I-90, take first Cle Elum exit. Turn right at sign for South Cle Elum and follow The Moore House signs.

J:　*At this writing one of the hottest shows on television is* Northern Exposure. *Its setting is a fictitious Cicely, Alaska, but the actual filming is done in Roslyn, Washington, about 5 miles from the inn. Whenever cast and crew are in the area for more than a day's filming, some stay at The Moore House.*

Olive Metcalf

The Captain Whidbey Inn
Whidbey Island, Washington
98239

Innkeeper: John Colby Stone

Address/Telephone: 2072 West Captain Whidbey Inn Road, Coupeville; (206) 678–4097 or (800) 366–4097

Rooms: 32, including 12 rooms in main building sharing 2 bathrooms; waterfront cottages and duplexes with private baths. Limited wheelchair access.

Rates: $75 to $175, double occupancy, continental breakfast.

Open: All year.

Facilities and activities: Lunch, dinner, full bar. Classic sloop Aeolus docked at inn available for cove cruises. Nearby: historic Coupeville's Victorian homes, museum, waterfront shops, restaurants; Fort Casey State Park; Deception Pass; boat rental, golf, tennis, Keystone Ferry to Port Townsend.

A funny thing happened to me at The Captain Whidbey. I blame it on the gray, drizzling weather the day I discovered it. I momentarily forgot that I'm a sunshine-loving, white wine–quaffing, nouvelle cuisine–eating Californian, and I had an overwhelming urge to have double old-fashioneds from the bar, toast my toes at the stone fireplace, and order steak—rare—with fries! In spite of Mr. Stone's dismay ("We don't have fries and haven't for the twenty-five years my family has owned the inn!"), it *still* feels like that kind of place to me.

The ambience at this funky, offbeat inn has been marinating

since 1907, when it was an ideal hideaway for guests from Seattle. On this dreary day, the wood-smoke smell from the fire, the creaky floors, and the warmth of the madrona log interior were cheering. The sense of being very remote, but in friendly hands, added to its charm.

The first floor of the inn is as it's always been: a comfortable sitting room and fireplace, with a cozy bar and dining room overlooking Penn Cove. The food reflects the Northwest abundance of fresh salmon, oysters, crab, and Penn Cove mussels, as well as steaks. The menu changes frequently according to what is fresh and in season and is limited to three entrees per night.

Up the stairway at the large landing is a library with such appealingly jammed shelves it almost forces you to browse. There are well-worn upholstered sofas and chairs to sink into, and funny old floor lamps. Continuing down the hall to the bedrooms will take some time. The walls are covered with family mementos— everything from John's father's grammar school diploma to his great-grandfather's naval uniform from the 1800s.

The twelve bedrooms are small (or cozy, depending on how you look at these things), with low log ceilings and furnished with antiques. All have sinks in the room, but everybody in this original building goes down the hall to use the bathrooms and showers. You can have private baths and fireplaces in the waterfront cottages. Newest accommodations are the twelve lagoon rooms with verandas and lovely views.

How to get there: From the Mukilteo Ferry landing at the south end of Whidbey Island, take Highway 525, to Highway 20, and go 3 miles past Coupeville. Look for sign on right for the inn; take next right (Madrona), and go approximately ³/₄ mile. From the north, cross Deception Pass Bridge, one of the most scenic spots in the Northwest.

J: *I confess a fervent bias for Coupeville. One of the oldest towns in the state . . . a waterfront setting . . . Victorian homes—it's enchanting.*

Olive Metcalf

Whidbey Inn
Whidbey Island, Washington
98260

Innkeeper: Richard Francisco

Address/Telephone: 106 First Street (mailing address: Box 156), Langley; (206) 221–7115

Rooms: 3 rooms and 3 suites with fireplace; all with private bath. No smoking inn.

Rates: $95 to $145, double occupancy, full breakfast. Rates slightly higher in summer.

Open: All year.

Facilities and activities: Nearby: beachcombing, bicycling, hiking the island, Langley's shops and restaurants, ferry to Seattle.

Here's a romantic, intimate waterfront inn on Whidbey Island. Open a picket gate, walk down a few steps, and you come to a freshly painted white deck hanging right over Puget Sound. Stretching the entire length of the building, the sun deck has lounge chairs, is decorated with colorful planter boxes spilling over with flowers, and has an entrance to each room.

Quaint lodgings tucked into vine-covered small places are terribly appealing, but once you're in them, it's especially winning when they open up to give you elbow room. That's the case at Whidbey Inn—cozy but not cramped, and very private. Dramatic views from the deck are a major attraction here: the Saratoga Passage, Camano Island, and the North Cascade Mountains beyond.

I fell in love with Langley. It's an enchanting "village by the sea," as it bills itself. There are no traffic lights, but plenty of historic charm and good restaurants, and the inn is tucked into the very heart of the town. The village motif is somewhat turn-of-the-century Western. Antiques shops, crafts, and homemade-clothing stores were notches above the usual.

Back at the inn after walking Langley, your room is a tranquil retreat. Provincial pastel linens, puffy comforters, clean, polished hardwood floors, and lots of fresh flowers give each a Country French feeling. Each of the three downstairs rooms has an entrance to the sun deck, which stretches the entire length of the building over the water. Three suites upstairs have a still more luxurious feeling. The Wicker Suite is light and airy with an atrium in the entrance and a white-brick fireplace. The Gazebo has a bridge to its own private gazebo in the trees. The Saratoga suite has bay windows, exquisite antique furnishings, a marble fireplace, and two sitting areas.

Down a brick pathway is a cottage garden where you can enjoy the flowers, read a book, and relax. As the innkeeper says, "This is a *very* quiet and peaceful inn. . . ." No television, no telephone. Doesn't it sound heavenly?

A full light breakfast is brought to your room in a basket to enjoy there or out on the deck: freshly ground coffee or tea, fresh orange juice, homemade muffins and croissants, and an egg dish.

This is a quiet, romantic inn with the kind of special touches that persuade you to slow down and enjoy—a glass of sherry, scented bath gels and shampoo, and chocolates on your pillow at night.

How to get there: From Seattle, go north to Whidbey Island–Mukilteo Ferry exit 189. Take 15-minute ferry ride to Clinton, Whidbey Island. Proceed on Highway 25 south to Langley. Inn is on the water side at the town's center.

❀

J: *Overnight or temporary boat moorage is available 1 block away at the Langley Marina.*

Indexes

Alphabetical Index to Inns

Inns with Restaurants or That Serve Dinner by Special Arrangement

Romantic Inns and Wedding Sites

Especially Elegant Inns

Rustic and Rural Inns

Architectural Treasures

Inns with Historic or Colorful Pasts

Inns with Fabulous Views

Inns near Water

Inns with Swimming Pools

Inns with Skiing Nearby

Mountain Retreats

Peaceful, Quiet Inns

City Inns

Inns That Especially Welcome Children

Inns with Small Conference Facilities

Inns with Wheelchair Access

About the Author

Julianne Belote claims she writes about country inns because it gets her out of the house and because she loves breakfasts that someone else fixes. A love affair with the West Coast and a husband's penchant for back roads began her inn discoveries more than twenty years ago. There were only a handful of inns then. Now she drives to hundreds every year from the Mexican border to the San Juan Islands north of Washington.

Her reviewing standards are firmly flexible. Solid comfort and a bit of charm are what she's tracking; and given her custom of arriving on an innkeeper's doorstep, often without advance notice, she says it's easy to see how deep the charm goes.

Julianne has lived most of her life on the West Coast and graduated from the University of California at Berkeley. She has written three other books and writes frequent magazine articles—when not getting her own breakfast.